Jon Anderson & The Warriors

the road to YES

David Watkinson

Sonicbond Publishing Limited
www.sonicbondpublishing.co.uk
Email: info@sonicbondpublishing.co.uk

First published in hardback in the United Kingdom 2019
This edition published in the UK and USA 2020

British Library Cataloguing in Publication Data:
A Catalogue record for this book is available from the British Library

ISBN 978-1-78952-059-0

Typeset in ITC Garamond & ITC Avant Garde Gothic
Printed and bound in England

Graphic design and typesetting: Full Moon Media

Jon Anderson & The Warriors

the road to

YES

David Watkinson

SONICBOND

sonicbondpublishing.com

Comments about the Hardback edition

Thumbs high up in the air to Dave, for an extremely enlightening book. I learned much more about Jon due to reading it, and I've known him personally for 55 years, now. Well done, mate. **Brian Chatton**

Looks great, well done! **Steve Nardelli** (The Syn)

Brill, I'm impressed, you're a star, Bless you. **Rodney Hill**

This is a great book. The amount of research done is very impressive. (We are) especially impressed with the family tree and photos, and the Germany experience is fascinating. A pat on the back for David. This is an essential book for any Yes, Jon or Warriors fan.
Kevin Mulryne and **Mark Anthony K** of the *Yes Music Podcast*

I hope it does well, many congratulations. **QEDG** (Yes Management)

Really enjoyable reading. Dad always spoke fondly of his band-mates. An entertaining insight into The Warriors early days.
Kelly Falkiner (Dave Foster estate)

What an amazing job you've done with the new book. It's meticulously researched; fascinating stories I'd never known before; brilliant visuals. Thank you for a simply outstanding book! I will treasure it.
Andrew Whitman (Yes fan)

I am loving your book - amazing! **Jon Dee** (Yes fanzine/Yes collaborator)

It's a great piece of work. I read half of it in one sitting. Good photos and some interesting interviews. A big well done. Along with the Yes Perpetual Change book this is a great addition. Many thanks for doing it.
Mark Watterson (Yes Fan)

Enjoying it a lot. The detail is amazing. Well done! Can see it's been a labour of love. **Geoff Bailie** (*The Prog Report*)

An important and indispensable part of the great Yes story.
John Bollenberg (*IO Pages*)

Dedicated to...

Charles David Watkinson

'I am very proud of you son. Love you always.'

Dad

What's in a Name?

Jon Anderson (Musician)

Johnny – Jonny Dean – John – Jony – Jonnie – Jon

For more than 50 years Jon Anderson's forename has been spelt Jon, without the letter 'h', which he dropped officially in the early 1970s, although he was still using it in the late 1960s. During the period covered throughout this book, the 1960s, he was known officially as John with the letter 'h'. However, I have chosen to spell his name as 'Jon', throughout the book, as most fans will know him this way. The one exception is the moniker 'Johnny', which was used by many who knew him in his earliest years in Lancashire.

Jon Anderson & The Warriors
the road to **Yes**

Contents

Thoughts from Jon Anderson

From an interview with the author in 2015

A book about The Warriors: that could be fun to talk about. On a good day, I can remember lots of crazy things that happened. The Warriors were a very silly, funny, crazy, 1960s band, an adventure into lots of amazing things. At the end, when I toured with The Warriors, after the last gig in Frankfurt - we had performed the Saturday afternoon show and evening show - I got up on the Sunday morning and was so excited about new music that I had in my head.

The wonderful thing was we travelled all over the British Isles and Europe. We had a great five-year period - a real baptism into the real world. Up until then, I'd never really left Accrington. The Warriors was something special for me; we became such a great band. Looking back, without those guys, I wouldn't be doing what I am doing now.

Maybe one day... when the moon is high like we were...

Above: Jon at the Rock & Roll Hall of Fame Ceremony in 2017. *(Alamy)*

Acknowledgements

During the many years I spent researching, writing and recording interviews for this book, I was given generous help by many people from all around the world. A big thank you must go to Stephen Lambe (Sonicbond), Sandra Wake (Plexus Publishing) and the book's designer, Huw Lloyd-Jones, for all their dedicated and patient work, and for sharing the same vision as myself.

A special thank you to Jon Anderson, who backed me throughout this long journey.

For the Yes logo: Daniel Earnshaw, Martin Darvill, Yes@QEDG.

To all the interviewees, especially to all band members of The Warriors: Tony Anderson, Rod Hill, Brian Chatton, Mike Brereton, David Foster, Ian Alveston, Tony Alveston, Gordon Kenyon, Graham Evans, Kenneth Borwick, John Howarth, Ian Wallace and Derek Thornhill.

Other interviewees and special contributions: Michael Tate (Yes, sound and lights), Brian Parrish (Badger), James Payne (Accrington Stanley), Kevin Parrott (The Big Sound), Lennie, Nikki Ragsdale, Marianne Evans, Angelika Granaht, Martyn Adelman and Steve Nardelli (The Syn), Peter Banks (Yes/K. Barroso/TheMarqueeClub.net), Billy James, (Billy@glassonyonpr) for the JA interview, Franny Franks, Dermot Bassett, Robert Kelly, Paul Gurvitz (Gun), Paul Rigby, Bob Hagger and Clive Bayley (Mabel Greer's Toyshop), Kelly Falkiner (David Foster) and Andrew Whitman for copy-editing.

Thanks also to Bill Bruford, Abbey Road Studios, FX Group, Decca Records, *Accrington Observer/Telegraph/Times, Lancashire Library Services*, *The Bolton Evening News*, Garth Dawson photos (Accrington), Raymond (Burnley), Ulrich Handl (Germany), Tony McNulty (Colne), Wood Photography (London), F. Davies (Bolton), Martin Standen, Dave Ridge, Margie Jones, Michael Ashworth, Nic Caciappo, *New Musical Express*, Dave Potts, Ken Crabtree, *Q magazine*, Yes Museum, Yestival, Mark Watterson, *Record Collector* magazine, dme.net, Tanya Coad, Henry Potts, Steve Sullivan, *Manchesterbeat.com*, Jon Kirkman, Chris Welch, Dan Wooding, *Melody Maker*, *Lankeybeat.com*, *perfectsoundforever.com* and Robert Packard.

Yes: Perpetual Change, *BBC Sounding Out*, Tim De Feu (*The Open Mind*), Kevin Mulryne (*Yes Music Podcast*), *Prog* magazine UK - Mark Blake, Olias of Bolton, Houses of Parliament, Jon and Yes for over 50 years of wonderful music and shows. Deidre (Dee) Nelson for editing, all-round goodness and understanding with this Yes obsession of mine and Mavis Watkinson, just for being mum, always there, whatever my plans.

You Came Along – at the right time!

This book would never have been written, were it not for a slice of good luck, and some amazing timing. I had lent my Warriors memorabilia collection to the Accrington Museum, following my Yes exhibition there, in November 2004. Ten years later, and I began to think about those early Warriors days again. With that thought, I phoned the gallery. It was a remarkable coincidence, or, some might even say, fate, that I rang them after all those years, at the exact time that they were doing a stock check.

'We are so pleased you have got in touch with us, as we had no way of knowing who all this material belonged to – we were going to throw it away any day now,' they told me. The material in question was around one hundred pieces of irreplaceable memorabilia. I instantly arranged for collection at the gallery in Accrington. With it all back in my possession, I began to think about how I could share it with Yes and Jon Anderson fans, hence the book, enjoy it...phew!

Above: Rod Hill, David Watkinson and Brian Chatton, taken in Bolton, April 2019. *(David Watkinson Collection)*

Forewords from Warriors guitarist Rod Hill and keyboard player Brian Chatton

When Dave approached me with the concept of producing a book about The Warriors, I was initially a little surprised, until I realised that the book would be about how our little Johnny became the iconic Jon of Yes. As I became more involved and drawn into the telling of the tale, I realised just how we (The Warriors) had influenced each other. I also began to reflect on how the band had changed my life and consequently what influences it has had on all of us. Dave worked hard on dragging the information out and frequently asked me to verify (or otherwise) the authenticity of the information he was collecting. It's frequently said that if you lived through the sixties you don't remember it. Whilst I understand the reasoning behind the statement I'm fortunate (touch wood!) that not only was I there, but I do remember it very well.

A lot happened over a very short period of time; as a band, we worked hard at our craft and had some success, some through luck but mainly through hard work and focus. Dave Foster was the original instigator, with Tony taking senior responsibility when he joined Dave, Mike and myself. Tony, in turn, then introduced Jon to the band and when we discovered Ian in Bury, the whole focus changed. After I wrote the van off and Mike and Tony left, the introduction of Brian was a touch of genius.

This book introduces the reader to how we – a bunch of northern lads – took on these challenges, how we discovered – through hard work – how to help one another. For those of us still here, friendship is still very important.

Thanks, Dave, for the memories this book represents.

Rod Hill, October 2019

I remember us being young lads who followed our own footsteps, rather than our parents, with all their northern sensibilities. We had the good fortune to continue being our father's sons, but also being paid to grow in the richness of other shores and lifestyles. I was the youngest member, so I became the brunt of the humour needed to survive the countless miles spent in the back of a van. Jon often found himself protecting me from the rest of the band, when he could see I had had enough. We continued our friendship in Los Angeles where we are presently observing the accolades and excitement of Jon's and my latest work, entitled *1000 Hands (Chapter One)*.

Dave and I have become close friends, so I have been anxiously awaiting the completion of his opus with great anticipation. I wish him well and think he truly deserves to enjoy success with what has become a terrific insight into a band that became known to Liverpudlians as the next Beatles – The Warriors.

Brian Chatton, October 2019

Introduction

As an admirer of Jon Anderson's work – and, of course, the legendary band Yes - and as a Lancashire native myself, I have long felt a need to put right the lack of documented history on The Warriors, Jon's band in the years before he joined Yes. Researching their history, I found that they had played gigs at a shop called *Wood's Pianos and Organs* in Bolton. As a young man, I started my furniture apprenticeship in this very shop, treading the same boards daily as The Warriors would have done some ten years earlier. Not shy of a challenge, I immersed myself in the search for information on them. With two 50th anniversaries recently passed - not only the end of The Warriors in 1967 but also the beginning of Yes in 1968, this work is well-timed.

Long before the progressive rock masters Yes produced wonderful songs such as 'Roundabout', 'Close To The Edge', and 'Awaken', or albums like *Tales From Topographic Oceans*, *90125* or even Jon's masterwork *Olias of Sunhillow*, Jon Anderson was formulating his musical apprenticeship in Lancashire in the North West of England. The 1960s music scene was overflowing with influences from America. There was a feeling that you could do anything you wanted, music-wise, and that anyone could join this musical revolution. The Beatles exploded onto the scene, knocking everyone sideways with their ground-breaking songwriting and performing, not to mention their winning personalities, to eventually become the greatest and most influential band of our time. The North West of England, from where the Beatles originated, was certainly a hotbed of possibilities. Jon Anderson and his fellow band members saw this potential and pounced. But his early learning years have mostly been glossed over up until now. I felt it was time to recognise Jon and his friends' musical roots – after all, two members of The Warriors went on to play in Yes and one in King Crimson. These hard-fought beginnings ultimately ended up giving the world Jon's unique voice, and a band unrivalled in its diversity, musicianship and musicality. Yes would go on to prove themselves the greatest progressive rock band in the world.

This book is based on my personal collection of Warriors memorabilia. With help from The Warriors band members, including Jon Anderson, this book delivers an authentic perspective on what life was like for young men starting out in the music business in the 1960s. My intention was to produce a unique book that would capture, in one place, the feelings of the people that were there at the time, establishing a historical document for the Lancashire music scene.

Although I have enjoyed researching Jon and Yes's history, it has often been challenging, especially when the information is over fifty years old, meaning that fewer people are around to recall those times. My task took me to the libraries of Lancashire, where I scrolled through hundreds of pages of old local newspapers. I tracked down band members, musicians, family and friends around the world, and met with many of them for a drink and chat, where they willingly dug deep into their memory banks. As they did so, their faces reflected their emotions as they recalled previously-forgotten memories of long-past days.

Throughout their apprenticeship in rock and roll and beat music, The

Warriors toured relentlessly, and for several of the musicians in the band, their dedication and persistence paid off in the end. Members of The Warriors would go on to play with bands such as Badger, Los Bravos, Flaming Youth, King Crimson, Meat Loaf, Jon & Vangelis and ultimately Yes.

I would like to give a big 'thank you' to all the musicians in the band, for being there in the beginning. You worked so very hard for years on end, in working men's clubs in Lancashire and beyond. Without your musical dreams, there would be no Jon Anderson *Prog* God (awarded in 2016) and no Yes.

David Watkinson
3 August 2019

Above: An excited Warriors show off their drum-head at the time of the single release. *(David Watkinson Collection)*

Band Introductions

Tony Anderson (Warriors - Vocals)

We were a good band because we worked so hard at it. We did a lot of travelling, and I certainly put the work in. We worked really hard. Not all the bands did TV and radio - they never got that far. Yeah, it was a very good band, The Warriors.

Rodney Hill (Warriors - Guitar)

On Friday 13th March 2015, I met with David Watkinson and Mike Brereton to discuss The Warriors, a band of lads who in the 60s performed as a group. During the few hours we spent together, I experienced a mixture of emotions. We weren't successful as a band, but more importantly, we were friends. The evidence of this is represented in the pages of this book. The memories of the memorabilia, which David produced, and the energy of Mike's responses, made me feel happy and sad at the same time. It reinforced the feeling that this was a formative time of my life; I joined the band at 16, and we folded in Germany six years later. My life with the band began in a church hall, we gained a recording contract, appeared in a film, performed on television and played gigs in iconic venues - to me this time together as a band was comparable to a degree course. I can most definitely state, 'I studied at the University of Life.' I have pondered many times on what may have been, and I have reviewed my memories to see what I had learnt during those years. This day with David allowed an opportunity to feel some of the emotions of that time with a colleague who had shared these experiences and a friend who is prepared to place them on paper. I was sad when the band had to finish, but it was great travelling around the countryside in a beat-up Bedford van with horns on the top. I had a ball.

Brian Chatton (Warriors - Keyboards)

In 1965, I met The Warriors by going to the Boneyard Club (Wood's Pianos) in Bolton for an audition. I did it and got the job. It was a growing-up-fast-experience from Kersley to Cologne, Frankfurt, Hamburg and Munich. There were hookers, drugs and music and many stories to tell. We knew, though, when we left the band that we wanted to be the best, it taught us to work hard and to practice more. Then it all split up. Jon and I went to London and look what happened then. But it was a fucking great training ground for us all.

Derek Thornhill (Warriors - Drummer)

It's five years I wouldn't have missed. When we started out, we were just some lads who had some fun, they were good times.

Gordon Kenyan (Warriors - Vocals)

The Warriors did well because we practised a lot. Jon once said to me, when I went to see him at a Yes gig in Liverpool, that if I hadn't left the band, then he would never have been where he is now. So, I'm afraid it's a success story in reverse, isn't it? Basically, I gave my place to Jon.

Ian Wallace (Warriors - Drums)

Nothing much came before The Warriors. They were my first professional band, six sets a night, every night and nine on weekends. This [band] is where I truly learnt to play the drums.

Dave Foster (Warriors - Bass Guitar/Vocals)

We became a very well-rehearsed band and began to build a good following in the local towns like Blackburn, Bury and Bolton. In 1967, though, we all said that was the end as we all had gone through a complete, total personality change. Jon had decided that he didn't want to sing Four Tops numbers anymore. I didn't want to play bass like I was doing anymore. Ian decided he wanted to play jazz. Everyone was messed up.

Tony Alveston (Warriors - Vocals)

They were fantastic times, really, to think what we were and where we came from. It was a hectic sort of five years. I can't believe what we did, I can't believe the distance we travelled, and all this in an old van!

Ian Alveston (Warriors - Guitar)

The most rewarding gigs were at the Accrington Conservative Club, where we played Monday evening dance night. We were young and just wanted to play anywhere.

Mike Brereton (Warriors - Guitar)

We played a lot with Gene Vincent and Bill Haley. Jon, well, he couldn't even play a bloody tambourine! What is still amazing, is that if you worked out everyone's talent in The Warriors on a scale of one to ten back then, Ian would be about a 9, Rod a pretty decent figure too, me about a 2 and Jon about a zero - he was just the harmony singer! When I think of Yes now, I can kind of see where it all came from - it was mostly 1960s, drug-induced rubbish.

The Warriors – A Family Tree

The band were also advertised as: The Warriors Rhythm Group, The Electric Warriors and The Sensational Warriors: the Decca Film and T.V. Recording Group.

Little John Skiffle Group - mid 1950s

Jon Anderson (Little John), Anthony Anderson (Tony, brother), Big John, friends and family at home

The Strangers 1959-60

Anthony (Tony) Alveston	Ian Alveston	John Howarth	Derek Thornhill
vocals	guitar	guitar	drums

(1) The Strangers become The Warriors 1960-61

David Foster	Tony Alveston	Ian Alveston	John Howarth	Derek Thornhill
vocals/bass	vocals	guitar	guitar	drums

(2) The Warriors 1960-61

David Foster	Tony Alveston	Kenneth Borwick	Ian Alveston	John Howarth	Derek Thornhill
vocals/bass	vocals	vocals/guitar	guitar	guitar	drums

(3) The Warriors 1960-61

David Foster	Peter Hibbert	Kenneth Borwick	Ian Alveston	John Howarth	Derek Thornhill
vocals/bass	vocals	vocals/guitar	guitar	guitar	drums

(4) The Warriors 1962

David Foster	Tony Anderson	Mike Brereton	Rodney (Rod) Hill	Derek Thornhill
vocals/bass	vocals	guitar	guitar	drums

(5) The Warriors 1962

David Foster	Gordon Kenyon	Tony Anderson	Mike Brereton	Rod Hill	Derek Thornhill
vocals/bass	vocals	vocals	guitar	guitar	drums

(6) The Warriors 1963-64 (11th May 63 was Jon's first gig)

Jon Anderson	David Foster	Tony Anderson	Mike Brereton	Rod Hill	Derek Thornhill
vocals	vocals/bass	vocals	guitar	guitar	drums

(7) The Warriors 1963-64

Jon Anderson	David Foster	Tony Anderson	Mike Brereton	Rod Hill	Ian Wallace
vocals	vocals/bass	vocals	guitar	guitar	drums

(8) The Warriors 1964-65

Jon Anderson	David Foster	Tony Anderson	Rod Hill	Ian Wallace
vocals	vocals/bass	vocals	guitar	drums

(9) The Warriors 1965-6 (4 or 5 nights only)

Jon Anderson	David Foster	Brian Chatton	Rod Hill	Kev Florintine
lead vocals	vocals/bass	keyboards	guitar	drums

Kev played in Scotland while covering for Ian, who was sick

Jon Anderson sang with The Koobas on stage on 1 January 1967 at the Storyville Club, Germany. Tony O'Reilly was on drums, The Warriors and a band called Thoughts made up the complete bill.

(10) The Warriors 1965-7

Jon Anderson	David Foster	Brian Chatton	Rod Hill	Ian Wallace
lead vocals	vocals/bass	keyboards	guitar	drums

There is a possibility that Jon also tried out with other groups, namely: The Open Mind, Les Cruches and possibly The Big Sound. These were most likely just a few gigs or one-off performances. At time of writing, Jon can't confirm that any of these happened. Another artist also appeared around this time who was also called JON. He is advertised playing a few evenings at The Marquee Club, then he disappeared. It's probably just a timely coincidence. After Jon left The Warriors, they did not carry on as a four-piece band as is sometimes reported. In fact, all the members went their separate ways.

These are the acts that Jon sang with before creating Yes with Chris Squire in 1968:

John & The Gentle Party - 1967

Known gigs on January 27/28 and in September with this band from Bolton.
Evidence of further appearances and details of the line up may be found in the future.

Hans Christian (Anderson) - 1968

March - Jon started as a solo artist in London.

Jon Anderson and Gun - 1968

Jon Anderson	Paul Gurvitz	Adrian Gurvitz	Louie Farrell
vocals	bass	guitar	drums

April - this band were his proposed backing group.

Mable Greer's Toyshop featuring Hans Christian (Anderson) - 1968

Jon Anderson	Chris Squire	Peter Banks	Clive Bayley	Bob Hagger
vocals	bass	guitar	guitar	drums

May to July - one or two gigs only with the band billed like this.

Mable Greer's Toyshop - 1968

Jon Anderson	Chris Squire	Peter Banks	Clive Bayley	Bob Hagger
vocals	bass	guitar	guitar	drums

Mable Greer's Toyshop / almost Yes - 1968

Jon Anderson	Chris Squire	Peter Banks	Clive Bayley	Bill Bruford
vocals	bass	guitar	guitar	drums

June - July

There were sporadic performances from May to July in London with this line up. By August Mabel Greer's Toyshop / Yes rehearsed at the Lucky Horseshoe Cafe in Shaftsbury Avenue. There is some doubt over Bill Bruford's participation in the band of that name as it transitioned to Yes, as Bill always states that he never joined MGT, only Yes. 7 June 1968 was Bill's first gig with Jon and Chris at the Rachel Macmillan College. It is often reported as the first Yes gig, but as Clive played guitar, it seems to be almost - but not quite - Yes.

YES

Jon Anderson	Chris Squire	Peter Banks	Tony Kaye	Bill Bruford
vocals	bass	guitar	keyboards	drums

From 3 August 1968 (Advertised as: Yes!, YES, The Yes)

The Warriors, what next?

The ever-changing Warriors line-up, which had as many changes as Yes, was in a state of perpetual change throughout the band's lifetime. There were also one-off, brief appearances made on stage. These included the occasional singer from other bands jumping up on stage for a jam. As Derek recalled, 'I think Jim Payne may also have joined us once for a song or two.'

The Warriors almost had a permanent saxophone player in 1967 added to the line-up as Geoff Peach auditioned from The Big Sound. In the end, an amalgam of the two bands changed their name to Sleepy, recorded a single for CBS and made their way to London. The Warriors band members came together outside of the band to play music in the 1960s with a number of other groups. The bands they played in were rumoured to be: Tony and The Tea Leaves (Leafs) although this is not verified by Tony himself, along with Tony and The Boys, purportedly featured Tony Anderson on vocals, Ian Alveston on guitar, John Howarth on lead guitar and the drummer Bill Armistead. The band had an unnamed bass player from the wonderfully sounding Lancashire local town of Oswaldtwistle.

A band called Wami (later Wammy) featured Tony Anderson on vocals and Dave 'Wammy' Walmsley on guitar, a friend of the Andersons, in 1969. Tony (Anthony) Anderson went on to play with the band Los Bravos, calling himself Andy by this time.

Following Los Bravos, Wammy sang in the follow-up band Los Zebra, joined again by Tony Anderson. A rare photo of both Jon and Tony working together again was taken in a Barcelona Recording Studio around 1969. It shows Jon, Tony, Wammy and Miguel Vicence (the original Bass Player of Los Bravos) singing in a Barcelona recording studio sound booth.

The band Sleepy (1968) featured Rod Hill (guitar) Dave Foster (vocals/bass guitar) and Ian Wallace (drums) and some musicians from The Big Sound. The band Accrington Stanley (1969) included Dave Foster (vocals/bass guitar) Jim Payne. (Drums) and Rod Hill (guitar).

Above: School day photos of a young Johnny Anderson. *(Lancashire Evening Telegraph)*

1. Beginnings

A Star is Born

The Lancashire mill towns of Bolton, Accrington and Nelson are not perhaps the most likely places to launch an internationally successful singing career. Yet for Johnny Anderson, these towns were the first stepping stones on the path to joining one of the greatest bands in the world. Born into a working-class family, little Johnny had ambitions in life and was never going to be satisfied shifting milk churns around forever, as he did in his early years of employment. Although Accrington itself was far from the hub of the musical revolution in the 60s, it was one of the many towns that knew a new musical scene was on its way. The effect of American music was filtering into the everyday lives of the working classes and changing the social environment. With the advent of music systems (radios and gramophones) becoming more accessible to the average household, teenagers were immersing themselves in music. It was an exciting time to be growing up. The enthusiasm and hype in the

Right: Kathleen and Albert Anderson. *(Tony Anderson)*

music scene were difficult to escape, especially when The Beatles, four cheeky Liverpudlians, began to make a name for themselves, and sold-out performances at The Cavern Club, so close by. It was almost possible to taste and touch the excitement.

It was a Wednesday on 25 October 1944 in Accrington, Lancashire, that Jon Anderson (John Roy Anderson) came into the world. He had three siblings: his oldest brother, Stuart, was born in the late 1930s, followed by another brother, Anthony (Tony), born in 1941, and finally a sister, Joy, who was the youngest of the family, arriving in July 1949. They grew up in what is still referred to by many, as a two-up-two-down terraced house, at 13 Norfolk Street. These small houses were so-called because they had two rooms both upstairs and downstairs. The house was set on a cobble-stoned row of terraced working-class houses, primarily built for the local workforce, each one exactly the same size as its neighbours. Built side by side, with no green grass in sight, they were small, but very well constructed brick buildings. These designs sometimes featured a little front walled garden of brick and stone, and if they were lucky, to the rear

Above: Jon smiling on the top row, second from the left at St. John's Infants School.

Right: Johnny in the centre, at St John's Church of England School. *(Accrington Telegraph)*

of the house, the residents would get a flagged, paved, yard area. This would be enclosed by high walls, and most likely, had an outside toilet. A gate led to an outer path or walkway which divided the houses.

Jon's home was only a short distance from the greener terrain of local farms and the Lancashire moors, which were windy and cold in winter, but a joyous escape into nature in the summer. The harmonious and friendly northern way created a feeling of a community. However, not everyone shared the same dreams. Johnny didn't want to follow in the footsteps of his contemporaries or his predecessors. He didn't want to go down into the pit or get an apprenticeship in the local area. He had bigger dreams.

Delving into their Roots

We need to go back to Jon's parents for clues as to what sparked his interest in a potential career in music and showbiz. Jon's father, Scottish-born Albert, was a hardworking man who had multiple jobs – as many did in those days – to make ends meet. He worked as a shop-keeper, a dancer, comic and salesman in the local town of Rishton. Albert was a sociable and outgoing man who had performed for the army entertainment section, ENSA (The Entertainments National Service Association). Indeed, Jon says that his father was essentially a show-off. Hard-working and fun, he worked for the family, making sure its life was as good as it could be in tough economic times.

Jon's brother, Tony, remembers his childhood fondly, recalling:

> As a family, it was tough for our parents, because the war years had taken their toll, and money was very short. We had no bathroom in the house, but had a tin bath in the kitchen, which was rather cold and unpleasant! We would have to heat up the water in a kettle to fill the bath up.
>
> It was hard for dad, as he would go out in the snow, wind, rain or (occasionally!) the sunshine, and travel to Blackpool, Blackburn or often even further afield, selling his wares door to door. With the bad weather to deal with, along with the smog – from chimneys and cars when he was out, from the coal fire burning at home – it was all too easy to get health problems. They affected Father badly – and as a result, the family income was also affected. Dad would get colds, the flu, and, eventually, much more serious illnesses, resulting in our mother having to care for him for over ten years.
>
> Jon and I were only farmhands. We were very close – and we still are. We had to work hard for the family. Father used to keep a scrapbook about Jon after he got ill. Jon's career was a big interest to him. He was proud of Jon, and his son's success and that kept him going while he was ill. I'm not sure who has that scrapbook now, possibly Jon.
>
> Growing up, Jon and I shared a room, and we used to sing ourselves to sleep. We had the room over the back door, which overlooked the small back yard. Stuart had the room to the left. I used to ride my motorbike up and down those cobbled streets in later years. It's still the same even now if you go there.

Jon's mother, Kathleen, also contributed to the upkeep of the family by working in the mills, as many had done before her. In the nineteenth century, the cotton trade had revolutionised and transformed the area. Cotton was moved by road, rail and river around the country and a century on, the giant industrial mills remained the principal employer for many in Lancashire. They were huge factories with hundreds of workers, spread across several massive floors, but with very poor working conditions. They were noisy, dangerous places, with scant regard given to the health and safety of the workers. Nevertheless, they were places where women could work hard, support their families, and be a part of the community.

It was a hard life with little spare money for the Andersons. But Jon's parents did have a means of escape from the grind of day-to-day living, in the unlikely form of ballroom dancing. They were talented as well as passionate about dancing, becoming East Lancashire County champions. Jon recalls the many cups and awards his parents won, which were proudly displayed on the mantelpiece over the fireplace at home. Although his parents were not musicians, it was clear that this theatrical part of their lives helped inspired him to pursue his career in music. Jon, as a very young child, recalls seeing his father on stage. He specifically remembers that he wore a kilt and was telling jokes, noting that entertaining people could be enjoyable, even at such an early age.

Time for School

Johnny attended St. John's Infants School, on Maudsley Street, not far from Norfolk Street in Accrington. He was a happy student, receiving good reports from his teachers, who said that Jon fitted in well at school. It does, however, appear that Jon liked to sing a lot, to the point that he would be told off. Surprisingly, though, he didn't display any real interest or talent in musical instruments. More interested in drawing, Johnny was reportedly a likeable young man, and friendly to his classmates. One of his teachers, Mrs Smith, recalls Jon, describing him as 'A lovely looking little boy with a happy disposition.'

Jon shared his memories of his old school and the surrounding area of Accrington when revisiting the town with his wife, Jane, in 1994. He visited the Accrington Stanley stadium, recalling:

> I remember running on here in 1955 – I was a mascot for Accrington Stanley. They got thrown out of the league because they went bankrupt. It sounds a bit like my life, really!

Jon remembered an occasion at school, during a pantomime, when he got up on stage and sang 'Rock around the Clock'. The singing bug clearly gripped Jon at an early age. He would always attempt to hit the high notes, but to no avail. Jon remembers:

> In the 1970s I was singing top E. I can't believe I was hitting all those notes all the way through. When I was young, I could never sing falsetto.

At choir, I would try to sing these top notes. The teacher would say 'Anderson, for God's sake, shut up! Turn it down or you can sing outside of the room!'

School's out!

Although Jon enjoyed school, it didn't fulfil him. He recalled his days at secondary school in a 1972 interview:

The school was called St. Christopher's Secondary Modern, it was a newly opened school when I went there. The school did nothing for me. They didn't seem to have any idea of what should be taught to children. They didn't tell you what the world out there was really like.

For Jon, by the age of fifteen, he knew his priorities lay elsewhere, and that he was needed at home to help with the family. He tried attending an agricultural college in St Michael's, but hated it, in spite of the years he had spent working on the farm. He was back at the family home within a week.

While still attending school, Jon had worked on the local Huncoat Hall Farm, becoming adept at all the farm duties, including mucking out the animals. This taught Jon the benefits of hard work, leading to an early understanding that it was the key to success in any field.

Jon recalled:

Me and my brother did a milk round for a local farmer. However, we had to go into the field and catch the cows, and milk them – it was a free workout too, moving the milk churns. That's when we started singing together: Everly Brothers, Buddy Holly. I worked on the farm getting up at 5.30am and did that from the age of ten, I was doing that till the age of seventeen. Memories of delivering milk, two pints to number 202, one bottle of cream, corner house, and so on - hands like icicles.

Interestingly, house number 202 was the home of another famous Accrington resident, writer Jeannette Winterson. Lower down at 139 was his mate David Lloyd, who played county cricket for Lancashire, and Test and One Day International cricket for England. David also played semi-professional football for Accrington Stanley.

A local Accrington resident called Taddy recalled:

Jon worked in a big hole in the ground, (Whinney Hill Quarry), with a big lad known at the time as Big D, when they were both in their teenage years. He would have been thirteen or fourteen at the time. His first job was at the Nori brickworks, where a lifelong friend of mine taught him how to turn the ginny wagons that ran under Whinney Hill from the now known as Whinney Hill quarry. The friend always remarks that his main claim to fame was instructing the half of Jon and Vangelis how to work in a big hole in the ground!

In the end, the love you take is equal to the love you make.
Paul McCartney

The Anderson family was a tight-knit one, with regular family gatherings at which music always played a part. They regularly listened to classical music, plus modern and dance music, because of mum and dad's love of dancing.

The author interviewed Tony in 2015, who remembered:

I was influenced by all the family, especially mum and dad, who exposed us to music and dance. My parents were champion dancers, so music was always in the house – we couldn't escape it! It was the days of the gramophone; our first family gramophone was a wind-up one, playing whatever was going on at the time, including songs like 'Little Brown Jug'. That was the first record I ever got, that one and Cyril Stapleton, who wrote 'Bugle Boy'. But then it went on from there, to Lonnie Donegan: also known as the 'King of Skiffle'. And then Elvis.

Long before The Warriors, we had what we called the Little John's Skiffle Group. Jon played the old washboard. I played the guitar a lot, though I hadn't a clue how to tune a guitar, so I didn't play any chords at all. I just hit the thing and sang as loud as I could, and Jon would join in. We had another mate who was also called John, who was very tall. That's why we called ourselves, The Little John group because my brother Jon is small, while Big John must have been six-foot-plus! This was before we ever got into The Warriors. I remember we cut a disc at someone's house – Jon Anderson's first recording! It was one of these discs where we sat in the front room, and he was in the next room with a gramophone, and honestly, it was one of these things where you peel the top off a 78 rpm record, a sort of a plastic covering, and you put the needle on and you've got just one take. And that was it, and we had that 78-size record for some time. I don't know what happened to it in the end, but that would be worth a mint now, wouldn't it? It was called 'Don't You Rock Me Daddy-O'. It would be fantastic to find that 78. Somebody's got it, probably in the bottom of a drawer. Jon would remember it. We often laugh about it. He's probably got it.

The birth of British Skiffle was marked by the release of two tracks by Chris Barber's Jazz Band, under the name of The Lonnie Donegan Skiffle Group, in late 1955. By the following year, the genre had really taken off, as Donegan's high-tempo version of Lead Belly's 'Rock Island Line' became the first debut record to go gold in Britain, selling over a million copies worldwide. Skiffle rapidly came to be seen as the main gateway into the music scene.

Another big musical influence was jazz, as Tony recalled:

My elder brother, Stuart, was a jazz fanatic. Every Sunday afternoon, after Sunday school, we would meet in the front room, and Stuart would get his music out. So, we had this diet of music: Johnny Dankworth, Gerry

> Mulligan, Stan Kenton. Whoever it was he was into, he would just play them all the time, and we would get into it, and we'd listen, listen, listen. Then eventually I started feeding my records in: 'Can we listen to Elvis, can you put it on?' Because we only had one record player, you had to make it known if you wanted your music on next.

Jon's siblings, Stuart, Tony and Joy would all join in with the singing, as well as taking their turn on the family piano. The front room was Jon's first stage, while his mates often popped over to join in the fun. Skiffle music was new and easily replicated, thanks to its basic construction and the instruments that were needed to play it. Home-made instruments like a washboard, a tea chest, a makeshift guitar, pots and pans from the kitchen and even a whistle, were all played by the likes of Tommy Steele, Cliff Richard and the Loni Donegan. Artists were airing this new sound on television programmes like the BBC's *Six Five Special* and ITVs *Oh Boy*, providing the first TV platforms for them to do so. Local bands that were hoping to be the next pop stars included the Rocking Vicars and the Lionel Morton Four.

We're all going on a Summer Holiday

For the struggling Andersons of the late 1950s, any holidays would be short and located not far from home. Money was not plentiful, so a long walk on the Coppice in Accrington – where Jon, Tony and Stuart spent many a happy hour – was like a mini holiday for them. They would just mess around, playing football, dreaming of better times and football stardom. The time away was brief and for the brothers a real treat came in the form of The Manor House building in Chorley, which came with a chalet where Tony and Jon spent time having a break. Although not a standard holiday location, the Town provided a welcome respite for those with not much money, and the Andersons would visit for up to ten days.

As many teenagers did at the time, Jon tried to earn a bit of money in whichever way he could. He would work in the mornings, delivering milk before school, and did a paper round on Saturdays, earning two or three pounds per week. He also started to work in a printing company that did art reproductions, staying with them for a year or two. Jon even tried working at Burco – a metal spinning factory, although he did not remain long. Although there were plenty of local jobs available at the time, Jon preferred to sing.

Jon was a big football fan, the Lancashire area being home to some of the country's biggest and most successful football clubs at the time, including Manchester United, Liverpool, Everton, Bolton Wanderers, Blackpool and Preston North-End. Preston's star player was the legendary Tom Finney. However, Jon was a loyal supporter of his local team Accrington Stanley. Regardless of whether they were in the upper or lower leagues, you tended to support your local side back then, unlike today, when you can follow a team from another country at the touch of a button, without ever needing to see them play in the flesh. Dreaming big,

Jon pursued a career with his Accrington football team, but he was rejected due to his diminutive stature - Jon is five feet five inches. As Tony recalls:

> Jon was into his football, big-time. He was really into playing for Accrington Stanley. He wanted to play professionally for them, but he was too small, so he used to get on the pitch about five minutes before the match and kick the ball about. The crowd would cheer him - I think he liked that feeling, so he became their mascot. I wasn't into football as much as him, but we used to sell match day programs together, at the bottom of Avenue Parade. 'Programmes, come and get your programmes', we'd shout.

Jon remains a fan of the club to this day. When I interviewed him, he immediately recognised my Northern accent.

'Where are you from?' he asked me.

'Bolton,' I replied.

'Bolton Wanderers… not as good as Accrington Stanley.' This was Jon's response, although he conceded to me that Bolton Legend, Nat Lofthouse was a great player.

Football matches in the 1950s and 1960s drew huge crowds. The terraces would be packed, as television was so limited in its scope, being a relatively new phenomenon in the UK. The matchday pint, a cigarette and a meat and potato pie were the staple diet of the working football fan.

Franny Franks, a school friend of Jon Anderson, and a teenage band member of the Accrington group, the Dappers, recalled his memories of Jon in 2016:

> I went to the same school as Tony Alveston from the first line-up of The Warriors. We played football together, and he was in my class. I lived in Barnfield, and Jon Anderson's family lived nearby - Jon went to St Christopher's school. Tony Alveston, though, was a real character. He was a bit big-headed, but nice with it. At one point, they were picking the under 16s inter-league side. Jon Anderson liked to play football a lot, and we were mates. They picked me for the side and not Jon. He wasn't happy about it, I can tell you, but there you go. Jon did go on to better things!

To this day Accrington remains a special place for Jon and his family. On their return in the 1990s, Jon and Jane explored their various childhood haunts. Jon became particularly nostalgic when rambling across the moors of nearby Pendle, from where it is said that the witches came. The Pendle Witches were twelve local women who were tried for witchcraft in the 17th Century. Sitting on the Coppice hill, overlooking Accrington and the surrounding countryside, Jon spoke of his love for the history and people of Lancashire, and of how this tied in with his fascination with the witches of local legend.

> They were really beautiful people, women with knowledge, who reminded me of the witches of the earth and nature and the healing powers of nature.

Above: Kathleen Anderson, probably taken in the late 1970s. Note the uncanny family resemblance! *(Tony Anderson)*

For Jon, returning to the moors stirred something within himself, and the childhood memories started to flood back: remembering school plays, the farm and football, all of them important in shaping the man he became. His roots kept Jon grounded throughout his life, as can be seen in the 1994 video of his return to Accrington, in which Jane and Jon are seen eating a traditional Friday evening meal of fish and chips, with Jon asking: 'Where's the newspaper wrapping?'

Living in California, Jon would become far removed geographically from his hometown, but he continues to keep up with the local football scores for his beloved Accrington, and when on tour in the UK likes to spend some time back in the town seeing family, friends and his old haunts.

2. Everydays

Following the demise of the musical family group get-togethers, in the late 1950s, skiffle, rock and roll and jazz became hugely popular. Like many young men of his age, when Jon finished his schooling, he wanted to travel further afield than Blackpool (a seaside town, some 30 miles away, which was the most popular location for the working class throughout Northern England), and do something different with his life. Music seemed the perfect means by which to do so. Among the local music community were the teenagers who went on to form The Warriors.

As founding member Derek Thornhill recalls:

> I was one of the originals who started The Strangers and The Warriors with the Alveston brothers, Tony and Ian. We all went through school together, up until they left school at sixteen. After that, we set about trying to form a band. I remember we once played together without a bass player, in the early days, when we were setting up the band. But we weren't any good!

The Alveston brothers had some instruments and wanted to put a band together. They took on a friend of Derek's called John Howarth, who played guitar. They were looking for a drummer, and Derek says: 'I was the only one with seven and sixpence in my pocket. No one else had enough to buy the drum kit, so I became the drummer because I had the money!'

The Strangers - the very earliest incarnation of the band that would become The Warriors - seems to have been born in the final months of 1959. They

Above: The Strangers just prior to changing their name to The Warriors. The drum head reads Gene Derek, a play on words as Derek Thornhill liked the famous big band drummer Gene Krupa. Photo taken at the Accrington Springhill Youth Club, 1961. From left to right: Ian Alveston, Tony Alveston, John Howarth, Derek Thornhill and David Foster. *(Derek Thornhill)*

were teenagers, young men searching for a future, knocking around the music shops and streets, with little to excite them but the thought of rock and roll stardom. They practised at home or anywhere they were allowed to. They learned their instruments and sometimes played in front of small audiences – it kept them moving forward.

Still called The Strangers, after about three months, they did a handful of gigs locally. At this stage they were copying all the hits, sounding rather like the Shadows, but with a little with a bit of everyone else from that era. At first, the band got away with this name. However, Derek admits:

> The original name The Strangers is what we really wanted, but unfortunately, we found out there was already another band of the same name, so we stopped calling ourselves that.

It is possible to see how young they were in the rare pictures that exist from that time. The earliest one of the bands shows the cross-over from The Strangers to The Warriors. They became The Warriors when John Howarth came up with the band's name and design for the bass drum head, a cartoon with some warriors on it. The Warriors' name came from John, who thought it was strong and memorable and it looked good on a drum kit, too. John Howarth was by all accounts well-liked. He was a fun character and a good player.

Little else is known about John other than that his family ran the local ironmonger's shop in Accrington. Derek recalls:

> He lived above the oil shop on Higher Antley Street. He was a nice bloke but John fell out with a few people because he was a stickler for stuff, and if it wasn't his way, then it wasn't the right way. He had a strong sense of self, but it could cause problems.

Ian Alveston remembers John as an immensely talented musician:

> John was a terrific guitarist and really should have gone onto much bigger things. He was very accomplished and used to teach guitar too. I remember at one of the gigs - most likely at the Accrington Conservative Club which was the best and most packed of the venues we played at - John cut his finger on something, but he played on with blood gushing all over the place on his guitar and the stage. He was a real trooper – the show must go on.

Another musician involved at the time was Lennie, of the group Lennie and The Teenbeats. He vividly recalls the hours he spent helping out The Warriors at a later date:

> I was the drummer of the band, and I introduced The Warriors to the dance halls where we played, by asking the managers if they could play during our interval. A work colleague and friend of mine, Nelson Thornhill, asked me if I could help The Warriors. I introduced his son Derek to his first drum kit, from the Reidy's music store in Blackburn.

With the band up and running, they played a couple of times a week at the start, when they could - in schools, halls and the church.

Although David Foster was in the band a very long time, he was not there right at the beginning. David originally came from Liverpool, moving to Accrington in 1951, when his father began work at the English Electric Works based there. As a teenager, David was heavily influenced by the exploding rock and roll scene, inspired by musicians such as Buddy Holly and Elvis Presley. After much practising and listening to records, David became a good singer and bass player. He initially joined the band as a backing singer and bass player, but soon began to do more, writing songs and adding stronger vocals. With David on board the band started to improve. Having the bands' various parents to act as managers, it gave the lads more time to practice, the band gigged locally in Accrington and the nearby towns. The full line-up at this time was: David Foster (Fossy) on bass guitar and backing vocals, Tony Alveston (lead vocals), Ian Alveston (rhythm guitar), John Howarth (lead guitar), and Derek Thornhill. (Drums). David Foster fast became a real driving force in the fledgling band and became recognised as their unofficial leader. Ian Alveston fondly recalls the formative years of the band:

> I was interested in music from when I used to listen to it at home. We had an old guitar lying around the house, which I picked up and played. With The Warriors we quickly managed to get venues, and more kids would come to see us, having a good night out dancing. The most rewarding gigs were at the Accrington Conservative Club where we played Monday evening dance night. You would get hundreds of kids in, ready to dance the night away and sometimes a crowd up to a thousand would get in. The big dance floor would have all the girls in the middle dancing around their handbags! Around the sides, all the boys would circulate anti-clockwise all evening, until they had had enough drink to buck up the courage to join the girls in the middle to ask for a dance.

Derek and David Foster would always be working on the material the band should play, leading the way in track selection and performance. As everyone knew each other in the town, other singers or musician would often look to join in. One such singer was Pete Hibbert, from Mark Day and the Knights (Mark Day being Pete's stage name).

It was said by many that David Foster was smart, taking after his intelligent and studious father who worked in Clayton-le-Moors on the outskirts of Accrington as a designer and was involved in the building of the Lightning jet, the famous fighter jet developed in the 1950s. David saw the potential of a career in music: he was ambitious, and academically he was very bright. He was passionate about music in these early days. Recalling his very first gig at Marlborough Working Man's Club, David Foster remembered:

> Actually, it was a bit of a makeshift effort; we played three numbers, and then rehearsed the next three during the break. The younger members [of the club] enjoyed it, but the older ones thought we made too much noise.

The band were focused on refining their technique. For Derek, there had always been more to drumming than simply making a lot of noise:

> I was taught by a local guy called Phil Trent. Unfortunately, he got run over by a horse and cart and lost part of his finger. Once I had a good grasp of it all, I softened my playing of the drums. I wasn't a beat drummer, as such, I was more of a sophisticated drummer – I wasn't a 'bang' merchant. I think the early band had a different feel to the one later.

The band were practising as hard as they could. By late 1962, the line-up consisted of David on vocals and bass, Derek on drums, John Howarth on lead guitar, Ian playing rhythm guitar, Tony Alveston as the lead singer and Ken Borwick also singing. Ken fit the bill well enough for a time until the inevitable band fall-out came. Derek recalls:

> We played the working men's clubs, at around the time when Ken was getting married. His mind wasn't really on the job, and he went and pinched an amplifier for the wedding! We all needed it, and it just got messy then. We got that sorted out, but that was the end of him and the old Warriors' line-up.

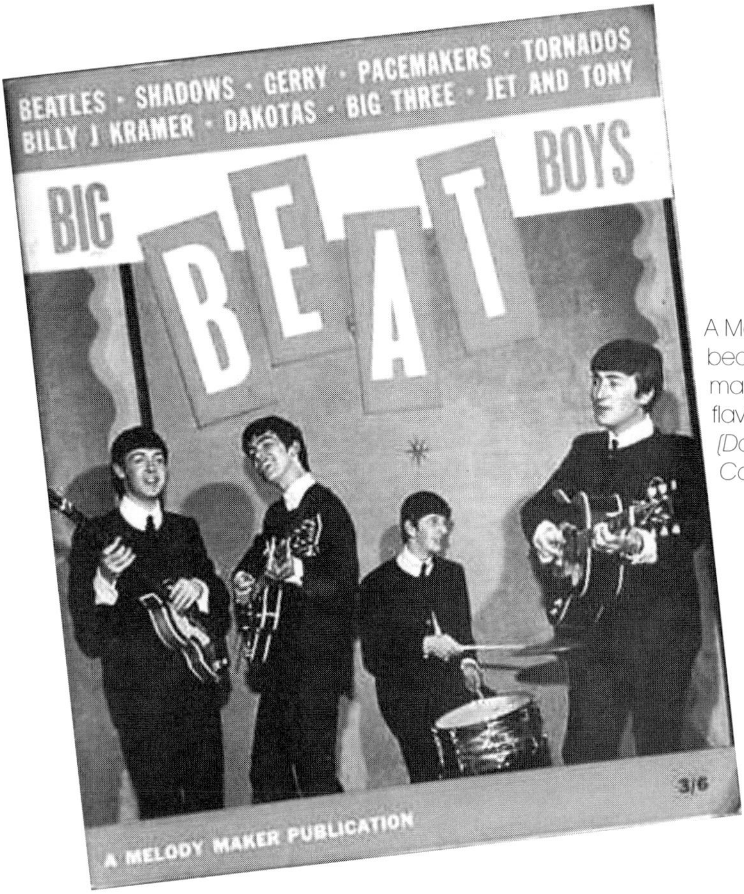

A Melody Maker beat scene magazine giving a flavour of the times. *(David Watkinson Collection)*

Another surprise change was that the Alveston brothers, with their exams coming up, decided that they were leaving too. 'Those were good, fun days,' Tony Alveston recalls. 'My brother and I were there at the start, just young lads looking to have a good time and playing some music. Ian was very good and really into his music. This has stayed with him all his life.'

October 1962 would prove to be an eventful month for the band, and it was a month in which the entire music world would change forever. The music charts at the time were full of relatively safe and unchallenging songs including The Beach Boys 'Surfin Safari', 'Sherry', by The Four Seasons, and Elvis Presley's 'Return to Sender'. Then The Beatles released their first single, 'Love Me Do', and the music industry would never be the same again. The North West of England – indeed, just about everyone who owned a radio – would soon be enthralled with the Fab Four. The Beatles were managed by Brian Epstein, who came to represent the archetypal new breed of band manager and had allegedly gone out and bought 10,000 copies of their first single to ensure it had a place in the top twenty. The commercial awareness of their manager aside, however, there is no doubt The Beatles were destined for stardom. When a young Jon Anderson, along with his brother, Tony, went to see the Beatles at the Cavern Club in Liverpool he, like so many others, was hooked. 'I just wanted to be a Beatle,' he would later recall.

Meanwhile, with John Howarth suffering from asthma and other health problems, the recent upheaval persuaded him it was time to move on. This action was something that would be repeated time and time again with The Warriors, the line-up changing regularly over the years. To Yes fans this will be very familiar too - Yes would do much the same throughout their fifty-year career. Yet these changes in personnel never seemed to hold The Warriors back. On the contrary they each change tended to lead to the band's next phase of development, with the new members enhancing the band's capabilities and sound.

Having said this, when the search began for replacements for over half the band in one go, Derek and David knew it would not be an easy task. Derek says:

> So, with all these crazy changes happening everywhere for The Warriors, we were left with me and David Foster. I did wonder if carrying on was the way to go, but with David on board, we had a great foundation. Mike Brereton was found by word of mouth. We asked around, trying to find out who was looking for a gig or a band. We met Mike, a guitar player and singer who could harmonise, and he was easy going – he joined us.

Mike, now in the band, was asked if he knew anyone else, and he said he had heard about someone in Accrington who was teaching guitar, a really good player, called Rodney Hill. Rod read music and was particularly accomplished at rhythm guitar and chords. He joined them, and this formed a basis of a three-guitar line-up plus a drummer. For Mike, it was a tough adjustment initially. He recalls being helped greatly by the presence of David Foster:

> When I first joined The Warriors, I had never played a song. I had only ever played instrumentals. I taught myself to play, and taught others, too, but they

Left: Tony Anderson in London. *(David Watkinson Collection)*
Above: Tony back stage. *(David Watkinson Collection)*

were doing songs with words, which I had never done. So, when we were on stage, David would shout out the chords to me – C and G minor, B flat, and so on. That's how I got through the first month, really. Until I eventually got the hang of it, I kind of relied on David.

Two other new members would also join The Warriors at around this time: Gordon 'Chinny' Kenyon, and Tony Anderson. Interviewed in 2015 for the very first time, Gordon was happy to talk about his time in the band.

I joined The Warriors overnight. They'd lost someone - Ken, I think - and I knew the lads well, so I joined the band for a while. I was a vocalist in the band with Tony. I was an apprentice hairdresser when I was playing in the group; I was a backup vocalist with them, part-time. I was doing music on the side, something to do in the evening, mostly. I was in two local bands before that, The Black Cats and The Vikings. We didn't travel very far. We were in Bolton, Bury, Manchester – they were just local gigs. It was only in about 1961-62 that we finally felt confident enough to branch out from the local venues we'd been playing at. We continued to play gigs in Accrington, but we began to spread out to other towns and cities like Sale, Blackburn and further afield.

The Warriors began playing at venues like The Boneyard Club and the Palais De Dance in Bolton's town centre. The Boneyard was on Manchester Road, opposite Bolton railway station - later, it turned into a music shop called

Wood's Pianos & Organs of Bolton. The Boneyard was decked out spookily, with coffins for tables. It later became the Caroline Lounge and was one of the best places to go, with people coming from all over to Bolton.

The Accrington of the early 1960s had become a lively town with a thriving music scene, with many clubs in which teenagers would dance the night away. There was the West End Youth Club, the Stanhill pub for pool and cards and Rhydings Park for football, crazy golf or live music. They were entertained by Jinx, Ian Alveston (The Warriors) and Phil Kubilius. R & B and blues jamming sessions took place in venues like the Derby Club or the Cavern while the Mecca was also popular, with groups such as The Searchers, Freddie and the Dreamers and The Hollies all playing there. It was after all Beatlemania time, so the girls screamed throughout these performances - there was mass-hysteria all night. The Warriors fancied a bit of this action, and this was to happen later in their career in Bolton, and even in Scotland when the band travelled further afield.

Above: Johnny back stage. *(David Watkinson Collection)*

In January 1963, the band asked Tony Anderson to audition for the singer position, at the Marlboro Club. They had heard he was mad about Elvis Presley and not only based his look on him but loved singing Elvis numbers. He wore a black shirt, black leather jacket and trousers and everyone thought he was so cool. As all he could sing was Elvis, that is what the band ended up playing. One of Tony's favourite songs was Elvis's 'A Fool Such As I', and it is very likely that this was one of the tracks with which he auditioned. Tony officially joined The Warriors on the 25 February 1963.

Although the band didn't have much money, the sense of camaraderie was always there, and they were virtually a family. The addition of Tony to the band made a huge difference. He was a good-looking young man, as well as an excellent and experienced performer. Moreover, it led to the addition of another member who would prove even more important in the band's history – his younger brother, Jon. There are many stories as to how Tony and Jon came to join the band, according to Rodney Hill:

> Gordon brought Tony along when we were practising at the Marlborough Club. We looked at this guy, and he had a leather cap on and a leather jacket.

Above: Jon and Rod at home in Accrington. *(David Watkinson Collection)*

> He looked like Marlon Brando. He had sideburns, and he looked rough, so nervously we all said he could join the band. Yeah, no problem… just don't hurt us. Then he sang, and we thought, 'bloody hell, he's good'. Then when Gordon left, leaving the music game completely, Tony asked if his brother Jon could sing and come and do some stuff.

The band were doing well, and changes to the band members only seemed to help them progress, so they decided to go professional. For Gordon, however, this was a step too far. He was a hairdresser by trade and music was a fun thing on the side. He decided he wanted to concentrate on hairdressing full time, so he stepped back, and Jon stepped up to the microphone. This was a benefit, making the band a better unit with brothers Jon and Tony singing close harmonies.

Mike remembers Jon's audition, 'We wanted to do Everly Brothers' songs, and this guy came over to Rod's house, and that was his audition really. We waited till little Jon buggered off, and then we had a vote on it, so he joined us.'

Another version of the story comes from David Foster:

> We knew his brother Tony, he was a rocker, and he had a Norton bike and all the leathers. We knew Tony could sing well and then he told us that his brother Jon was a singer too. So, I waited for Jon to deliver the milk to my house and asked him to join the group.

Tony himself recalls how first he, then his brother, came to join The Warriors.

> As boys, Jon was always a natural harmoniser to me. We used to sing Everly Brothers songs at night all the time. When we delivered milk, we used to sing out loud walking down the streets. I even waltzed a lady up and down her path, when delivering the milk one day. Jon and I went to an agricultural

show nearby in Lancashire on my motorbike. On the way home, it started pouring down, our wellies were overflowing, and of course, we sang 'I'll do my crying in the rain!'

I joined The Warriors when I was working on a farm, and I had a motorbike. There was no way I'd have gone for an audition or jam or whatever; I wouldn't have done it. I was just very shy. I couldn't have done an interview of any kind.

Rod adds:

Gordon asked Tony one day if he could have a lift on his bike. Tony agreed, and he went with Gordon to a pub. A soon as he saw the microphones, he was in his own world. Tony joined The Warriors and soon after Gordon's hairdressers' shop took off. He decided he could not do both hairdressing and music, so he gave up music. Tony asked the guys if he could bring his brother, Jon, along because he was great at singing. And that's how Jon got in.

The start of Jon's musical career began differently according to Rodney Hill, who remembers:

Jon was standing in my doorway in some big working boots, saying, 'My brother said I can join the band?' Gordon and I all went to the same school. The first time I ever remember seeing Jon and Gordon was in the art room at 4 pm, in the art club. I was a bit older than them. That was how I remember him, with his school uniform on.

Rodney says that Tony was a real character:

He was the gaffer (boss) really, he just knew stuff and was more experienced. It's thanks to Tony that I learned about Chet Atkins. Tony was a grammar school lad and listened to lots of music. A great guy, very intelligent, we used to give him more money because it was tough for him with a family. We didn't want to lose him – he was the leader in the band, leading in a good way. He'd done more. He used to go to the Ace Cafe in North London with all his biker mates. He would tell us about riding back from London taking over three hours in the rain, snow, or hail, on his Norton Dominator bike!

Every musical 'great' has to start somewhere, and with Wembley Arena a few years away yet, Jon stepped up to the mike-stand for his first ever gig on 11 May 11 1963, at Burnley Padiham Working Men's Club.

When interviewed in the UK by *Prog* magazine about these early gigs, Jon vividly recalled his nervousness at performing in some of the seedy places such as the Devonshire club.

We came on after the bingo but just before the stripper. I was a young lad, about seventeen years old. It freaked me out when this woman walked past us naked. It was enough to put you off sex forever - she was frightening!

Above: An early signature by Jon. *(David Watkinson Collection)*

Left: The Chelsea-type boot from Shaftesbury Avenue, London. *(David Watkinson Collection)*

In these formative years for the band, the possibilities felt endless as the influence of the Beatles began to take hold of the teenagers everywhere. It wasn't just Jon and Tony who idolised The Beatles, but everyone. Many years later Jon met Paul McCartney.

> I shook his hand, and I couldn't talk! I used to go on stage thinking, I'm Paul McCartney. I'm going to sing 'I'm Down'. I used to scream it out. I enjoyed the idea of the girls and the travelling. There was an element of escapism, I think.

Expanding their repertoire, the Anderson brothers worked well together - no other band had that sound. They also added a couple of instrumentals in their set to break it up a little. The first song Jon learnt with the band was an Eddie Cochran song which they played it at the Padiham Club.

'I was standing there singing and no one was taking a blind bit of notice, just drinking and talking.' Jon remembers. But he loved the whole atmosphere of it all and stayed with the band, learning more songs. Jon remembers being the band dogsbody in the beginning.

> They said all you got to do is carry this, and put that together, and carry the drums. And as a second singer, you had to carry everything - a dogsbody, as you call it. Just being in a band and playing gigs in and around Accrington and places like Blackburn Mecca ballroom - those early years were really the most interesting times. All we wanted to do was learn and get some Cuban heeled boots! The Beatles had them, so we wanted them.

Jon joining the band made a big difference, the band's fortunes began to improve and then everyone had to get a little bit more serious. With more

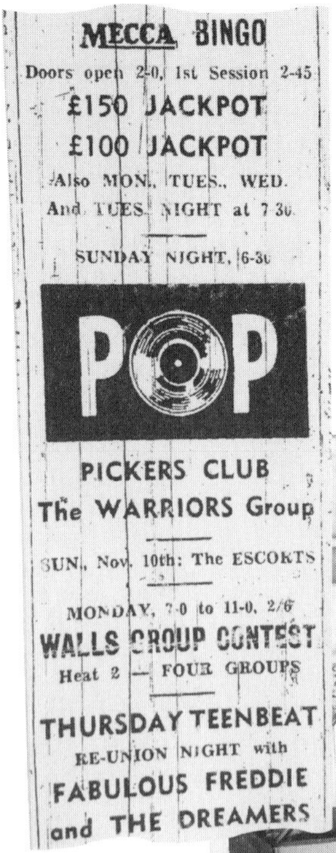
MECCA BINGO
Doors open 2-0, 1st Session 2-45
£150 JACKPOT
£100 JACKPOT
Also MON., TUES., WED.
And TUES. NIGHT at 7 30.
SUNDAY NIGHT, 6-30

POP

PICKERS CLUB
The WARRIORS Group
SUN., Nov. 10th: The ESCORTS
MONDAY, 7-0 to 11-0, 2/6
WALLS GROUP CONTEST
Heat 2 — FOUR GROUPS
THURSDAY TEENBEAT
RE-UNION NIGHT with
FABULOUS FREDDIE
and THE DREAMERS

Left: Local paper cutting for an early Warriors gig. *(David Watkinson Collection)*

Right: The big venue – The Bolton Palais – packs them in on another night. *(David Watkinson Collection)*

THE TREKKERS

PALAIS, BOLTON
TONIGHT
BIG BEAT NIGHT
THEY'RE BACK
THE WARRIORS
TOMORROW NIGHT
LONG EVENING DANCE
8 p.m.—1 a.m.
Tickets on sale until noon
SUNDAY NIGHT — From Belfast
THE PEOPLE

Above: Jon looking incredibly young as they wait in the working men's club for the call to play. *(Garth Dawson – David Watkinson Collection)*

Left: Tony back stage with the silver suit hanging up. *(David Watkinson Collection)*

Right: Jon on the far left here with Dave in the middle and Tony on the right performing at the Blackburn Mecca. *(David Watkinson Collection)*

discipline and focus the band strove for more practice, more gigs and more money. Tony adds:

> When later the lads from Bury joined: the drummer, Ian Wallace, and then Brian Chatton, the band was just fantastic. We supported lots of big names and then recorded at Decca. It was a good band but the problem was we were just in a sense, a copy band. We could do lots of material, and whatever we did, we did well, but we had no original material as such. We weren't writing. It just wasn't going to go far.

The Warriors had ambition, and they were committed to making the most of their talent. Rodney praised Dave Foster's drive in particular.

> He was great. Let's face it, in the beginning, it was his band. He was a founder member and his family backed him, which helped a lot. Dave was a very good bass player. He could come across as arrogant in those days. But you know what? He really could do it well: play well. He knew his stuff.

With a hectic schedule for the band, it fell to Rodney to keep a record of bookings and contacts, phone numbers and addresses, and to make calls. 'I used to do all the bookings for the gigs and keep the only record of it all in diaries I had. We worked proper hard at it all, they were long days.'

Tony Anderson admitted that although Jon went on to be a huge star with Yes, during this period, Jon was just the harmony vocalist – it was Tony himself who was the lead singer. However, Jon certainly showed glimpses of his ability, as Tony points out:

> I do remember one time when we were playing at Mecca Ballroom, and Jon asked to do a solo song. I remember that when he was singing on his own, he made such an impression, especially with one of the managers who was looking after the band. I think you could see the cogs going around with them thinking that he was good on his own and had a nice voice.

Not making it in the business was a distinct possibility, given the number of young people with similar ambitions. Music as a career was never considered a likely, or even a possible way to make a living, until the breakthrough of The Beatles.

The band played the working-men's sporting clubs and small halls in and around the Lancashire. The competition between new bands was fierce, as they fought for the best gigs – and the girls. Among The Warriors' main rivals were The Lionel Morton Four, Herman's Hermits and Atlanta Roots. The Warriors would play just about anywhere at that time, just to scrape a living, playing music. Heavily influenced by the big names of the time, they played covers of big hits to a quickly-built fan base. The Warriors did have the benefit of being unusual in that they had two good frontmen in Tony and Jon Anderson.

For Jon, one thing he will never forget is the sheer volume of gigs the band had to play to keep afloat.

WALSHS Ford MAIN DEALERS

Lancashire

Evening Telegraph

No. 23,821 THURSDAY, OCTOBER 31, 1963 4d

The Warriors 'make a hit'

HUNDREDS of teenage girls skipped lunch today so that they could scream all the way through their break. For they were watching The Warriors, the beat group which won the "Lancashire Evening Telegraph's Big Chance contest, singing and twisting at a special appearance at Mullard's Blackburn Works canteen. When the screams, stamping and clapping had died down after the show, the group got a surprise gift—a cake from "M" block girls, who followed their climb through the heats of the Big Chance contest. Dorothy Hester, who made the presentation along with Pauline Cash and Aileen Darroch, told The Warriors: "I'm sure you can get to the top."

● PICTURE shows Tony Anderson, the group's leader with the cake. From left: Derek Thornhill, Michael Brereton, Dorothy Hester, Dave Foster, Tony Anderson, Rodney Hill, Pauline Cash, Aileen Darroch, John Anderson.

Above: Front page news with some girls and a cake after local success in a competition. Jon is on the far right. *(Lancashire Evening Telegraph)*

Mr Gordon McIntosh, Promotions Manager of the "Lancashire Evening Telegraph" presents trophies to the winners of the talent contest after the finals at Blackburn Locarno. Left to right: Miss Eileen Nicholls (of Don and Donna); Mr G. McIntosh; Tony Anderson (leader of the Warriors Rhythm Group); Don Williams (of Don and Donna).

Warriors win Big Chance

ACCRINGTON rhythm group The Warriors and duettists Don and Donna from Wigan have won their "Big Chance" of fame and Blackburn Orphanage has been given a sum of money—all as a result of the final of the "Lancashire Evening Telegraph"-Mecca Dancing talent contest of the year!

The cash gift came from "Big Chance '63" Beat group section winners The Warriors. It was part of their prize and they decided to give it to the the Orphanage because, as leader Tony Anderson (20) said: "We did not enter this contest for monetary gain—it was for the prestige value."

'Telegraph' trophies

Talent section winners in last night's final at the Locarno Ballroom, St Peter Street, Blackburn, Don and Donna, sang "Wreck of the Old John B," and, like the Warriors, received "Lancashire Evening Telegraph" trophies, and will get a recording test, television audition, and ballroom bookings.

Runners-up in the beat section were: The Dynamites from Haslingden (second), the Phabulous Phantoms also from Haslingden (third). Both received long-playing records, cash and ballroom bookings.

Second on the talent side was George Livesey, a pipe fitter's mate from Brierfield who sang "In the Beginning," and third was David Reeve, a "pop" vocalist from Blackburn. They also received LPs and cash.

Prizes were presented by Mr Gordon McIntosh, Promotions Manager of the "Lancashire Evening Telegraph."

The Warriors, comprising lead guitarist Mike Brereton (19), rhythm guitarist Rodney Hill (17), drummer Derek Thornhill (18), bass player David Foster (17) and vocalists Tony (20) and Johnny Anderson (19), played "Sabre Dance," "Will You Still Love Me Tomorrow," and "She Loves You."

Accrington boy, a

THE WARRIORS, from Accrington—formed only three months ago. Now — the Continent.

ROY LONDON and the Nightriders—have been playing "beat" for 18 months.

An extra day of life

Mrs Mary Voight (80), died at Willard, Ohio, 20 hours after an undertaker, who was about to embalm her, discovered that she was alive.

A doctor said that her heart might have been jolted into temporary action when the ambulance taking her to the undertaker's struck a bump in the

FROM PUBS TO THE EUROPEAN CLUBS

ELEVEN young melodymakers from Accrington and Blackburn will shortly be giving up their jobs to make a 12-month tour of two Continental countries—as professional musicians.

'Sweater'

Above: News of both The Warriors and Blackburn's The Nightriders embarking on European jaunts. *(Evening Telegraph)*

Right: A happy Tony Anderson with the Big Chance trophy. *(Lancashire Evening Telegraph – David Watkinson Collection)*

We used to play the Beachcomber Club in Bolton every week, driving everybody crazy. It went on for about five years. We travelled around Scotland, Wales and all over England, north and south. Then we went to Germany.

Looking back at some of those defining moments, Jon, speaking in 2015, said:

We were rehearsing one day in Avenue Parade, in a club. Two guys from Manchester came to see us. They were salesmen types. Apparently, they had figured out how to get a record in the charts, and they were going to make The Warriors into stars with a hit and get us onto TV. They invited the band to Manchester the following week for an audition and to meet the people who were going to finance them. There was much excitement at this prospect until Tony reminded them that they had already booked a gig at Padiham Working Men's Club in Burnley. The band had been seen three times before by these agents - these salesman backers - but they wanted one more free audition gig. The backers asked them to cancel it, but Tony would not do that, saying they had to honour a gig and get the money in. This led to these guys becoming angry, and they told The Warriors to forget it, they would find another band who wanted to become stars.

When nineteen-year-old Jon Anderson was asked by the local Lancashire paper what instruments he played, alongside being the band's joint lead vocalist, Jon said he would play anything he could get his hands on. Jon would go on to play the tambourine and learned both the saxophone and guitar. Ten years later, Jon Anderson would amaze fans with his epic solo album, *Olias of Sunhillow*, on which he would play all the instruments,

A packed house again for the band, with Jon furthest away. *(Garth Dawson – David Watkinson Collection)*

including the harp, in the manner of Mike Oldfield's seminal work, *Tubular Bells*. For now, however, he would mainly have to be content with bashing a tambourine in time with the music.

The band were a tight and well-honed unit: they were the product of countless hours of perfecting their craft on tiny stages. Thoughts of playing at Madison Square Gardens, the iconic arena in New York, seemed a long way off. The Warriors very much lived day-to-day and focussed on one gig at a time. Listening to their earliest live recording 'I'm Down', one gets that sense that not only were they playing great dance music, but the band were also having a fantastic time. They performed with a solid belief in themselves and their music. They were teenagers having fun, but equally, they already played very well.

Far Left: A flyer poster with the band Warriors at the bottom of the bill. *(David Watkinson Collection)*
Left: *Beat Scene* Magazine advert. *(David Watkinson Collection)*

On the 22 and 23 of October 1963, the band played in a regional competition to find the best band in the area, and all of their practice paid off, with The Warriors finishing in first place. The band featured on the front page of local paper the *Lancashire Evening Telegraph*, where they are shown accepting a cake from the workforce at the Mullards factory, for winning the paper's *Big Chance* contest. This led to them being entered in a national competition, sponsored by the *New Musical Express*, and they reached the finals in London, ultimately finishing in fourth place. However, their lack of commitment to signing a contract with the promoter of the competition put their future in jeopardy.

In December 1963, Phil Solomon, a businessman, and the then head of Decca Records, Dick Rowe, watched The Warriors perform at their Salford Southern Sporting Club gig. Liking what they saw, the band were invited to London to audition in the following January, with the view to signing a record deal.

London would be an exciting trip for the band and a great start to the new year. They travelled down on the overnight train on Sunday, 12 January 1964, arriving early for their big day on the 13th. The band's drummer, Derek, recalls that this first audition went down brilliantly. The Warriors were signed to Decca on the 28 January 1964.

Follow-up dates were planned for recording sessions, scheduled to take place 26 - 27 February. Once again, after a long day travelling, the band played

services each fortnight, or once a month.

REV J F RICHARDSON

'Warriors to record their own songs'

After a seven-hour session at Manchester reco[rd]ing studios "The Warriors" have signed a 12-mo[nth] contract with the Decca Recording Company.

Next week, they will go to Decca's London studios, ... and Northern Counties f...

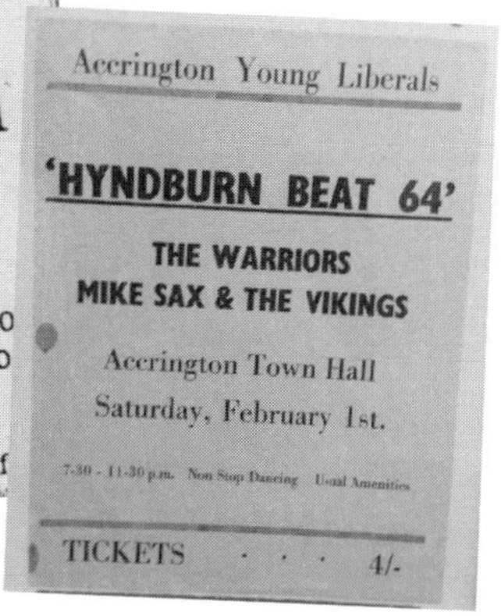

Above Left: Lancashire Evening Telegraph headline. *(David Watkinson Collection)*
Above Right: The earliest known poster or flyer. *(David Watkinson Collection)*

their usual set, which was well-received, and everyone was happy with the sessions. Pretty pleased with themselves, and obviously excited at the fact that they were seemingly on the verge of real success, they returned up north. In the following weeks, the band received a new song from Decca called 'You Came Along', written for them by Mason and Reed, professional songwriters. With renewed vigour, the band practised the song. However, a B-side was needed, and so Dave Foster made his first foray into songwriting, with 'Don't Make Me Blue'. This was written while travelling all the way to London, a few of the guys threw ideas in for it, but some years later, David Foster would describe it as 'absolute rubbish'!

This was undoubtedly a huge leap forward for the band, and the exciting news was reported in the *Accrington Observer* in an article on the 4 February 1964. Headlined 'Warriors to Record their Own Songs', it read:

> After a seven-hour recording session at a Manchester, Salford recording studio, The Warriors have signed a 12-month contract with the Decca Recording Company. Next week they will go to Decca's London studios where they will cut two discs, the first of which will be released in March. Now the band has turned semi-professional, this next step will be an important one. Three of the numbers they will record are with vocals written by themselves – 'I Found You', 'Don't Make Me Blue' and 'Will She', the fourth being an instrumental version of 'The Sabre Dance'. The road to success started a few months ago when they won the area final of the All-British 'Beat Championships', sponsored by the New Musical Express. Following that they went on to win the Lancashire and Northern Counties finals and secured fourth place in the national finals in December in London.

The band also recorded the song called, 'Anything that's a Part of You', or sometimes called 'Only You', going to a studio in Manchester, the Salford side of town, paying around twenty pounds for the privilege. They recorded an early Elvis track, 'Anyway You Want Me (That's The Way I'll Be)', making it on a soft plastic record, along with an acetate with the 'Sabre Dance' on it.

Left: The Warriors. Mike, Rod, Derek and Dave. *(Garth Dawson – David Watkinson Collection)*.

Below: Mike, Tony, Derek, Rod and Dave with Jon taking the photo at Trafalgar Square, London. *(David Watkinson Collection)*

Above: Mike, Dave, Rod, Derek and Jon wearing the 'W' enhanced jackets in London. *(David Watkinson Collection)*

Above Right & Left: Jon and Tony in Trafalgar Square London. *(David Watkinson Collection)*

The article continued that the band had been together for a year, and they listed the members, quaintly adding their addresses.

> David Foster (17), bass guitar and songwriter, 1 Downham Drive, Fern Gore; Rodney Hill (17), rhythm guitarist, 11 Pilot Street; Derek Thornhill (18) drummer, 2 Malham Avenue; Michael Brereton (19), lead guitarist, 34 Slaidburn Drive and Tony (21) and John (19) Anderson, the two vocalists, 13 Norfolk Street.

It noted that Nelson Thornhill and Edwin Foster were the group's joint managers. David Foster was quoted as saying, 'We have had a lucky break with winning the competition and we hope that this contract is just a promise of an even brighter future.'

However, with an uncanny similarity to the Yes of the future, the line-up began to break up, and the revolving door of personnel changes continued. Only a month after having been signed up to Decca Records and still gigging hard every week, Derek was finding the commitment and uncertainty of a musical career challenging. The Rock and Roll business was certainly fun, but tough work. If not fully committed, then one could easily become disillusioned.

Derek commented:

> One Saturday night when we'd finished playing, someone came to see us because they had heard we were good - the best in the area. It was when we were on with Wayne Fontane and The Mindbenders that showed how good and tight a band we were. We showed them up big time, we really did. Alan Lewis, a band promoter, wanted to see us at the Salford Devonshire Sporting Club in Manchester, to talk about making us successful.

Burnley Express
29th Feb 1964

MECCA
LOCARNO · BURNLEY
TO-NIGHT 7-0 to 11-45 — 5/6
LEAP YEAR
CUPID CARNIVAL
Cupid Charm to the Ladies and
ONE OF SOLID GOLD
TO-MORROW (SUNDAY
6-30 to 11-0 p.m. — Members 3/
Guests 4/- — Come early
THE WARRIORS
THURSDAY NEXT

CASINO CLUB
CROMPTON WAY,
BOLTON
Tonight all star cabaret show featuring as top of the bill that crazy comedy couple
SYD and EDDIE
Members Free. Guests 2/6
THURSDAY
Beat Night
Two Great Groups
The Warriors
Also
Three Dots and a Dash
Plus DJ Time and top twenty records,
Members 1/-. Guests 2/6
Don't forget next Monday
THE FOUR PENNIES
The Big Three

Left: Sunday night advert at the Mecca 6.30-11pm. *(David Watkinson Collection)*
Right: Mid placed in the pecking order in Bolton as the northern comedy act headline with local rivals featured coming next week. *(David Watkinson Collection)*

Packed house at the dance hall. *(David Watkinson Collection)*

It was Tony who reportedly declined the offer to play just one more time for Lewis. He had his reasons, of course, the importance of being paid to play being the main one. It seemed Lewis, the band promoter, really wanted to champion them, believing they had what it took, but after doing a few free auditions for him, they walked away from the situation as they could not afford to keep doing free gigs for him as well as their regular shows. Then, a few months later Alan Lewis made Lionel Morton successful with a hit record with The Four Pennies group, which got them to number one. It could have been The Warriors: they were that close! Jon always remembered how close it all had been, but that's the music business. Many fans had said that the group were perhaps the next Beatles, maybe that was a little bit optimistic. What Jon went on to do with Yes was pretty mind-blowing and led to music that was influential, timeless, creative and would last fifty years and more.

Just missing out on that big break led to unease in the ranks. Perhaps they had missed out on their moment of stardom was a career-changing event. Just as it seemed the band were getting somewhere, Derek, the founding member and drummer, decided to leave the band. In what was potentially the start of exciting times for the band, this was bad timing, to say the least. With the band damaged but determined to continue, Derek hung on for a short time, making sure they could find a drummer to replace him. During this time, they travelled to the Decca Studios in London, for the recording sessions.

BEAT DRUMMER DEREK PLUMPS FOR SECURITY

By Daily Mail Reporter

BEAT drummer Derek Thornhill turned down a £500 film part for a nine till five office job.

Derek, who is 18, said: "There is no security in the beat business. It's not worth risking everything for a very outside chance of reaching the top."

This week Derek's group, The Warriors, went in front of the cameras at Shepperton Studios — alongside The Bachelors, Freddie and the Dreamers, and The Applejacks.

Hobby

Derek, still at his desk in an accountant's office in Blackburn, said: "I had the choice of staying with the group and taking part in the film or getting this job. I'm training to become an accountant, which might seem dull, but I'll be sure of a good future."

Derek went on: "It was a hard decision to make. There's plenty of go and glamour in beat. The group has just got its first big break. The film *Just For You* should get them well known. I had to decide now whether it was worth going on, and I chose security."

His father, Mr. Nelson Thornhill, said at their home in Malham-avenue, Accrington: "Beat groups are all right as a hobby and for the few who reach the top. But the most important ... to earn a living."

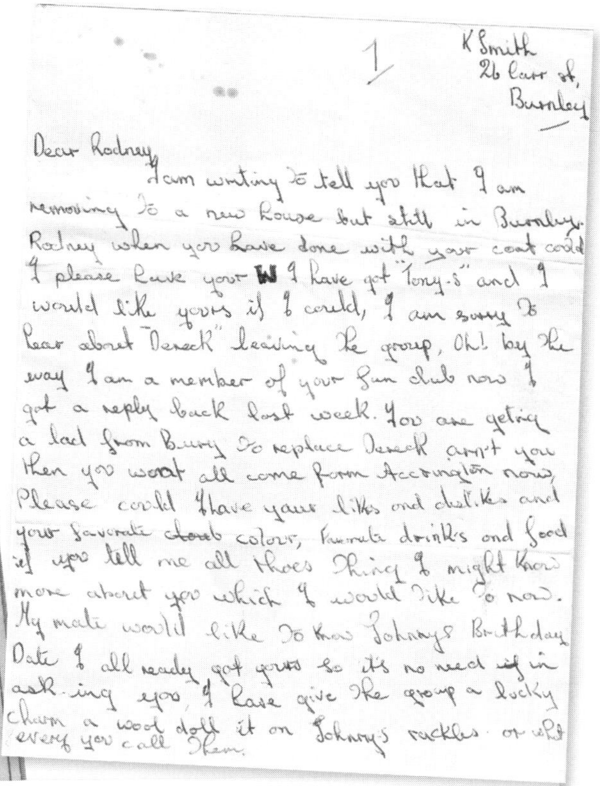

1

K Smith
26 Carr St,
Burnley

Dear Rodney
I am writing to tell you that I am removing to a new house but still in Burnley. Rodney when you have done with your coat could I please have your W I have got "Tony-s" and I would like yours if I could, I am sorry to hear about "Dereck" leaving the group, Oh! by the way I am a member of your fan club now I got a reply back last week. You are geting a lad from Bury to replace Dereck arn't you then you wont all come from Accrington now, Please could I have your likes and dislikes and your favorite clorb colours, favorite drinks and food if you tell me all thoes thing I might know more abort you which I would like to now. My mate would like to know Johnys Birthday Date I all ready got yours so it's no need of in ask-ing you, I have give the group a lucky charm a wool doll it on Johny's rackles or what every you call them.

Top Left: Derek leaving the band makes the *Daily Mail* national newspaper. A steady job is what's recommended, instead of the music business.
(David Watkinson Collection)
Top Right: A fan letter about clothes, Derek leaving and something for Jon!.
(David Watkinson Collection)
Above: More back stage messing about in this energetic photo.
(Tony McNutty – David Watkinson Collection)

Derek recalls:

When we went to London for the studio session for the single, although Ian Wallace was on the track they recorded, I was on the backing track and, it was me that was under contract with Decca. I'd only just left the band, but I'd also started working. It was my second day at work so I pretended to be ill and travelled down to London at three o'clock in the morning so that I could be there at the studios. I got back at six o'clock in the morning the following day to go to work. I went to Decca about four or five times. We were also in a competition at Tooting Granada in London, NME ran it. We did ok, but because we had already been for a test with Oriole Records (which became CBS Records in 1965) it discounted us [from a prize in the competition].

The band were disappointed to hear that although they were awarded second place, they did not get any prize money. For Derek, all that effort needed some reward, as he was under pressure to move on with his career outside music. He chose the latter for the rest of his life - he had other ideas for his future.

Derek's last gig with the band was at either the Bolton or Bury Palais. Although not noted in any of the diaries, it was thought by band members that during Derek Thornhill's last gig, Ian Wallace was in the audience and was asked to join there and then for their next gig as the new drummer. This was either extremely well planned by band members or a bit of good fortune. Most of the band knew each other in the local scene and so finding replacements was not that hard. Indeed, the fact that everyone knew each other, led to real camaraderie between bands. If your van broke down or needed some equipment there was always some musicians nearby to help you out. As a result, musicians' paths crossed frequently. Ian Wallace had been playing in the band The Jaguars and was known by the band to be a good drummer. He was from the town of Bury, very near Bolton, which was about twenty miles from the rest of The Warriors guys, so it required some dedication to keep travelling over to rehearsals and gigs on public transport. But he was well-liked and always had a smile on his face. He was also a tight drummer and managed to keep the band solid and in time. Joining The Warriors was a step up from his last band, and his ethos and dedication to practising was unquestionable, taking the big step of leaving his job as a clerk in the NHS, quitting The Jaguars and becoming a full-time musician. Even though he was only 17 years old, his recruitment was seen as important enough for the local newspaper the *Bury Times* to feature it in its *Teen Topics* section, headlined 'Local Drummer Joins Professional Group'. They reported that the band were soon to be off to London to cut a record and make a film.

Derek commented that the band did well to capture Ian Wallace:

The band changed, and the way it was going wasn't my style. When I left and Ian Wallace joined, the drum sound changed again, and he took the softness away. It became more like R'n'B and louder. The band went a bit heavier when I left. I thought we were quite classical, really. We did our own versions of stuff and we were making a living. On the track, 'Heh Baby' I played an independent and off-beat rhythm which changed later. Ian Wallace was the right person to take them forward doing a straight four-four.

I get around

Getting to these gigs was the same for any band at the time. They would undertake lengthy, manic trips up and down the country in poor quality vans - that was the norm. Everyone did it. Imagine the sheer hell of travelling on icy, wintery days in basic transportation without functioning heaters. The vans were usually painted in bright colours decorated with bold designs. Pink Floyd had a wide stripe on their Bedford van. The Warriors had a rusty and very basic Bedford, brightly painted and with menacing bull horns attached to the roof. With little creature-comforts, these vehicles were cold and unreliable, but most were modified to become little worlds where the rock 'n' roll lifestyle could be indulged. Imagine up to six sweaty young men drinking beer, sleeping, singing and laughing while sitting on all their gear. It was not an easy lifestyle. One of the band's vans had a settee in the back instead of seats, while their second van (bright green and cream) had proper seats in it and a little mascot rubber Indian (Warrior) which they placed on the van's aerial.

Stories abound of van adventures. One tale has the van's silencer blowing until it fell off at one o'clock in the morning, making the vehicle so loud that the police would stop the band all the time. The Warriors also had a car for a while, but mostly hired vans - as they kept breaking them.

The Warriors felt they had to stand out and they certainly got noticed in an old orange Bedford van that Tony found - the sort with sliding driver and passenger doors. They embellished it with a great paint job plus the legendary

Above: New member Ian Wallace (on the right) with Jon and one of the many vans used to go around the UK. This one is a Bedford. *(David Watkinson Collection)*

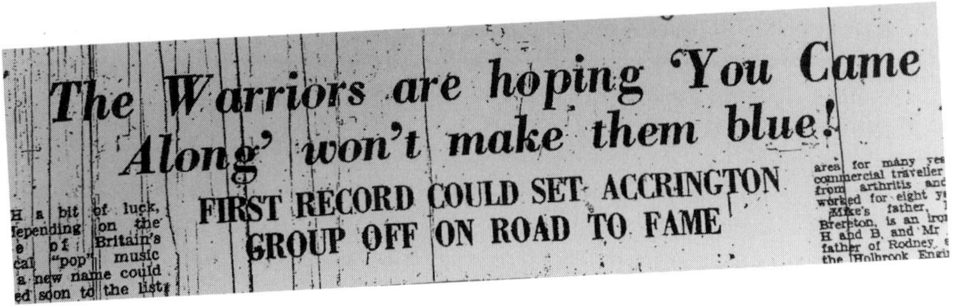
The Warriors are hoping 'You Came Along' won't make them blue!

FIRST RECORD COULD SET ACCRINGTON GROUP OFF ON ROAD TO FAME

Above: Headline in the Accrington paper. *(David Watkinson Collection)*

Above: Fan postcard main photo. *(David Watkinson Collection)*

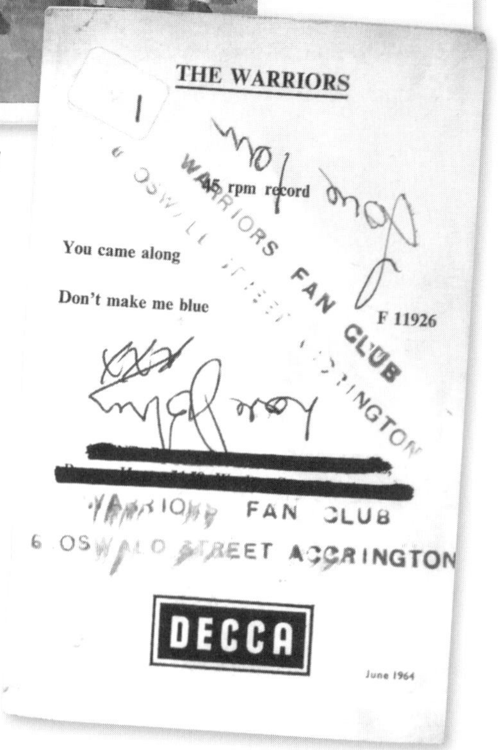

Right: The other side of the fan postcard signed Love John XXX and Love Ian. Notice the old fan club address crossed out – Renown House, 54-58 Wardour Street, London – and the new one stamped across. *(David Watkinson Collection)*

horns on the roof along with long aerials. Jon enjoyed the driving, but like the others experienced various difficulties from time to time, including a flat tyre, icy roads, or being stopped by the police. Speaking in August 2015, Jon Anderson explained:

> We had the van - it was dangerous and orange. We were crazy driving that thing! We would speed through Bury to get to Manchester to do a gig, and we didn't think about speed limits or anything like that. And with those horns on the front: we could have impaled people on them!

Jon recalled how he was driving the van once and heard this strange noise.

> We were driving to the local town of Blackburn, and there was a chugun-chugun-chugun. It got louder and louder and louder until we got to the top of the hill and I thought I'd better stop at the top, so I did, and the front wheel rolled down the hill! The van tipped over. We realised it could have happened when we were going fast down the hill! It's a wonder we all survived at all.

Apparently, after a gig, school friends would go to Jon Anderson's house and clean all the lipstick messages off the side of the van that had been left by fans. Oh, the Rock Star life!

The Rock Star Life

The Warriors, under the leadership of Tony Anderson, really did try to be professional. They had lurex jackets made for them. The way they presented themselves and the shows they gave were important. On stage, Jon would wear a red jacket, Tony would wear a white one, with gold jackets for the rest of the band.

After recording at Decca Studios, and two months of gigs around Lancashire, The Warriors managed to gain a star-studded spot in a pop music-orientated film called *Just for You*. These sorts of films would promote up and coming bands and established stars to the larger cinema audiences throughout the UK. In April 1964 they all travelled to London, a little nervous but excited nevertheless, for their initial chat with agents in Wardour Street.

Rod recalled travelling to begin filming at Shepperton Studios the next day in West London:

> I remember the morning we went to do the movie. Tony and Jon in the van were arguing big time about all sorts of things. The weather was bad; it was pouring down. It was like six o'clock in the morning, and we were on our way to Shepperton Studios, and they were falling out like cat and dogs! They were really having a go at one and another. But that's brothers, they all do it, I suppose.

When they arrived, managers Dick Roe and Philip Solomon were discussing business concerning the likes of Sid and Eddie Little, Jimmy Tarbuck - both UK comedy acts - the singer Johnny Moore, who had a hit with 'Saturday Night at The Movies', and another singer, Johnny Theum. This was another new and exciting world for the band. Pretty wide-eyed and new to the business, they were open to any suggestion about how to improve their careers.

However, Rodney says, 'We were not stupidly wide open, and I think we knew when we were being conned - or at least Tony did - as he was a couple of years older than us and just that little bit wiser.'

It was Phil Solomon, sitting behind his Wardour street office desk, who said they needed to change their look, arranged for the band to have a trip to Savile Row to get fitted out. He paid for complete outfits - shirts, suits, socks, boots and ties - for the film shoot. Rodney adds, 'yeah and that's all he paid for.'

As is common in filming, what appeared to be a quick shoot, took much longer than expected. The band, being inexperienced, did not help the situation by messing around. Asked to get out of a car with their guitars - not an easy task - they ended up doing umpteen takes, as much as anything because they thought it was a stupid idea anyway. They would drive the big car onto the set, and someone would get a leg stuck or a guitar strap wrapped around the gearstick.

The film was directed by Douglas Hickox and Vincent Scarza, and featured Sam Costa as a disc jockey, lying in bed operating the first push-button hit

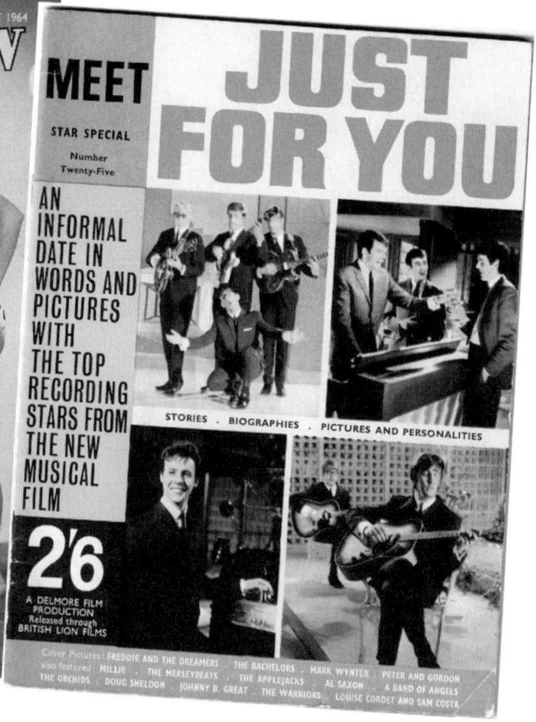

Left: Film Review magazine, which features the movie Just For You, in which The Warriors featured. Elvis is on the cover. *(David Watkinson Collection)*
Right:. The special magazine that came out about *Just For You* with The Warriors mentioned on the cover. *(David Watkinson Collection)*

parade machine. This electronic device provides not only the performers, the music, plus vitamin and pep pills but also a girl to go with them! The band were excited by the filming process, though. Mike remembers:

> The beginning of the movie has a bed scene [Sam Costa's]. During filming, being bored, I went up to the remote control on the bed. I was intrigued by all these knobs. I was just going to touch them when I was told in no uncertain terms that I was not to touch them as it would throw the whole continuity [of the film] out!

d NOW ACCRINGTON 'BEAT' GROUP IN FILM

ACCRINGTON'S popular "beat" group, The Warriors, are to take part in a film.

Next week they begin work at Shepperton Studios on the film "Just For You," which is expected to be released in June.

Also in the film will be Freddie and the Dreamers, The Bachelors and The Applejacks.

Climax

This latest rise to fame is the climax of three months' good fortune which has seen The Warriors play in a church, a cathedral and a recording studio.

A record they made earlier in the year is expected to be released in the near future.

The film contract has been negotiated by their personal manager, Mr Johnny More, of Salford, and their business manager and agent, Mr Phillip Solomon.

Mr Solomon is also manager and agent of The Bachelors.

The contract was signed by all concerned in Manchester.

The Warriors will travel to London next Monday and begin filming the following day.

At church

The Warriors are well known in the town for trying to get young people back into the Church.

In conjunction with the Rev J. Fletcher Richardson, minister of Antley Methodist Church, Accrington, they have taken part in two "pop" services at the church.

A fortnight ago they appeared in a service at Manchester Cathedral.

Left: The word is out for the exciting movie project for the band called *Just For You*. *(David Watkinson Collection)*

In the movie, The Warriors, looking very young indeed in their silver suits, perform the track 'Don't Make Me Blue', the B-side of their single. They drive a cream coloured Ford Zodiac car around and onto the set of a cafe bar. Pretty girls drape themselves over the band as they attempt to mime to this rather poor, albeit catchy, song.

Seen now, it's a slice of innocence and jollity, but they do all look desperate to be The Beatles and Jon Anderson looks like he's in the way, as much as anything. In one shot, while Tony is singing to a girl with sunglasses, Jon almost gets knocked over. It is also interesting to note is that the drumming on the track doesn't always link with an actual drummer on-screen. Indeed, the song is halfway through before Ian Wallace sits at his kit at all. It is miming at its best!

The band took advantage of the waits between takes, by chatting to anyone who was famous. David Foster spent many an hour with Dusty Springfield, apparently driving everyone mad with their joint impressions of BBC radio show *the Goons*. In the released cut of the film, The Warriors ended up with a slot mid-way through the second half of the film, along with their Lancashire contemporaries, The Four Pennies.

The Warriors' guitarist Mike Brereton adds:

> We were at the Burnley Cinema for the release of the film. The bloke who was running the cinema was quite forward-looking, and he said we should go on and play before the showing. We did! When we all went to Manchester to see the film, we got into trouble: the usherette told us to shut up because we were all shouting, 'That's me! Look it's me! Yeah!'

Above: Posing just before the cinema gig on the opening night of *Just For You*. *(Garth Dawson – David Watkinson Collection)*

The Warriors' first record 'You Came Along' was released on 5 June 1964, by Decca, performing very well in Lancashire, in the local charts. A few days later, the band were featured on the front page of the *Accrington Observer & Times*:

> A new record jumped to the top of the Accrington music shops 'pop' charts yesterday. Not by The Beatles, The Four Pennies, Cilla Black, Roy Orbison or any of the other top-line stars whose discs have been selling like hot cakes for so long, but by Accrington's own group The Warriors. Their first record 'You Came Along' backed by 'Don't Make Me Blue', was issued only last Friday, and already there are indications that it is going to be a winner, not only locally but throughout the country.

The article goes on to mention the band's hectic schedule and how they had jumped from obscurity to near national fame in just twelve months. It was an exciting time for the band: within the week they had been on ABC's *Thank Your Lucky Stars,* and they had toured the local music shops all week.

Tony told the paper:

> I must have signed hundreds of autograph books. We feel great about how the record is going. Naturally, it's too early yet to say if it will make the national charts, but we're hoping.

Above: The band in town on the banks of the River Thames in London. *(David Watkinson Collection)*

Right: One of the few fan club postcards made, image on one side and address details on the back. Taken in TONY'S, The Record Centre Ltd, 110 Blackburn Road, Accrington. *(David Watkinson Collection)*

THE WARRIORS

This group, the Warriors, are a six-strong vocal and instrumental group from Accrington. Their first disc is called "You Came Along". The Warriors have a very strong local following in their home area up North, and have been together now since February, 1963.

And here's the group line-up. There's Rodney Hill, 17, on rhythm guitar, and he also plays banjo, piano and harmonica. Rodney was formerly an apprentice toolmaker. Next we have Johnnie Anderson, 19, on lead vocals, and he was formerly a long-distance lorry driver. Following him we have his brother, Tony, he's 22, and also on vocals, also harmonica, and formerly was a fireman.

Dave Foster, their 17-year-old bass guitarist, was actually born in Liverpool, but was educated in Accrington. Dave also wrote the flip-side of their first disc, "Don't Make Me Blue". Mike Brereton, aged 19, is on lead guitar, and Ian Wallace, 17, drums, completes this new big beat group that is destined to go places.

Above Left: A press release giving Johnnie's job as a long distance lorry driver. *(David Watkinson Collection)*
Above Right: A local newspaper advert for the 'You Came Along' single. *(David Watkinson Collection)*
Right: Imperial Ballroom in Nelson Lancashire. Big names headline in the 60's again, no jeans allowed, and ties must be worn.
(David Watkinson Collection)

Mary Mortimer, the local music shop and club owner, and a big promoter and friend of the band, said:

> It's doing fabulously well. We are selling far more copies of The Warriors' release than anyone else. We sold over 200 since it was issued. I'm sure it's going to be a winner.

She was right, as it went on to sell 40,000 in a matter of days! Tony Woods of the Record Centre in Blackburn Road remarked:

> The first lot I ordered went in no time, I'll have to get another supply. Any record that sells one hundred in a week is doing really well. All the photographs of the group have gone, too.

On 13 June 1964, Jon commented in the local paper about the Mersey Sound that was gripping everyone:

> I think we may have got in on time. In any case, we have not stuck to one brand of music and are not stereotyped like a lot of other groups. Now that the trend is turning more in favour of ballads, we are quite happy about it. Of course, the vast majority of our fans are teenagers, but we also go out and try and please the older set.

The Warriors head local pops list

MEET-THE-FANS PLAN AFTER TV SUCCESS

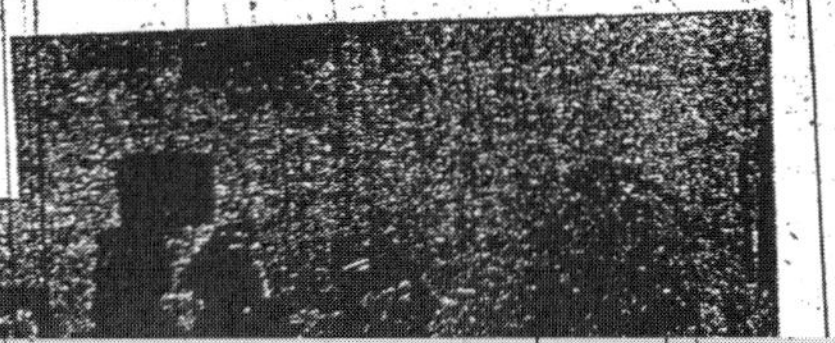

A new record jumped to the top of the Accrington

Warriors mobbed after 'Lucky Stars' TV date

Popular Accrington group The Warriors had their name in lights 25 years ago.

They were mobbed by adoring fans in their home town after appearing on the television show,

1964

crington.

Under the revolutionary syst devised by Sir James Pitman, of Sir Issac Pitman who inver the shorthand system, child would be learning ITA instead

Thank Your Lucky Stars

INTRODUCED BY
BRIAN MATTHEW

TV's top pop show presents another all-star bill. The *Lucky Stars* hit parade brought to you tonight by
PETER and GORDON
THE FOUR PENNIES
DUSTY SPRINGFIELD
CRAIG DOUGLAS
THE MIGIL FIVE
THE MODS
ANDEE SILVER
THE WARRIORS

JANICE NICHOLLS
heads a panel of teenagers who comment on the latest American releases in
Spin-a-Disc

GUEST DISC JOCKEY
TONY HALL

DESIGNED BY TONY BORER
DIRECTED BY MARK STUART

ABC Weekend Network Production

Top: More headlines for the band. *(David Watkinson Collection)*
Above: Mobbed as the fans go crazy!. *(David Watkinson Collection)*
Right: Details from possibly *The Radio Times* magazine or a local paper. *(David Watkinson Collection)*

54, Green Lane,
Blackburn,
Lancs,
9/8/64.

Dear Pill,
Please will you ask Tony if he will take us to the Mecca in the van with you from rehearsal the saturday after next.
We told Tony we might be going to St Augustine's on Wednesday night to see you but we don't think we'll come because it ends a bit late.
If you get any photos taken of yourself please send us one each.
We want to know what kind of lacquer you use because your hair is lovely. You wore some fab shoes on saturday and you know we think your fab also.
Please write back before we see you again.
Wish Tony luck for us.
All our loving we send to you
Linda & Val

P.S. Get this!
We love you Warriors
O yes we do
We love the songs you sing
We love you too.
When your not near to us we're blue
O Warriors we love you.

Above: A fan letter addressed to Pill – a nickname for Rodney. Asking for a lift to a gig. *(David Watkinson Collection)*

British TV was growing as a product and for a young band to get a slot on any of the programs was certainly a coup. It was considered vital to get onto the very popular panel music show, *Juke Box Jury,* hosted by the charismatic David Jacobs, with large audiences tuning in every week. Mike Brereton recalled: 'When we did *Juke Box Jury*, it didn't get a good vote. You had either a hit or miss given by the panel. We got a miss!' Mike recalled that following their appearance on the *Thank Your Lucky Stars* TV show, 'The press said, "The Warriors were a grand team of lads."'

As Jon remembers it:

> An agent [the same agent that had wanted to promote The Warriors the previous year] came across The Lionel Morton Four in Blackburn and persuaded them to rename their band to The Four Pennies. With the backing of that agent, Phillips Record company took them on board which lead to them having a hit record 'Juliet', which went to number one in the charts. Overnight they became famous! It could have been The Warriors' lucky break. They were so close, yet so far away.

The Warriors head local pops list

MEET-THE-FANS PLAN AFTER TV SUCCESS

A new record jumped to the top of the Accrington music shops' "pop" charts yesterday.

Not by The Beatles, The Four Pennies, Cilla Black, Roy Orbison or any of the other top-line stars whose discs have been selling like hot cakes for so long — but by Accrington's own group, The Warriors.

Their first record, "You Came Along," backed by "Don't Make Me Blue," was issued only last Friday, and already there are indications that it is going to be a winner, not only locally but throughout the country.

What a hectic few days it has been for the five Accrington lads — Tony and Johnny Anderson, Mike Brereton, Rodney Hill and David Foster — and their Bury pal, Ian Wallace, who have jumped from obscurity in the "pop" music world to near-national fame in 12 short months.

On Saturday, they had the top spot in ABC's "Thank Your Lucky Stars" show . . . yesterday they were kept busy signing autographs for fans, many of them armed with newly-bought copies of their record.

HOPING . . .

"I must have signed hundreds of autograph books," Tony told the "Observer."

"We feel great about how the record is going. Naturally, it's too early yet to say if it will make the national charts, but we're hoping."

Record dealers in Accrington reported a brisk demand for "You Came Along."

Mrs Mary Mortimer, of Mary's Music, Whalley-road, said: "It's doing fabulously well. We're selling far more

Picture by courtesy of ABC Television

Above: The local newspaper front cover The Warriors appearance on the TV show *Thank Your Lucky Stars* and their single success. *(ABC TV – David Watkinson Collection)*

Left: The band on a high with the single out and an appearance on TV, captured in this local newspaper advert. *(David Watkinson Collection)*

Above: A concert likely to be either, December 26th at the Rawtenstall Astoria or the 31st at the Bolton Navada Ballroom. Dave Foster said 'we played on New Year's Eve at a ball. I think we did "Won't Be Long" by the Beatles – they were very influential to us'. *(Garth Dawson – David Watkinson Collection)*

Mike added: 'We were on [the show] with the Four Pennies of all people. Bearing in mind what happened to them and us, just our luck: it was a proper kick in the ribs, that was!'

About a month later the band received their first royalties. Plans were afoot to record a second single. Their manager at the time, Philip Solomon, also arranged for them to tour with The Bachelors - a three-piece pop group from Dublin, who have enjoyed a career of sixty years and are still touring today. Reflecting on that year, Rod remarked:

> In 1964, I remember we did the Burnley Miner's Club, that was one of the big ones in those days. We did Y.M.C.A. too and some other biggies, like the Blackburn Y.M.C.A. I do distinctly remember standing on stage playing the fast Shadows' number, 'Savage'. When I saw The Shadows do it, after the fast bits you could see Bruce go, phew-thank-god-for-that, while he rested his hands for a moment or two. I couldn't do it now, but back then we would practice all day till four, get a bite to eat, then set off to do a gig.

The Warriors' recording contract was for a few recordings, perhaps four or five, meaning actual recordings rather than releases. It will have been standard practise at the time. The record companies would try and sign as many bands as they could in the hope that one would make a hit. Then they could recoup their investment. Decca promoted The Warriors with some publicity, photos, fan cards, and a radio show here and there.

Top Left: A fan club postcard signed by five members with Jon adding Johnny XXX. *(David Watkinson Collection)*
Top Right: The Bolton Beachcomber Club saw many performances from the band, this one was captured and used for the Bolton Live CD.

The trouble with the record that was released, was that not everyone was convinced of the choice of songs. The band were given The Applejacks song 'You Came Along', and it did not go down well with the band. It was quite wrong for them, many had thought. To add to their sheer lack of control, they were also given the B-side of the single to play in the movie, and not the A-side. Jon and everyone else thought it was crazy and did not understand why this choice had been made.

On a more positive note, though, Jon remembers that:

> In the early days, we did a lot of shows in Glasgow. We were treated like real rock stars there. All the girls would scream at us. Only up there though, that's the only place it happened, for some reason. Maybe it was because of Tony, who was a very handsome guy. Me? I was just hanging around banging my tambourine.

Behind the scenes

In an interview, Rod chuckled as he spilt the beans: The Warriors were a party band. They all enjoyed a drink or two, and in later years in Germany, they tried light drugs too. However, they were never ones for the punch-ups or throwing TVs out of windows like The Who were. Unless they were cornered at Mortimer's dance hall in Blackburn that is. Joe Morts (as it was known), was owned by the effervescent Mary and Joe and was a massive club that had a reputation for a good night out, but one which could turn into a fight swiftly. The landlord of this private club had two very

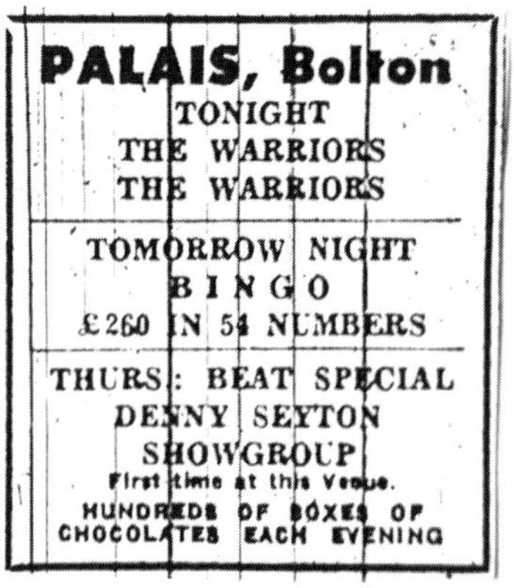
PALAIS, Bolton
TONIGHT
THE WARRIORS
THE WARRIORS
TOMORROW NIGHT
BINGO
£260 IN 54 NUMBERS
THURS: BEAT SPECIAL
DENNY SEYTON
SHOWGROUP
First time at this Venue.
HUNDREDS OF BOXES OF
CHOCOLATES EACH EVENING

Above: The Bolton Palais loves The Warriors, and they are giving chocolates out too!. *(David Watkinson Collection)*

Teenagers will hear pop stars in two churches

ACCRINGTON teenagers will be able to go to two church services ... Sunday and still see their "pop" idols.

In the afternoon, Antley Methodist Church, who started "beat" services ... town, will once again feature The Warriors, and in the evening Cotton Street Unsectarian Mission will have The Rave-Ons rhythms group topping the bill.

These services are part of a campaign to get young people back into the church. Antley's minister, the Rev J. Fletcher Richardson started the idea more than a month ago. At the first "beat" service more than 500 teenagers packed the pews and nearly 100 had to be turned.

Leaflets

They came from all over East Lancashire. Later, Mr Richardson told the "Lancashire Evening Telegraph" that he hoped to hold a similar service every month.

Members of Antley Youth Club will be issuing leaflets advertising the service tonight outside the Conservative Club, Accrington, where Wayne Fontana is appearing.

They will also be issuing them outside the town's two cinemas.

The difference between the two services will be that Antley will use specially-written modern hymns, while the Unsectarians will use "pop" tunes with the words of hymns adapted to them.

Mr Jim Connor, the superintendent of the mission, will do the adaptation.

Mr Connor was organist and choir master at Cotton Street before the last war when Edward Holgate's Majestic Dance Band went there to play.

The Warriors recently made a record which is expected to be released next month, while The Rave-Ons are a new group which started last Christmas.

Above: The local paper features the church performance in Accrington. These gigs proved to be a massively popular couple of events which drew young fans from afar. *(David Watkinson Collection)*

WHEN THE WARRIORS COME SWINGING IN, OUT GOES A CATHEDRAL TRADITION

The Warriors taking part in the cathedral service yesterday

Express Staff Reporter

A CHAPLAIN whispered "O.K., boys!" and a new sound shattered the quiet of a cathedral yesterday.

It was the first "pop" service in the history of Manchester Cathedral.

For 700 schoolchildren, it was an 80 - minute Sunday service with Saturday - night over tones.

Difference

For The Warriors, a six-man beat group from Accrington, it was a date with a difference—a solid session with no teen-age squeals, no shake—and no fee.

The service, to mark the 21st anniversary of the Student Christian Movement in schools, followed a two-way pop-trad pattern.

The cathedral choir sang six traditional and contemporary numbers.

The beat group followed up with "He's Got the Whole World in His Hands" . . . "Blowin' in the Wind" . . . "All Things Bright and Beautiful" . . . and (to the Z - Cars' theme) "Father Hear the Prayer We Offer."

Said 21-year-old Tony Anderson, one of the group's two singers: "We have had two rehearsals in the cathedral to get the sound right. We had to tone it down a bit, but otherwise it was just plain sailing."

Whisper

A tea party followed the service. The group didn't make it. In mid-service, they packed guitars, mikes, drums and amplifiers, and tip-toed out.

Whispered Tony: "Sorry we can't stay. We've got a big beat show at Blackburn at six o'clock."

Above: 700 fans turn up at the Manchester Cathedral for a 'beat service'. *(Daily Mail – David Watkinson Collection)*

Above: Headlines for the band's controversial church gigs. *(David Watkinson Collection)*

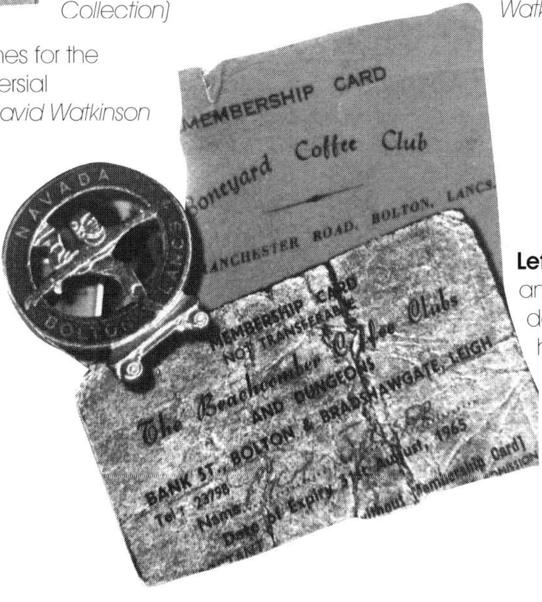

Left: Bolton Boneyard and Navada dance club and hall memorabilia. *(David Watkinson Collection)*

large German Shepherd dogs, which would greet you as you walked in. The floor was of sawdust and it is said that the Teddy Boys (Britain's original teen subculture) would on occasion show off their knuckle dusters and bicycle chains. All in all, it offered a dance night with an edge! Joe and Mary were always really good to the band, helping them out. The band bought their instruments from them, with Ian Wallace buying his Ludwig drum kit and Rod buying at least two guitars.

> I never went there because I was a bit younger then. We all went to meet the girls, drink and have good time. We would also go to the Springhill Club: the girls there were fun, lots of fun. We all liked the girls. I can remember meeting a fan called Eileen there and learnt how she had changed my mates Jim's life one evening too if you get what I am saying! At one stage we worked with The Hollies, and David went out with their guitarist's sister, Maureen. He went out with everybody really, if he could get his leg over!

Gigging is fraught with pitfalls. On one occasion, when they played at The Beachcomber Club in Bolton, Dave Foster's bass was stolen. The band surmises it was either stolen by a roadie or by a well-known member of another band. Mike recalled one of the bands' numerous trips to London:

> We were staying in London, while we were recording for Decca Records when we met Chas Chandler of The Animals. We were quite pleased with our recording session, and while we were getting our stuff into our van afterwards [a group of lads] were there standing around chatting. We asked who they were. Chas said they were called The Animals. We all thought that was a stupid name for a band, and they would never make it called that!

Gigs and more gigs - that's what the band wanted, and if possible, a residency anywhere would do. The manager of the Bolton Palais, Mr Booth, recalled the band in 2000 saying:

> The Warriors were the only group to ever get the offer to play [at the Bolton Palais] every Monday night because they were so popular. They would play about two half-hour slots, on our revolving stage at the Palais. It was just like the London Palladium. One side of the stage would have the local DJ on it and when it was time for the group's turn, we would turn it round, and they would be ready waiting behind the dividing wall. After the gig, which would always finish at 11 pm, as there were no late nights in them days, the band would go to Mr Smith's in Manchester for a drink. I do remember Jon and the other guys going all the time. They were a very good group.

The band developed a great following in some towns. Jon reminisced:

> The main thing, in those days in Bolton, was the fact we had so much support, with great fans. We had the best time ever. We used to drink a lot and play The Boneyard Club (Bolton). We went to play in Newcastle one day and a great story from those days was the support band, called Listen - who

Right: A meeting before one of their church beat services gigs. Jon to the left with Tony on his knees. *(David Watkinson Collection)*

'THE WARRIORS' AGAIN – AT CENTENARY SERVICE

To mark the second day of centenary celebrations at Antley Methodist Church they had one of their now famous "beat services" with the "Warriors" providing the beat.

The morning opened with service conducted by Rev. Ernest Hardy, of Windermere (Chairman of the Carlisle District) and the "beat service" was in the afternoon.

The evening service was also conducted by Rev. Ernest Hardy.

The collection was £10 and it will go to Christian Aid Week. Over 30 young people pledged themselves to work for the Christian Aid Week after the service.

The celebrations began on Saturday evening when Accrington Townswomen's Guild Choir gave a concert.

They sang songs from various musical shows and solos were given by Mrs Headley, Mrs Garth Dawson, Mr R Gee, Mr H Dugdale, Mrs Boardwell and Mrs Lomas.

The conductor was Mrs A Spencer.

The Rev F Richardson (standing extreme left) and church officials, chat with "The Warriors" before the afternoon "beat" servic

'The Warriors' say thanks in music

As a gesture of appreciation for being allowed to practice in the Church Hall, "The Warriors" — Accrington's latest recording stars — gave their services free of charge for a youth club dance in St Augustine's Church Hall, Huncoat, last Wednesday.

The group's manager, Mr Edwin Foster, told me that they had been using the hall five days a week for several months without charge, and hoped that by saying "thank you" in this way they would be helping the Youth Club in repayment for the help they had received.

It was the first dance the Club had organised, and their leader, Jack Scott, described it as a complete success.

"Our intention was for everyone to enjoy themselves, and they certainly appear to have done so. The dance has really gone down well," he remarked.

About 100 young people jived, twisted, "did the monkey" or merely stood watching their favourite group, but those who were hoping to hear the three numbers written by the group themselves and recorded, met with disappointment.

The response to "The Sabre Dance" — the instrumental which "The Warriors" arranged themselves for recording — left no room for disappointment with either fans or the group, however. Judging by the teenagers' enthusiasm, the disc should shoot into the local hit parade almost immediately on its release early next month.

With engagements throughout Lancashire keeping the boys busy almost every night of the week, it is good to know that "The Warriors" have not forgotten the friends who helped them on their way to success.

Pictured doing one of the latest dances are (from left to right) Pauline Campbell (15), Elaine Campbell (12), Olwyn Savina Fulcham (13), and Catherine Towner (13) and Catherine Woodcock (15)

(Picture: Garth

Left: A press cutting for the thank you gig played at St. Augustine's Church Hall. Around 100 fans did the 'Monkey' dance while the band played their version of 'Sabre Dance'. *(David Watkinson Collection)*

supported The Undertakers. Listen were a serious big party band, who had this singer with long hair. His name was Robert Plant, [later to become a huge rock star with Led Zeppelin]. It was he who gave me my first smoke of marijuana! I didn't know what it was.

Robert offered it to me, 'Do you want to try a funny cigarette? It's grass.' I replied, 'We have tons of grass on the farm.' Robert giggled, 'No not that kind of grass - weed!' He was stoned.

We had a wild weekend, and I don't remember it all now, but The Undertakers were the funniest band ever. Listen were from Birmingham, a place more cool than funny. We didn't talk to bands from Birmingham then, because they would break your legs!

Above: Jon and the band looking extremely cool and serious in this promo shot. *(F. Davis - David Watkinson Collection)*

Right:.Yet again a group shot, this time one taken in a stately home in Lancashire. *(David Watkinson Collection)*

• One of the first groups to emerge in any sort of prominence on the Mersey scene was CASS AND THE CASSANOVAS. They disbanded some years ago and their vocalist CASEY JONES left for Germany to form a group

ALAN CROWLEY has written a number which the new "Terry Hines Sextet" hope to record for the R.C.A. Victor label. The composition is titled "Tomorrow". He has also written a number "It's Like I Said," which may be TIFFANY'S next "A" side for Parlophone.

"LIVELY and headed for the big time" — that's readers' verdict on THE WARRIORS, a group fast building a big reputation. The group's managers are the proprietors of the successful Beachcomber circuit of clubs in Leigh, Preston and Bolton.

Y.O.R. CLUBS
PARR HALL

JONATHAN KING

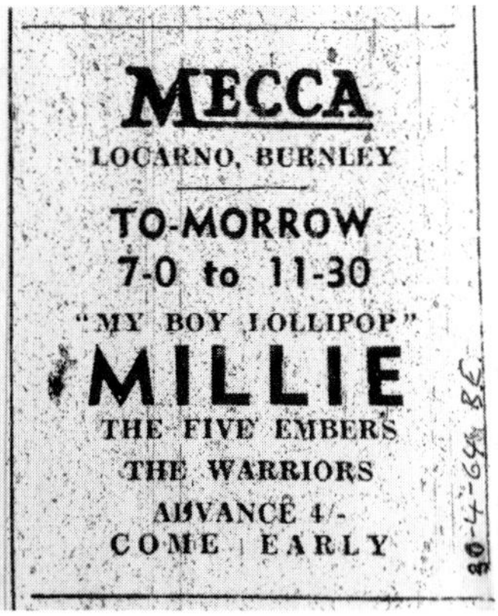

MECCA
LOCARNO, BURNLEY
TO-MORROW
7-0 to 11-30
"MY BOY LOLLIPOP"
MILLIE
THE FIVE EMBERS
THE WARRIORS
ADVANCE 4/-
COME EARLY

Above:.Bottom of the bill at the Mecca club supporting 'Millie'. *(David Watkinson Collection)*

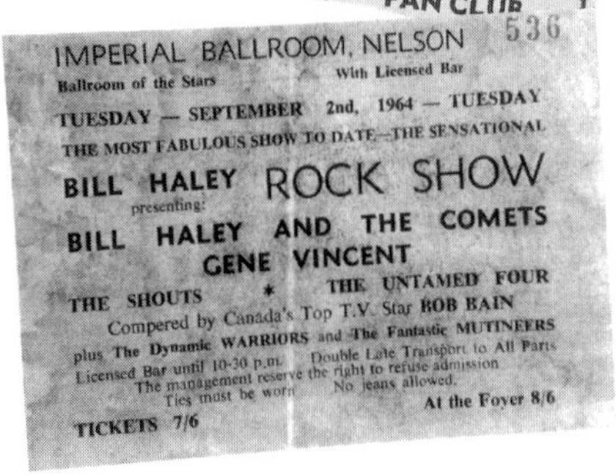

IMPERIAL BALLROOM, NELSON
Ballroom of the Stars
With Licensed Bar
TUESDAY — SEPTEMBER 2nd, 1964 — TUESDAY
THE MOST FABULOUS SHOW TO DATE—THE SENSATIONAL
BILL HALEY ROCK SHOW
presenting:
BILL HALEY AND THE COMETS
GENE VINCENT
THE SHOUTS ★ THE UNTAMED FOUR
Compered by Canada's Top T.V. Star BOB BAIN
plus The Dynamic WARRIORS and The Fantastic MUTINEERS
Licensed Bar until 10-30 p.m. Double Late Transport to All Parts
The management reserve the right to refuse admission
Ties must be worn No jeans allowed.
TICKETS 7/6
At the Foyer 8/6

Right: A Nelson Imperial Poster showing The Dynamic Warriors on the bill with Rock and Roll legends Bill Haley and The Comets and Gene Vincent. *(David Watkinson Collection)*

On the back of all this stardom coming their way, the local community grew to like and support The Warriors. A big backer and an unusual one came in the shape of the local vicar, Fletcher Richardson at the Antley Methodist Church. He became a friend of Tony's, helping him through hard times and guiding him spiritually through many tough moments, which would be something that stayed with Tony all his life. Fletcher was not your average vicar. Nicknamed 'The Rockin' Vicar', he dashed about in a smart sports car and later in life, he became a popular DJ on *Radio Lancashire*. He was good to the whole Anderson family. He allowed the band to rehearse in the church for free and it's likely that due to his influence that the band went to Manchester to do a gig at the Cathedral. Covered by the local paper, The Warriors played 'All Things Bright and Beautiful' plus a number of other pieces. The band used to practise in the church with Fletcher on Sundays. These rock-goes-to-church gigs were very popular indeed with hundreds of young fans attending them.

The Warriors were a tight-knit band, both musically and - especially with brothers involved - emotionally. Rod Hill and Mike Brereton say of Tony Anderson:

> We would never have been as successful if it hadn't been for Tony. Because he was much more experienced and had better musical knowledge [than the rest of us], he really led the band well. We looked up to him as he knew so much more. We only have good things to say about Tony.

Replying to these kind words (on my visit to see him on the Isle of Wight) Tony replied:

> Well, you see, they were able to do it. Whatever I asked Mike Brereton to do, whatever song, he meticulously copied the solo, so it sounded like the record. I think that that's why we were a very good live band because when we got a great song, we did sound like the people we were covering.
>
> We did lots of stuff, a mixed repertoire. Sometimes when we went on as support with the bands, such as The Hollies. [Audiences loved] that and we'd go down just as well - if not better than them - the main act! They really liked what we were doing, we just needed that 'break'. But, perhaps the problem with us, was that we didn't play anything original and I think that's why we never really became big.

On the road again

The band played at The Beachcomber Club in Bolton often and in many other locations travelling about Lancashire. Bolton was just down the road for the band - a short trip over the moors. The town had a love for the band, and The Warriors felt like it was a home from home and they played there regularly. There would be quite a few different groups on at The Beachcomber every week, and it was here that the band met Scottish singing star Lulu (later to become a legend) for the first time. Lulu and The Luvvers band went down well, as Lulu was a strong and determined singer. The lads managed to have a photograph taken - Jon and Dave together with Lulu.

Jon would happily drive the van and loved doing so. Only a couple of the band were able to drive onto the next gig, so tiredness would be a hazard, particularly considering the miles they had to cover. A gig in Edinburgh at a place called *Bungies*, just off Princes Street, which was a hive of fun nights out, would be the furthest drive they had to endure. They spent hours on end chugging up the M1 motorway to a Beat Music night there. The Warriors would play a lot of 'doubles' as they were called. They would play an early evening gig, and then go on and play somewhere else later on the same evening, quite possibly in another county. The second gig could easily have been miles away, a real trek. Long days were always on the cards, consuming food on the go, drinking a few beers and getting some sleep if they were lucky. The band would start loading up their gear at eight or nine o'clock in the morning, drive to their venue and play. Then do it all again at another venue or perhaps even at the same venue later, playing well into the early hours. The band used to say that in those days if they drove only 1000 miles a week, they had been playing locally.

BLACKMAIL CORNER

WELL, NO response from the Yes office following last week's highly entertaining shot of Chris Squire, so here it is as promised — Jon Anderson in a suit! The band is The Warriors, and that's young Jon second from the left.

THE peace of our village is shattered each weekend by gangs of youths riding their motor-bikes round the green.
What can we do to get them to keep down the racket?
B. O. F., Chester

A genuine letter from the Daily Mail, 2-11-77. Sent by N. Cadillac of Pontypool.

N.M.E. Nov.12/77

THE END

Above: The Warriors press photo, which was taken at the same time as the photo used on the front of the sheet music for the single, around June 64. This seems to be a kick at prog bands like Yes by the *NME* in the 70's. *(David Watkinson Collection)*

Right: June 1965 and once again The Warriors are on the bill with Tom Jones. *(David Watkinson Collection)*

Inspiration

The band had open minds to other types of music at the time. On his visit to Decca Studios, Mike says:

> I remember hearing a Walker Brothers' backing track, and thinking how good it was with the string arrangements and the horns. It really turned me on to using an orchestra and the big sound that was created, I think they are some of the best backing tracks ever done.

Jon also enjoyed this larger-than-life, grand production sound, with great vocal harmonies. All these influences were being gathered up and stored for a later time. Jon, speaking in August 2015 said:

> In 1964-65, I remember playing the small clubs like the Manchester Sporting Club, the Salford Southern Sporting Club and Northern Clubs. We would set up the equipment and play. We opened for Bill Haley and The Comets, Little Richard and Gene Vincent. [We had a] fifteen-minute spot. It was amazing to see these professionals and one day we saw The Hollies. They had a big hit record then and played the Nelson Imperial. At that point, we thought it would be great to be famous pop stars.

Years later, Jon was in a reflective mood when interviewed for *The New Musical Express* music paper in May 1974. The headline article began, 'In the tranquillity of the mid-seventies, the Topographic Mariner recollects the halcyon days of a turbulent youth.' Jon spoke fondly of his tender younger days, 'In the studio things were difficult. You had one 3-hour session during which a band was expected to do not only a sound-check but crank out two A-sides and their respective flips.'

He went on to explain how after a couple of sessions, they just might be given a whole day to record the debut album, featuring just the highlights of their stage-act, a few covers, and anything else that would not take more than half-an-hour to complete.

The Warriors were fortunate that they could just about live off the money they made from the music. But like most bands of that era, they were copying the more successful groups. In the five years The Warriors were together, they only ever wrote two songs, for the simple reason that there was an incredible mass of good material around. They used to look up to The Beatles and all the fabulous American songwriting teams because they were so great at what they were doing.

Jon admitted that although they didn't stop to think about it at the time, being in a band like The Warriors was great schooling.

> All those chords and notes that you hit, really came in handy later on, because you'd learned your trade by practising on the very best material available. Unless you were an incredible live performer, it was invariably the song and not the singer that was of paramount importance. Anybody could get hold of a bunch of musicians and push them into a studio with

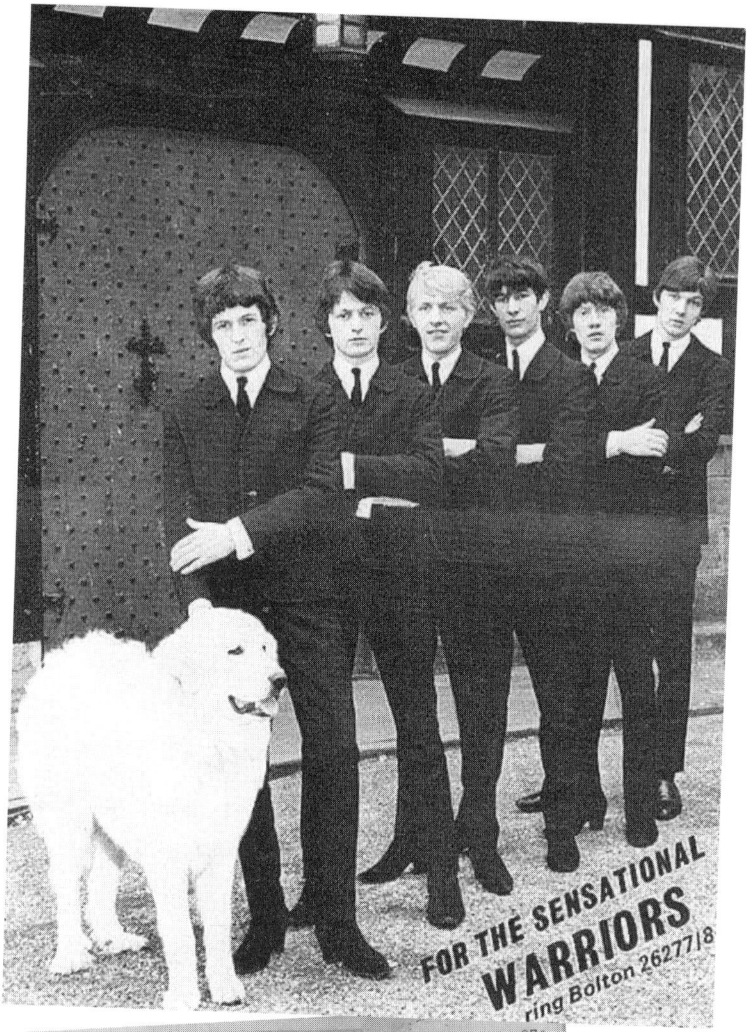

EVENING NEWS, Wednesday, December 18, 1963

274

A peep at Bolton's night life . . .

Town's new teenage night spot extended— to the Dungeons . . .

Beachcomber Coffee House

THE Beachcomber Coffee House in Bank-st. is fast becoming Bolton's most popular teenage night spot.

Hundreds of young people crowd into the club every night and dance to the music of local beat and jazz groups.

Because of the outstand-

1737

★ IMPERIAL BALLROOM ★

Ballroom of the Stars —— With Licensed Bar

SATURDAY NIGHT IT'S STAR NIGHT

JUNE 12th, 1965 7-30 p.m. to 11-30 p.m.

presenting the Fabulous

Donovan

plus THE WARRIORS

and the QUARE FELLOWS

Licensed Bar till 10-50 Ties must be worn.

Treble Late Transport to all parts. No Jeans

TICKETS 7/6 AT THE FOYER 8/6

Next Week — THE SEARCHERS

Top: A promotional poster with the band's contact details included. The dog was not a new member! *(David Watkinson Collection)*

Above Left: Local newspaper cutting about the Bolton Beachcomber Club. *(Bolton Evening News)*

Above Right: Donovan headlining the evening. Twelve years later on he would support Yes and Jon on the *Going For The One* tour. *(David Watkinson Collection)* equipment they'd never seen and really didn't know how to operate. It was songwriters like Les Reed and Barry Mason who were the important people because they wrote the hits. The groups never really mattered.

As a band they copied everyone, but Jon and Tony were especially influenced by their idol, James Dean. On at least on one occasion, Jon and Tony Anderson sign autographs as Johnny Dean and Tony Dean!

Back to reality

All the bands were in the pockets of the agents, and they had no control of where they would play nor the setlist to be played. Agents were seen as a necessary evil, only interested in their cut of the proceeds. They booked gigs all over the country with little thought for the lack of creature comforts involved in travelling from one part of the country to the next. The Warriors had, like most bands, more than one agent. They had one in Scotland, a few down in England, and some in Wales. They were constantly travelling, and while they were travelling to a gig their agents would often be trying to find them another gig. And then, of course, there was practice and rehearsals with The Warriors rehearsing on Saturday mornings for a while in the old church hall at St Augustine's on Bolton Avenue in Huncoat.

At this point, the band were really enjoying the limelight, even if the hysteria was mostly local. All the local youth bought the single, and their management seemed to be fully behind the band. Phil Solomon was excited by their prospects and promoted them widely.

However, one-hit-wonders come and go. Would this be The Warriors' fate? Despite all the promotion, the single flourished only in Lancashire. Not to be put off by this, the band went into the studios to record what they had hoped to be their next single, 'I Found You'. However, it has been said that you only get one shot at stardom. If you don't make it, you are out. Management began to lose interest in them a little, as they did with any new band that was not a complete success straight away. But the lads had plenty of fight left in them and success was their goal. Having a 'look', along with the talent to impress, was as important as always. The record company supplied the lads with blue jackets with a Warriors' 'W' on them. The group loved the look, and it seemed that the girls did too. Publicity photos were taken by Garth Dawson who worked for the *Accrington Observer* newspaper, was a local photographer who would capture most of their important moments.

1965 seemed to be a tough year for the band, however. Some gigs were played but not as many as the previous year. There was a slow-down in work and it seems that their peak had been reached and the moment had passed for a nationwide hit single. There was much waiting around for work to come in, and for agents to get in touch with any work that might come their way. The year seemed slow.

Despite the hard work and dedication of the band, the management company and Phil Soloman finally announced that they would not book anything else for the band after the 1 August 1965: it was a shock. They never heard from him again. Around this time, the band did an interview at a

London radio show in Earls Court. Missing their train at the last minute they drove all the way to Edinburgh for a gig at Bungies the day after. Around this time, Ian became ill, and a cover had to be found for four to five days, and Kev Florintine was called in. Rod says: 'We travelled to Scottish gigs via Shap [a village in Cumbria] in the snow, following snow ploughs many times. The one with Kev was the worst'.

Parents of the band angrily set about getting the situation put right, even considering legal proceedings. But as a band, they had been dropped, and the families were told to get lost. The band, now in limbo and without a schedule to work towards, hired a Mini car. Tony, Dave and Jon went off up north to get some gigs. They went to Carlisle, way up to Edinburgh and then back down through Newcastle to Birmingham and back home. They took posters and promotional material with them and sold themselves as a band. It worked. They came back with a load of gigs which earned them the backing of different promoters like Drunken Duncan from Scotland, who was rumoured to put whisky on his cornflakes!

The band were offered a residency at The Beachcomber Club in Bolton, partially through their persistence, and partially because they had a good following and were known by the local agents and club managers as a reliable act. This saved The Warriors at this stage.

Tony Moves On

In late 1965, Tony Anderson was finding the work-life balance difficult. He had a new 'little family' to take care of, and the lack of gigs and income meant it was time to move on. Speaking in 2016, he recalled his leaving the band.

> I felt the band wasn't going to make it, and I understood that. I was the only married one, plus they wanted to go off to Hamburg, and I didn't. So, I dropped out. They got one or two new guys in and went off to Hamburg eventually. And it all petered out there. They did the London thing, and Jon tried hard… and then along came Yes'. The rest, as they say, is history.

Tony's decision to leave was a big loss for the band, as he was so much more than just a lead singer to them. He had become a mentor, a leader and spokesperson. He was a charismatic and handsome singer; the fans loved him. Jon was losing a brother to sing and harmonise with, and while it was a necessary move for Tony, it was with sadness that the band now decided to move on with Jon as lead singer.

When Tony left, Mike also began contemplating his future in the band. The driving sagas of the band began to rattle him, 'Rodney crashed [a van] on the way back from Nottingham University. It was an icy road, wintertime and crunch! Andy, a driver mate, crashed one too.'

Mike did try to continue with the band, by going to gigs on trains, as he really wanted them to be successful, but eventually, it became too much. Mike added, 'When Andy just lost it and Crunch-Crash-Bang-Wallop, I nearly died!' He was quite badly injured in this incident and this set in motion a feeling of panic. Mike told the band:

Left: Liverpool in 1966 and the band are still languishing at the bottom of the bill. It is still only 3/6 to get in, which is about £3.00 nowadays. *(David Watkinson Collection)*

> I've had enough. I'm leaving because I can't do this anymore. I don't want to die in a van crash. We were zooming around the country all the time, getting home late into the mornings. It was a hard life, I enjoyed it while I did it, sort of. A better memory, though, was that the last time I played was in Liverpool, at Levinson's club - good times.

The band now had a new line up. Jon Anderson said, 'Everybody has a different picture of what a band is, it changed when Tony and Mike decided to leave. We decided to get someone different because we still had Rod there doing great guitar.'

1965 had become quite an eventful year for the band. They finished it with the line-up of Jon Anderson, Rodney Hill, Ian Wallace and David Foster. To continue, though, they needed new blood, new members. What The Warriors did have, however, even at this disrupted stage, was a fantastic backline of Ian on drums and Dave on bass. Solid and thorough, Rodney on rhythm guitar could reproduce anything ever played so far by any of the leading bands of the time. He happily switched to lead guitar and relished the new challenge.

Jon moved to lead vocals, and so now they needed 'that something special' to complete those changes. Jon was soon in control of plans for the band, moving quickly to become their spokesman and leader too. The Warriors invited a young keyboard player to play with them after a short search. Joining in November 1965, Brian Chatton was to play as the keyboardist to help

expand the band's sound at a time when more and more artists were bringing in keyboards to add colour to their sound. Jon remembered meeting Brian Chatton previously and noted how good he was.

> We decided to get a keyboard player in. We met this kid Brian, who we had seen play in Bolton. I said to Brian, there were only two reasons he got into the band. [Firstly] he was good looking, and [secondly,] he could play 'Green Unions' (one of the greatest tracks of the time by Booker T. and The MGs which had a great keyboard solo, a Hammond organ). I said, 'ya good looking and you can play that! You're in the band, shut up, ok'. We are brothers from a different mother, that's what he is. He has the best stories and is not afraid to tell them either.

With Brian joining the band, not only did they now have great musicians, but Brian could add wonderful vocal harmonies too. Brian recalls joining the band:

> When I started my first band, The Three Jets, we were managed by my dad. We had Barry Reynolds, a good guitar player and Johnny Pickup, on drums. The Three Jets, well we had had enough really after a short time - we weren't kids anymore. It just fell away, really. I loved music, and while I was on one of our gigs, we met The Warriors at the Boneyard Club [later called Woods Pianos & Organs, where the Author began his apprenticeship] on Manchester Road in Bolton, just opposite the old train station.

Brian was recommended to Jon and he was invited to meet the band. The Warriors were playing at The Boneyard as were Brian's band, The Three Jets. His keyboard was already set up. They asked Brian if he could play 'Green Unions'. He played it for them and got the gig in ten seconds.

Brian adds: 'I was seventeen when I joined The Warriors - far too young to go to Germany with them, so they smuggled me over!'

Not everyone remembers meeting him for the first time quite like that. Rod recalls meeting Brian: 'I remember him on stage with a band we had seen. We went to a party somewhere in Bolton, and he was in bed with Wendy, and I was with another girl. That's the first time we spoke! Very rock and roll!'

Brian loved his football, as did Jon, Brian's team being Bolton Wanderers and Jon's Accrington Stanley. For many decades to come, that would be a source of teasing for both. Brian's musical interest started when he was about five years old. His father played the piano, although not very professionally. Brian chuckles and remembers:

> Dad could play anything in 2/4 time. He'd use full sustain pedal and use lots of bass notes and volume. He would play all the melody on the black keys, plus the odd white note and often get that wrong! Mum would sing and want something in 3/4 time and dad could only do 2/4 time so they would start and finish at different times. My granddad played piano in pubs. He told me to do myself a favour and not grow up like him. He said I should learn to play the

piano and I would never be without food or friends. He was right. I have him to thank.

The band were also given an introduction to the agent Don Reed which resulted in a meeting with the famous producer Joe Meek. Brian Chatton, speaking in 2015 recalls:

> We went to Joe Meek's studio to do an audition. He did the famous Telstar record. His studio was on the top of this four-story building, with really [treacherous] steps - it was not easy to get up there, especially with Ian and his drums. He spoke in a very high voice, like a woman, and he was so squeaky saying 'come on boys'. We were just killing ourselves with laughter so much. We kind of messed up, because me and Ian were laughing that much, so he cancelled it all. We had just carried it all up and set up the gear and then he said, 'No No No! I've have had enough of you all, take your stuff'. Jon wasn't too happy with that!

Above: August 1966 and The Warriors play in London at the Tiles club on Oxford Street. *(David Watkinson Collection)*

Developing their own style

Jon Anderson and The Warriors were at this point a very well-rehearsed, practised band. The rigours of the road had been mastered, and agents and management had come and gone. Some band members had seen enough and left to join the 'real' world again. Some members just had the music business deeply engrained into their beings.

The band felt they were as good as anyone on the circuit at this time. The only thing missing was that elusive hit record to take them to the next rung on the musical ladder. Tony Anderson comments that the band were a formidable, professional band and ready to be at the top. There was certainly no stopping Jon Anderson's drive and vision. People liked Jon's persona, his sound and his movement. Watching Jon Anderson with The Warriors in the few clips that still exist, he looks rather smooth and has a bit the style of the great James Brown going on in his movement. He is fond of a shoe shuffle, a twist and a fluttering of the arms. However, Jon knew that it was all about his voice and not the gyrating of his hips. He would never be a Mick Jagger, Tom Jones or even a James Brown. If anything, he was more of a 'cheeky chappy', with a sweet smile, just like Jon's musical hero, Paul McCartney. Brian continues:

> Jon always moved well. Tamla Motown was popular and the great song 'I'll Be There' was a big hit. He could dance like the black guys, and he taught me how to dance, which is hilarious when I think back. He made me move well. I could never move that well, being a Bolton lad not caring about fucking Come Dancing (the British TV program about Ballroom Dancing) and all. He just moved naturally like a black American guy. He'd be swaying and clicking his fingers and turning around, in his inevitable fashion.

The music scene was full of successful British acts with smash-hit records, and The Warriors emulated them, note for note. The Animals, Manfred Mann, Wayne Fontana and the Mindbenders, and The Troggs, they played all their hits - they were a fine copy band indeed.

It was in the early part of 1966 that the band had one of their musical highlights. Jon recalls the time when a young, enthusiastic singer joined them on stage one evening:

> We were playing a gig in a place called Sheffield, and the manager of the club asked if we would mind if a friend of his got up and sang with us. The band all agreed, so this young sixteen-year-old guy with a bottle of whiskey shouted out that he wanted to sing in our band. And in a flash, he joined us on stage and asked us to sing 'Hit the Road Jack' by Ray Charles. We started singing it, and he joined in, and it was amazing! He sounded just like Ray Charles.

Afterwards, having blown them away with the talent, the kid announced: 'My name is Joe Cocker. I'm sixteen!'

It's not every day your path crosses with a future world-class vocalist,

Above: A visit home, with Jon back on the farm in his finest Warriors outfit. *(David Watkinson Collection)*

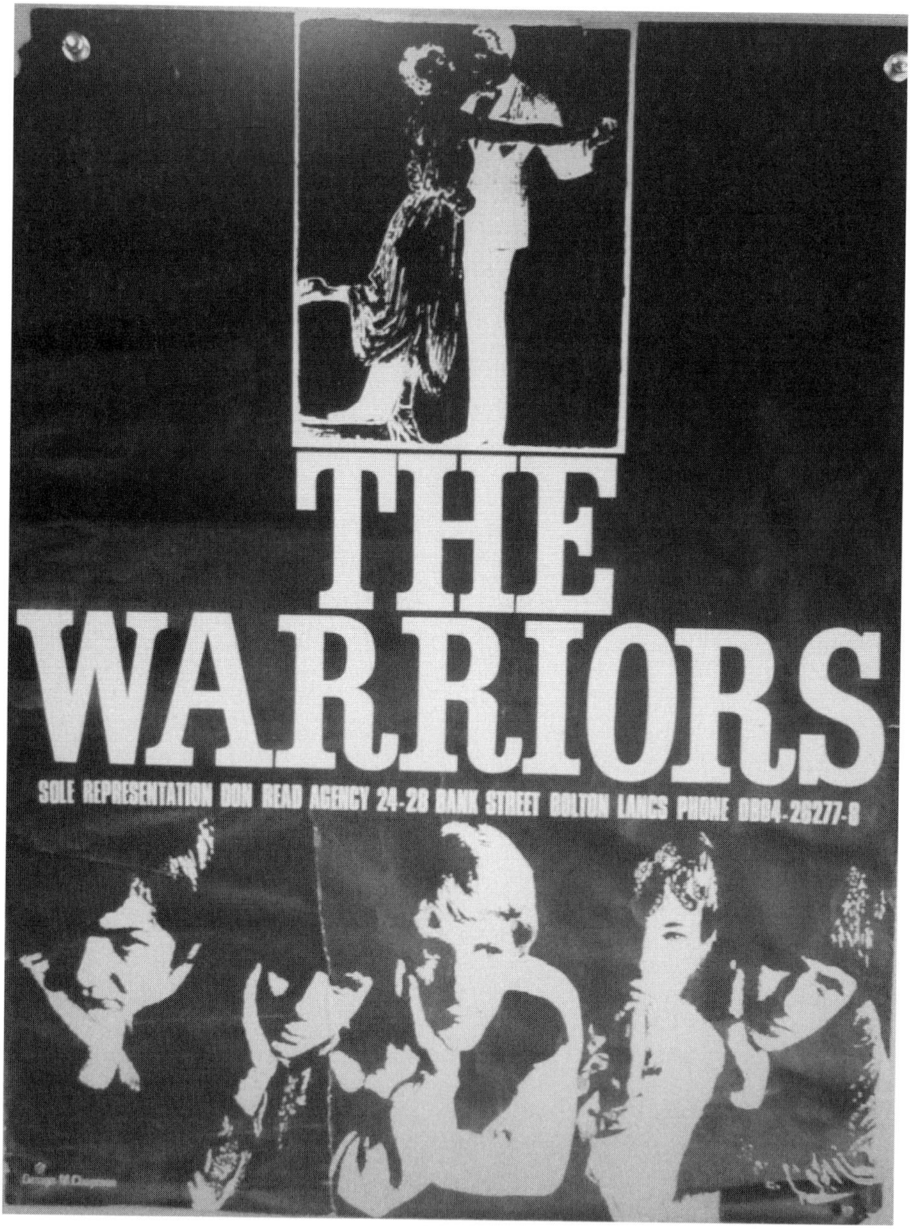

Above: A fabulously rare Warriors poster from around 1966. This is believed to be the only one left and the earliest known poster with Jon featured on it. Large in size, it is rumoured to have been produced at the art school in Bolton. Designed by M. Chapman. *(David Watkinson Collection)*

one unique in their performance, sound and influence. Brian Chatton also recalls this moment:

> It was at the Sheffield Esquire Club, and Joe Cocker got up on stage with us and sang. He was totally mind-blowing, with an enormous voice and so down-to-earth, like most Northerners. He would wave his arms around like a madman, and pretended to play the guitar, look at Rod, and point to indicate it was his turn to play! We weren't ready for this and wondered 'what the fuck is going on here'! Rod played his heart out that night. Then he pointed to me to play the keyboards, and he pretended to play the keyboards! I hadn't seen this before, but I think it was the best solo that I have ever played on my Vox Continental. I played the shit out of it. He was so inspiring. Jon joined in singing harmony with Joe. The guys in the band said 'should we open some windows' as he was swishing his head and his arms about, and spit was flying about. It was like he was having a fit!

The Warriors were a good, live band and they knew it. If Jon and the band were going to progress, though, then what was the next step? They wanted more success. In May 1966, at the Bolton Palaise gig, they met an agent from Hamburg who had been very impressed by them that evening and this led to an invitation to play in Germany a few months later. Jon says:

> We wanted to go to Germany, but none of us had passports. We went to do an audition to determine that we could get the German gigs and as we did alright, we were good-to-go to Germany. 1966-67: there was much 'peace-love' in the air!

3. The European Adventure

Following in the footsteps of their heroes The Beatles, The Warriors set off for Germany in June 1966, on their big money-making, fame-and-fortune adventure across Europe. They started in Cologne.

Jon says: 'The Warriors went to Germany because it's a tradition: English musicians have been going to Germany since [the time of] Beethoven, so we went too.'

Germany had a thriving music scene, and plenty of offers of work came in for the band. Playing gigs to similar-sized audiences as at home, it all went smoothly, but they didn't change the world. They were one little band among hundreds doing the circuit. The funny thing was, though, that they did have someone special upfront as the lead singer. It's just that no one knew it yet. Perhaps Jon was starting to believe it, though.

Sex, songs and smoky venues

Showing everyone the way, The Beatles toured Germany, Japan and the Philippines between 24th June and 4th July 1966. The Warriors were soon following suit, with John Marshall, The Warriors manager, booking the band plenty of gigs. In the beginning, they played their UK set, but it soon became clear that they would have to learn just about everything that came into the charts every week to keep the punters happy. The smoky venues were full of hardened music-lovers, big drinkers and girls looking for a pop star to latch onto, for drinks and more. The band were playing a steady schedule with showtimes starting at about six o'clock in the evening and ending at two in the morning. Really earning their money, they were given a very short break of 5 - 10 minutes, to have a swift toilet break and a fast beer, plus maybe a pill or two and then they were back on stage.

Musician and friend of the band, Brian Parrish, shares his memories of The Warriors and Germany in the late 1960s:

> I met and knew all of them. I was in Germany at the same time as The Warriors for the whole of the mid-60s. It was a time of unbelievable energy. You have to remember the atmosphere [where] the music was so much more important to people, not just musicians, but to everybody.

Popular culture was changing, and a lot of that change came through rock 'n' roll music. The post-war younger generation had, for the first time, a disposable income and a burning desire to be part of an anti-establishment movement. Musicians began to express their emotions for them - in their lyrics. The teenager was born out of Rock 'n Roll music, and the younger generation developed a new identity.

Although post-war Germany had a stigma attached to it, the teenagers were not fazed by it. They wanted an escape, and rock 'n' roll music helped to change everyone and everything. Germany was just a playground of booze, birds, drugs and music for these lads from Lancashire. Indeed, for the band, having a good time was pretty high up on the list of what they wanted to achieve while they were in Germany. Brian captures the moment: 'Our hormones were bouncing around, and sexually everyone was in and out of each other!' If fun was the name of the game, then music was the way it was paid for. These were new music styles for the next generation, and being in Germany, well, that gave it that extra thrill.

When British bands came to Germany they were celebrated. The German bands were covering songs that they had heard from the American artists, but not quite well enough. It wasn't their first language, after all. One of the key figures in kick-starting the music scene was Manfred Weissleder, who opened the Star Club in Hamburg. It was his idea to do something no one else had done, which was to open a club and book all the big artists from America to come over and play. He was a real trailblazer. Open from six in the evening to six in the morning, these big, superstar acts had to fit the bill. With the German acts not quite cutting the mustard, they looked to the American and English bands to step in and fill the gap. Ray Charles, The Everly Brothers, Eddie Cochran, Chuck Berry, Little Richard, he had them come over and play for one or two weeks at a time. He also had acts like Cliff Richard, and Johnny Kidd and The Pirates. Bands from the Liverpool scene was soon snapped up,

Left: Brian, Dave, Ian, Jon and Rod in Munich in 1967. *(Urich Handl – Brian Chatton)*

with good acts such as Terry Sheridan, Rory Storm and later, of course, The Beatles. Our intrepid Warriors were one of many hopeful bands to be invited over. Package tours had been big at the time where six or seven artists a night would perform short sets, so no one in the band had done a residency like this before.

Weissleder paid some of these artists handsomely. Ray Charles was reportedly paid in the region of 100,000 DM, which was a huge amount of money at the time.

It was felt that the UK bands played better versions of the hits of the time, that were truer to the originals, than the German bands. But what happened after a while was that bands started to look for more obscure songs to play and then change them a little. The Beatles led the way, emulating the most famous bands, and mixing the standards with some of their own compositions. Other bands saw this happening, and they began to write their own songs, too. The bands themselves expanded. Some would have roadies, some horn sections, some jazz musicians. The possibilities seemed endless - this was such an exciting time to be in music.

Shenanigans

With the bands like The Beatles playing long sets late into the night, some of the shifts early in the day led to people doing silly things to keep awake and to keep everyone interested. Once, it was said that John Lennon came on in his underpants, another time with a loo seat around his head. All the bands got up to shenanigans to get through their sets. There was a lot of drinking and the odd massive food fight. One of a band's members once faked a fit, where they had set up a stretcher to run on and take the lead singer off. Oh, and doing a striptease to keep the crowd awake was all part of the fun. Then they would all go down to the Reeperbahn - the famous street in Hamburg, known for its nightlife - to party. The Warriors were the same as the rest of the bands. These were 'crazy, silly times' as Jon Anderson has called this period many times.

Partying was common with the guys in the band. They would mingle with the other bands into the early hours of the mornings. Germany had a different feel to it. It was artier and freer, with a lot more travellers and hippy types and - of course - more drugs. Dope, acid, pot and LSD were prevalent. These were crazy times, the like which the bands had not seen before.

Jon confirms: 'While hard work sums up the band's ethic, what also went on was lots of partying and drinking.'

Jon chuckles about Brian Chatton: 'He chased all the girls a lot. It must be something to do with the water up-north in Bolton [Brian's home town] - it makes you horny!'

Mike remembers touring Germany:

> There were a few members of the band that would be affected by the girls. I know we were all young, but I couldn't do what a lot of them did in Germany, it wasn't my scene! The bars were full of dancing girls, forward girls who weren't exactly like the ones back home. Go-Go-Girls were a big favourite at the PN Hit House in Munich. There was temptation all around.

Above: Rod in Hamburg at the Top Ten Club in July 1966. *(Lis Klowe Pedersen)*

With the amount of work over these long days and evenings, somehow the band had to be kept up and awake. Energy was often severely lacking, and a boost was needed. Rod recalls:

> We had to get a kick to help us do the gigs and play into the night. We just used it for a for the pick-up and to keep us going. We started on the blue-ees (blue coloured pills), for the kick, the buzz. It was different then. We used to buy it in London, and you could get cough medicine that was forty per cent morphine. I remember driving in London one time, through the underpass and getting pulled over by the police and hadn't a clue I had even been done! I just carried onto the gig. Until mum said, 'What's this!' when a letter came in the post. I hadn't a clue - I couldn't remember.

The band's escape from the gigging routine came in the form of trips to the coast. Either Jon or Rod would drive the band to Lübeck, taking all their friends and musicians to go and sit on the beach all day to drink and laugh. And then they would go back and play all night.

The band meets Jimi Hendrix

If you are going to meet any famous rock star from the 1960s then right up there would be Jimi Hendrix. Synonymous with that era, he did cross paths at various times with Jon Anderson, The Warriors and Chris Squire.

Brian Chatton recalled his Hendrix moment:

> Hendrix stepped over me in Germany! We were playing the PN Hit House club, and he was playing the Big Apple club, which was four doors away. It would have been 1966, and he was in his prime. We had heard about this Jimi Hendrix Experience band, but we never got the chance to see them because we were playing seven days a week. We could never see any other bands because they were playing when we were.

They sent a message out to Jimi and invited him to a party, telling him that they had heard great things about him. Brian continues:

> We finished our set at two in the morning, and they finished later, so we went around to Ursula (Uschi/Ish), who was Jon and mine's girlfriend. We used to share her, never together but he would be with her then I would. We never fought about it; we were too close for that. So, we went to her place, and I got as smashed as hell, I was drinking this cheap drink and smoking some strong shit!

Brian remembers crawling to the bathroom, which was next to the front door, to throw up. The front door opened and in came Jimi Hendrix and his

THE OBSERVER, Tuesday, August 9, 1966

Our younger readers' OWN page

Teenage TOPICS

'THE WARRIORS' ARE BACK FROM GERMANY –With a return booking

The "New Warriors" have just finished a highly successful tour of Germany — two weeks in Cologne, two weeks in Frankfurt — and have earned themselves a return visit to these two cities in December.

Their continental agent phoned the Don Reid Agency in Bolton after they had been in Germany only a few days in order to book their return dates.

BUSY

Their "new sound" has made the Warriors, who originated in Accrington, one of the busiest groups in the country, with their diary fully booked to the end of the year.

It has been noticeable that their popularity is strongest in the Tyneside area (home of "The Animals") and in both Glasgow and Edinburgh.

During the next three weeks they will be in London to make their new record written specially for them by the top Radio Caroline disc jockey "Ugli" Ray Terrett and it is hoped that the record will be released in the autumn.

The new sound is provided by Brian Chatton, an organist from Radcliffe, who was brought into the group to replace the lead guitarist and singer.

The new line-up is completed by John Anderson (vocalist) Rodney Hill (bass guitar) Dave Foster (lead guitar) and Ian Wallace (drums).

The group are to play at the "Miss Accrington" dance, which will be held at the Town Hall on Friday, September 2nd.

AT YOUR LOCAL CINEMA ACCRINGTON

NEW PRINCES: All this week Tony Curtis, Jack Lemmon and Natalie Wood in "THE GREAT RACE", one of the funniest comedies of all time.

It is a story of the death-defying rivalry which exists between the unscrupulous Professor Fate (Jack Lemmon) and that dashing knight-errant the "Great Leslie" (Tony Curtis). This reaches a climax in the year 1908 with the Great Auto Race from New York to Paris. Fate, everlastingly foiled in his efforts to outdo Leslie in deeds of amazing daredevilry, is sworn to beat his rival in this the greatest of all their adventures.

Fate builds himself a malevolent black car with nose-cone cannon to compete against Leslie's gleaming white brass phaeton.

Maggie Dubois (Natalie Wood) a determined young woman who smokes cigars, and who campaigns — vociferously — for women's rights, joins the race as a reporter for the "New York Clarion". While Fate quickly eliminates other competitors by mysterious explosions and flying wheels, Maggie eliminates herself when her "Stanley Steamer" roadster breaks down. She persuades Leslie to let her accompany him and his associate, Hezekiah, on a temporary basis and brings along her pigeons with which she is going to send back her dispatches.

The Great Race has begun. The cast also includes Dorothy Provine, Vivian Vance, Arthur O'Connell, Keenan Wynn and Peter Falk.

ODEON: Showing until Wednesday night is the film version of the Peter O'Donnell book "MODESTY BLAISE", starring Monica Vitti, Terence Stamp, Dirk Bogarde, Harry Andrews and Michael Craig.

It is the tale of a female super-agent, Modesty Blaise, and her Cockney side-kick Willie Garvin. They are recruited by Sir Gerald Tarrant of the Secret Service to protect a shipment of diamonds on which could depend a vital Middle East Oil concession.

Far away in his op-art island castle, arch-villain Gabriel plots to purloin the diamonds and ruin Britain in the Arab world's estimation.

In Amsterdam Modesty makes contact with British agent Paul Hagan, in whose flat she is captured by the enemy. Willie and Tarrant hurtle to the rescue. The dia-

HS RACE FROM KEMPSEY

Results of the Accrington and District Homing Society race from Kempsey: 1 Roberts and Watson 1273.26 ABCD; 2 Anderton and Sons 1269.53 BCD; 3 J Marshall 1263.29 E; 4 C Firth 1260.16; 5 G Lupton 1252.13; 6 J Marshall 1245.76; 7 J R Greenwood 1243.46; 8 C Firth

Let's see what's in the Classifieds

You can often find the article you've been looking for in the classifieds.

Someone may have things in the house they no longer want—a cycle a piano a pram, a camera, a washing machine, a cooker, a radio, a sewing machine, or a piece of furniture.

You may be able to buy what you want, at the price you want to pay, through the classified columns.

It will pay you to advertise

In the 'Observer'

Left: The local paper welcomes the lads back from Europe. *(David Watkinson Collection)*

Above: The band playing in Koln in May 1967. *(Urich Handl – David Watkinson Collection)*

two friends. Jimi, Mitch Mitchell and Jon chatted for an hour after Jimi had stepped over the incumbent Brian like a doormat!
Brian says:

> I saw him later at the Speakeasy Club, and he had heard that I could write music. He didn't know anybody who could do it, and he would write all these riffs and stuff, and he said he couldn't afford to go to the studio every time he did stuff like that. He said he just needed to put it down and he had heard I could do it. I'd have a vodka and tonic, and he would have a beer. He wanted it written down - but this was Hendrix! You can't write 'WHYYYYEEERHHHHUUUOOOO' down as a Hendrix lick, can you? You couldn't write down what he played!

Note: Uschi Obermaier was a famous groupie/model/ film director, who also went on to be a girlfriend of one of the members of Krautrock band Amon Duul, at the famous Kommune 1 in Munich. She followed that by dating Keith Richards, Mick Jagger and Hendrix. She was, and many would say still is, the beautiful face of Germany's chaotic 1960s era.

At the 1994 Yestival festival in the USA, Jon spoke of his time with Jimi:

> I met Jimi Hendrix in Germany, and he was such a gentle soul. This guy was wild on stage and amazing. We spoke while we were recouping from a load of drugs! I was in a jazz club called the Ronnie Scott's Club, and Rahsaan Roland Kirk was playing. He was one of the greatest saxophone players ever - he used to play two or even three saxophones at the same time. Unbelievable!

He told me a lot about music. Jimi walked in and got up on stage, and they both just played together without speaking to one another. They created spontaneous jazz, and it was amazing.

Rod Hill recalls meeting Jimi too: "I saw Jimi Hendrix play at the Bolton Odeon with The Walker Brothers when they toured together once. I saw him set fire to his guitar! Wow!"

But everybody wanted to be a Beatle. Rodney recalled a fan comment which he could never forget: 'The Warriors at The Cavern Club were great and all the people who saw The Beatles every week said that we were the next Beatles.' While there has never been 'the next Beatles', Brian Chatton adds:

We became like The Beatles because they played in Hamburg at the Star Club. They would do the ten hours a day: that's how they became that good. There are no overnight successes. It takes time.

Left: Jon, Dave and Ian in Koln in 1967. *(Angelika Granaht)*

Above: Dave and Rod, Koln in 1967. *(Angelika Granaht)*

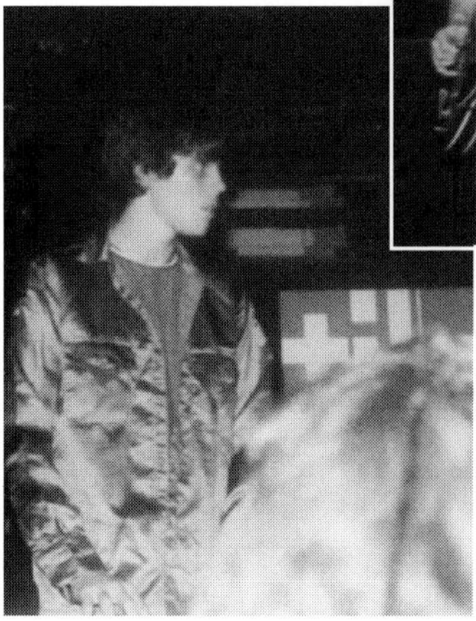

Left: Brian and his organ, Koln in 1967. *(Angelika Granaht)*

Die Krieger kommen

Vor zwei Wochen spielten sie noch in Frankfurt im "Storyville": die englische Beatgruppe The Warriors (Krieger). Ich lege Euch die Karte bei, die ich von ihnen bekam. Könnt Ihr nicht mal etwas über diese Band bringen? (Ja, gern! D. Red.) Barbara Rosing, Bad Vilbel

Left: An article about the band's Storyville appearances. *(David Watkinson Collection)*
Above Right: At the Storyville in Cologne in 1966. *(M. Evans)*

Jon Anderson's obsession with The Beatles is confirmed in an interview with Jon in 2011 by Dan Bond of *Geeks of Doom*. Jon said:

> I wanted to be a Beatle. [Adopts Liverpudlian accent]. I used to talk like that a lot, like this! My mum smacked me over the head. [Puts on very broad Lancashire accent] 'Stop talking like that, we don't talk like that up here!' [Back to Scouse] 'I want to be a Beatle, mum!' [Back to Lancashire] 'Well piss off then!' my mum would say. Everybody wanted to be a Beatle. I dyed my hair black, and it looked terrible! I bought the boots; we wore the distinctive grey jackets with red leather buttons and half belts. That's life. You try things out; you keep going.

After a solid, non-stop, gruelling tour of Germany, in April 1967 the band decided it was time for a break so headed back to the UK, taking a rest for a few weeks, before returning to Cologne to do it all again. An article in the local Lancashire newspaper covering the return of the now-famous Warriors, said:

> Even though the band were brewing up a storm on the continent, it seemed not all teenagers were up to speed with the new beat scene and maybe a bit behind the times. It has been a hard job but through their persistence and professionalism The Warriors, with their slick and dynamic presentation of Tamla Motown material, are getting heard and recognised as one of the best English bands.

Led by their excellent millionaire manager John Marshall, who has been associated with such artists as the legendary Humphrey Bogart, Frank Sinatra and Ava Gardner, rumours began circulating about possible TV and film work to promote them further. It was said that with their dapper outfits they really would look good visually, too. The wonderful songs out there in the charts would supply the band with more than enough material. But it appears that The Warriors lost out on at least one good song. Cliff Richard had a hit record with 'It's All Over'. However, before Cliff recorded the song, the band had asked their agent if they could release it, but he refused as he thought it was not commercial enough. The Warriors were not enamoured of that decision.

The relentlessness of the gigging in Frankfurt, Cologne, Munich, Hamburg then Copenhagen was tiring but fun for The Warriors. They played each venue for four weeks, performing four and a half hours a night with a fifteen-minute break every hour. Over weekends they did two-hour matinees in the afternoons and ended at midnight on Sundays.

The low-down on the Ladies

During these lengthy stays in Europe, the band met and formed relationships. Dave Foster was with Nora, (Sex Pistol Johnny Rotten's future wife) for a long time. He stayed with her and went on to record an album with her, which has since been lost.

Jon was going out with his girlfriend Uschi (also known as Ish). Parties were held both at Uschi's flat and at a favourite bar called Stubchen in Koln. Tagging along were Helga, Nanni and Rosi, who liked Brian Chatton. Rod and Nanni were great friends too. While in Cologne, the band met sisters Renate and Marianne, also Angelica, the three of whom were close to the band all the time after that. Marianne eventually married one of the members of the band Badfinger, Tom Evans. The band's story is almost too hard to hear, so let's just say they suffered the stresses and strains of the music business to the end. It became a shocking story of how poorly the band had been managed. Rock 'n roll at its worst. It was said that Renate was as innocent as the day was long. In the end, all the girls followed the band across Europe, and some came back to the UK with them. The fun time girls with long hair and mini-skirts, loved their music, dancing, drink and cigarettes.

Marianne, a long-term friend of Jon's from the late 60s, spoke in 2016 about the exciting Warriors days and her relationship with Jon in London and Germany up until the very early Yes days. She reminisces:

> I was a Warriors fan from the very beginning, as were my friends. Brian Chatton liked his women - he was such a good-looking lad. When he and Jon slept at my parent's house, my mother would tell us girls that we had to stay in the living room and the boys had to stay in their room. They slept in one bed, and we slept on the settee! They stayed just a few days, I think. Jon and Brian went sightseeing up in the mountains. I still have letters from those days from Jon, and I have one from Jon's parents who wrote to me when I sold Jon a cape to wear on stage. It was a black cape, and it looked great on him. Jon once wrote a ten-page letter to me about dreams he had, but they got destroyed by my husband, who was jealous of our pen-pal relationship. That's all it was, never any more.

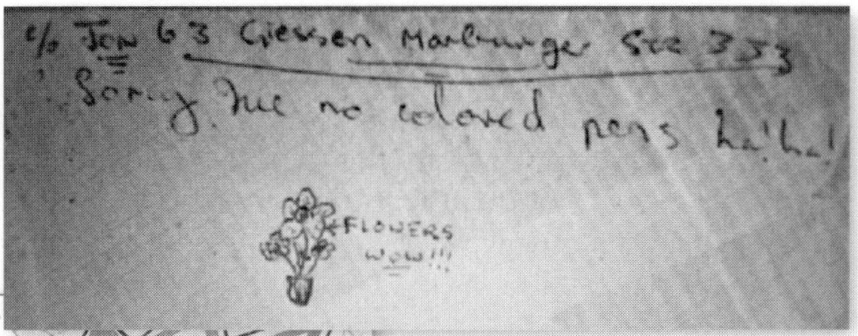

Top: This envelope dates from around the first time that Jon used the spelling 'Jon' as a forename. Often thought to have started doing this much later, these were the early days before Jon went public with the change. Jokingly, he commentates that he ran out of the coloured pens he often used in his decorative letters and envelopes to friends in the 1960s. *(N. Ragsdale)*
Above Left: Jon and the girl fans *(M. Evans)*
Above Right: An envelope to Jon's hotel in Koln 8 December 1966 *(N. Ragsdale)*

She also recalls a trip to the Storyville Club, Cologne:

> I had a large Phillips tape machine and with it made a tape of one of The Warriors' gigs. I went over to see Dave Foster, and he asked if he could borrow that tape. I lent it to him, and never got it back. The Storyville club was a great club with a good atmosphere. I would sometimes get on stage at the end of the show and sing the 'Edelweiss' song with Jon. Jon was a little shy on stage and was working on what kind of showman he was going to be, which was nice - endearing. The Warriors had great harmonies, the best around and Jon was the best.

Rod has a random memory about Brian and one of his ladies:

> Brian was going with a girl who was about seventeen, and we had a police raid on a flat. We hid this girl in the fridge, and then we all forgot she was there for about an hour before we remembered her and got her out! She was freezing, but she was ok. We celebrated that we hadn't killed her, we drank the place dry.

The melting pot of change

The Top Ten Club was a popular place on the Reeperbahn, and it was here that The Warriors met with The Remo Four, whose keyboard player was Tony Ashton, who went onto be the band Ashton, Gardner and Dyke, and later Paice, Ashton, Lord. They also met and played with the band The Artwoods in Copenhagen, who had Jon Lord on organ. He would go on to become part of Deep Purple.

It was only a few years since skiffle had been gripping teenagers. The music scene had changed drastically, with many bands creatively feeding off one another, and being influenced by a variety of music genres. Meanwhile, The Beatles were working on *Sgt. Pepper's Lonely-Hearts Club Band*, which contributed hugely to this era of rather more arty and experimental music. Hendrix, The Who, Jefferson Airplane and The Moody Blues all added their unique blend of music into the mix.

In January, The Beatles recorded a fourteen-minute avant-garde performance which was known as 'Carnival of Light', and is considered the holy grail of missing Beatles' songs. The Beatles were really the first progressive rock band, in the sense that they planted the seed in all others that you can do anything in music. All these fascinating musical changes and experimental works showcased the light and shade, the mystical and classical. There was a blending of comic moments and light-heartedness with serious lyrics. Boundaries were broken by stretching music away from the three-minute hit song. Jon was captivated by it all.

This era was shining a light on how music culture was changing. The Monterey Pop Festival surprised everyone by being attended by around 100,000 people and with the release of *Sgt. Pepper*, a new era of psychedelia was ushered in. The mass appeal of the Beatles meant that the album was played virtually everywhere. No longer would this out-there music be hidden away in the underground scene. This was the future. Jon Anderson was as amazed as anyone with the new sounds and possibilities, often describing the album as a huge influence on him.

Rodney, the guitarist, saw changes happening to their arrangements of songs which had pretty much been set in stone: 'What we decided to do was to stick an extra verse or a bit of another song into the piece or do a solo and so we would extend songs. If you look at what Yes did later, Jon had a lot of that organised in The Warriors.'

The band had the same management as The Kinks for a while, supporting them at the Rawtenstall Astoria. By then, in 1967, the Kinks had had eleven top twenty hit singles. However, when The Warriors met the dashing, trendy Kinks, and they noticed them wearing their red riding jackets with stains and spills down them, they were not impressed. Mike Brereton says:

> [The band] liked them at first when they did The Everly Brothers numbers. But then they went on and did the 'crap stuff'. The Kinks, managers, Robert Wace and Grenville Collins, apparently related to royalty, looked after The Warriors too. The Kinks, well, we didn't think much of them. To tell you the truth, The Kinks were crap.

Above Left: Rod and Ian enjoying some backstage time. *(David Watkinson Collection)*
Right: Fun in the Seven Hills with Jon (in cape), Brian and Rosi. *(M. Evans)*

One of the formidable bands at the time also from Liverpool and with links to The Beatles were The Koobas. They were playing in Germany over Christmas and New Year in 1966, at the same time as The Warriors. The Koobas had a short career but probably had one of the greatest support band slots in history - with The Beatles on their final tour, as well as The Who and the Jimmy Hendrix Experience. They played in Germany in January 1967 and it was at this point that Jon met Tony O'Reilly, their drummer, joining Tony and The Koobas on stage at The Storyville Club. On that night the line-up was The Warriors, The Koobas and the band Thoughts. Tony would later play a role, albeit a minor one, in the history of Yes. The Koobas, who were a very accomplished band indeed, never quite got that break that they deserved. For readers knowing nothing about them, a YouTube visit will provide something of a surprise. The band changed style but disbanded in 1968, having given it their best shot. In Rodney Hill's diaries of the band, Tony has his phone number listed, so clearly, they were in touch, as they would be with other bands. Indeed, The Warriors gigged along with bands such as The Small Faces and many of the other Mersey-beat bands.

Christmas Blues

December 1966 was their first Christmas away from home. For Jon and Brian, being away from family was a big deal for them. But meeting the girls who were really hardened Warriors fans helped. Marianne let both Jon and Brian stay with them in The Seven Hills, Bonne. Brian says: 'I really missed my mum and when they put on the Bing Crosby song 'White Christmas' I just flooded. Jon said, "Come on Bryson, (his nickname for me) you will be home soon." I was gutted.'

Enjoying the late-night Christmas air, both Jon and Marianne would often walk down the streets singing 'Kling, Glöckchen, Klingelingeling' (or 'Ring, Little Bell', a German Christmas carol from the 19th century), and Marianne reports: 'crazily people threw sweets and chocolates out of the windows at them'. On leaving the Storyville Club one night, Jon could be heard singing 'Edelweiss' as he walked along the streets, with friend Angelika, no doubt fortified by their favourite German beer, also called Edelweiss.

They drank till late all the time, Angelika remembers, fondly:

> Sometimes Jon drove me home. We sat in the van just talking, sometimes till the sun came up, and for me, it was time to get to work. They were lovely times and memories. I loved the band and it is Jon who I remember most. He was - is - a special person. He's a little bit of an angel - or fairy-like - living on another planet! On stage he did his songs his way, in his own style singing with his heavenly voice. He kept his style the same for 50 years, although the band Yes and their instruments were more advanced! Jon has his own way to live. He was a kind of a dreamer.

THE OBSERVER, Tuesday, April 18, 1967 7

Our younger readers' OWN page

Teenage TOPICS

THE WARRIORS TAKE A SHORT BUT WELL-EARNED REST

(Picture: Garth D...

After brewing up a big beat "storm" on the continent, the Warriors are back in Accrington.

The lads are enjoying a well-earned holiday before going to Cologne in a few days time.

Although the group are proving explosively successful with teenagers abroad, certain sections of the continental pop fans are a little behind the times.

In Cologne for example, Bill Haley, the original "king" of ... popular ... Accrington's best ... group, with their slick and dynamic presentation of Tamla Motown material, are rapidly winning fans over to the best in contemporary beat.

The boys have a good manager in John Marshall, a millionaire who has been associated in the past with such artistes as the legendary Humphrey Bogart, Frank Sinatra and Ava Gardner.

The group's line-up is John Anderson (vocals), Rodney Hill (bass guitar), Dave Foster (lead guitar), Ian Wallace (drums) and Brian Chatton (organ).

TO MAKE FILM

When the lads get to Cologne they will make a film which is to be shown on German television.

The film will no doubt highlight the group's exciting new act, which lays more emphasis ...

AT YOUR LOCAL CINEMA

ACCRINGTON

ODEON: One of this year's best British films, "GEORGY GIRL", starring the likeable Lynn Redgrave in the title role, is showing today and tomorrow.

Interest in this tremendously enjoyable film has been aroused by the hit recording of the title song by the Seekers.

The recently married Miss Redgrave, sister of Vanessa and daughter of Sir Michael, ... nominated for an oscar ... her portrayal of "an ugly ... in the film.

... of the characters ... meets during the ... of the film are a ... businessman who has designs on her played by popular James Mason and an affable rogue portrayed in admirable style by Alan Bates.

According to critics and audiences alike, "Georgy Girl" is a film you cannot afford to miss.

The supporting film, an exciting thriller called "RAGE", stars Glenn Ford.

On Thursday, and for the rest of the week, one of Britain's top male stars, Michael Caine, can be seen starring in "GAMBIT", a sophisticated and exciting yet amusing thriller.

The plot centres around the attempted robbery of a statue from one of the world's richest men (Herbert Lom).

Caine's attractive accomplice in crime is Shirley MacLaine.

The young Mr Caine first gained fame in "Zulu", and followed this success with "The Ipcress File", "Alfie" and "Funeral In Berlin".

A western, "THE PLAINSMAN", starring Don Murray, completes the bill.

NEW PRINCES: A stunningly good film, "WHO'S AFRAID OF VIRGINIA WOOLF?", is showing all week.

Based on top American play... successful Broadway production, ... George and Martha, a couple whose marriage is, to say the least, a little stale.

Raw nerves are exposed as argument follows bitter argument between the pair.

Eventually George, a college professor, and his wife entertain a young teacher and his young wife with shocking results.

Probably the world's most famous married pair, Elizabeth Taylor and Richard Burton star as Martha and George.

Anyone expecting Miss Taylor to be at her most beautiful will receive a surprise when they see the film. She plays a ...

ANNIVERSARY

Gospel hymns and songs were played with a modern beat by the Nazarene Crusaders at an anniversary weekend at ... Church.

The Saturday rally was supported by friends from other denominations.

The Convener was Mr Stephen Jackson and the accompanist was Mrs Coates.

Pastor Norman Wade, of Rainhill, a former minister of the Church, gave the address.

Pastor Wade conducted the services on Sunday, accompanied by his family.

Local police win soccer cup again

CLIMBER LECTURES ON HIS TRAVELS

... Gray, paid a visit to Accrington last week when ... lectured to an apprecia... library audience about ... travels and expeditions.

His topics included the ... city of the Incas and the ... beautiful cities in the wo... He also gave an account ... his recent expedition to P... to climb the north side of ... Alpamio. The talk was ma... concerned with So... America, a part of the wo... which Mr Gray knows w... having been the leader of ... Andean expedition in 1966.

The lecture was illustrated ... slides including ones ...

Left: Newspaper article about The Warriors resting back in the UK. *(David Watkinson Collection)*

Memories of January 1967

Jon had a great social life alongside all the hard work, building up the good reputation of the band. In the age before mobile phones, Jon was a keen correspondent, writing many letters. Not only did he write, but he drew and painted too. Former German club scene DJ Nicky speaks about the letters she still owns from Jon: 'I have a few after all these years. They are personal, about Germany life, low key, day to day stuff, living in the same house or nearby as friends. Jon liked to write a lot.'

Most of the German clubs, like the Top Ten Club, The Star Club and others, used to have bands sign up to play nightly for a month at a time. The clubs were a haven of activity where you met friends and fellow musicians. Jon's first encounter with the band The Gentle Party, from Bolton, happened at the end of January 1967. The diary entry shows them (possibly) playing at the Star Club. He got on well with them, and this was an important encounter, as he would go on to sing with them after The Warriors split up.

The Jon Anderson moves can be seen on YouTube, via The Warrior's track 'Mr Nobody Nothing'. Jon does indeed move well. This style of performance would eventually disappear, along with the music it accompanied, as Jon moved forward and presented a different image to the world. But still loving the harmonies and style of The Everly Brothers, Jon would copy this, along with a mixture of all kinds of music.

Changing visions

By late 1967, Jon Anderson's visions of the future were changing. Often dreaming big and talking to other bands about music, his plans were slowly gathering speed and beat music, and top twenty hits were waning from priorities. Jon spent more and more time reading. One of those influential books was by Lobsang Rampa, the controversial author of books such as *Wisdom of the Ancients* (1965), *My Visit to Venus* (1957), and *The Third Eye* (1956). Buddhism was being explored by many of that set at the time, and Jon found all of this influential on his changing vision. He found quiet moments to indulge in these fascinating, challenging areas, enveloping himself in reading and thinking a great deal. Jon bought some white moccasins and wore beads and flowing white tops, and because he did, others copied. The straight-laced suited-and-booted, neat and tidy, look was on the way out.

Jon was once asked if organised religion played a part in his life and he answered:

> Not necessarily, no. I was christened Catholic, and I was in a Church of England school. When I realised, I had been a Catholic, I thought, 'well that's cool! I can't believe that!' Now and again, it's just funky. But after a while, it just became so disorganised in my own mind. I haven't studied very many religions at all. I just come to terms with what's presented, and if I can enjoy and sustain it, I'll enjoy and sustain it.

Still mighty proud of their work and their single as The Warriors, the acetate demo they recorded was taken along everywhere to parties and played repeatedly in rented rooms to friends and anyone else who would listen. However, much was changing for Jon and the music scene – the bands and sounds were developing fast. Jon was looking to experiment in all areas and being the lead singer in the band was not enough for him.

Brian Chatton says: 'Jon used to play the saxophone in those days. He played it on stage a few times near the end of the life of the band. He picked it up, deciding that he didn't just want to sing.' As many musicians could play an instrument as well as sing, Jon wanted to achieve the same. He played it adequately, apparently. Impressed by the soul records, it was Jon who had wanted a sax player in the band. The band, The Big Sound, also had a sax player and had impressed Jon.

By 1967 flower power had infiltrated the music scene in a big way. Clothes, design, artwork, substances, the influence of this new scene was everywhere. The summer of love was having an effect on the band, with many followers off their heads. Drugs, sex and drink, were easily available; life was crazy but good. The music in Jon's head was changing, and it affected what The Warriors played, or more importantly, how they played it. They would be doing the usual three half hours or two three quarter hour spots as usual. However, making the music played match the time requirements given to them required them to be clever, forcing them to improvise. Initially, they added solos and extra verses. Then Dave Foster and Jon began writing together, which meant they added snippets of other songs to existing songs that sounded similar. They began rock 'n' roll medley-style arrangements.

Above: A very casual Warriors, wearing it well. 1966-67. *(Brian Chatton)*

Brian Chatton elucidates, 'For the first few months, this worked fine, but eventually we began to tire of the whole thing. We fell out, made up, fell out with someone else, made up. It was becoming a different relationship to what we'd intended.'

During what would be their important final last month, they met up with Mitch Mitchell (formally the drummer from The Georgie Fame Band). Mitch was now with Jimi Hendrix, and they were playing in the club next door, so the band went and watched them. Later, they partied through the night. In Copenhagen, they met up with The Spencer Davis Group. A couple of guys from the band went for coffee with Spencer, and he explained his band was splitting, as Steve Winwood intended to go out on his own. This is what was happening to many of the bands at the time including Brian Poole and The Tremeloes and The Animals. There were dramatic changes all round.

The Warriors too were not immune to this sharing of band members. Kevin Parrott of The Big Sound Band, who went on to have a hit record as Brian and Michael, a British music duo, best known for their 1978 UK number one hit single, 'Matchstalk Men and Matchstalk Cats and Dogs', reminisces about The Warriors at the end of their Germany tour:

> I remember the band coming to see us, and they were all smashed, stoned out of their heads on dope - that was the first time I met them. I have a photograph of Jon and Rodney leaning out of the window, both wearing GI helmets that they borrowed from some guys who were at the local army base. In Cologne I recall The Warriors doing 'Good Vibrations' on stage, and they were totally brilliant. I remember Brian Chatton (who was the good-looking bloke) would often go missing, and we would eventually find him, inevitably, with a woman. He was a bit of a lad, he was.
>
> I remember we had two front line saxophone players Jeff Peach and Phil Ramsbottom and Jon liked the sax. Over the winter our drummer got bad flu, and as The Warriors didn't have a lot on, we swapped drummers. Ian joined us in Sweden for about 4-5 days. Our drummer, Graham, sat in with The Warriors because the doctor said he wasn't fit enough to travel far. Our saxophone player was later offered a job with The Warriors but turned it down.

Final recordings

In May 1967 in Munich, The Warriors were approached to do some recording in a small studio. After playing a gig, the band went to the studio and recorded some songs through the evening and into the morning, free of charge. The songs included, 'She's Gone', 'Mr Nobody Nothing' and 'Marianne Bell'. The latter two were on tapes believed to be held by David Foster, although these haven't been heard of since that date.

The track 'She's Gone' was recovered in 2017, found in a suitcase in a band member's loft, where it had been languishing for 50 years. The track 'Marianne Bell', as of the time of writing, has not yet been found, although the author did inform Marianne that a special track had been written for her, which she never knew about.

Above: Jon in December 1966. *(M. Evans)*

Ian Wallace produced the sessions, but as the band were in such a tired, drunk, stoned state they ended up not sure of what they had done. As they listened back to the session, they realised that at one point Ian had got so involved in listening to the backing track, that he had missed out a full verse of the vocal. One of the tapes of 'She's Gone' from this session was dated 30 May 1967, meaning that this would be the last recording by Jon Anderson with The Warriors.

It was June 1967, and the gigs carried on as usual, but one important event was to happen which influenced both The Warriors and Jon. While playing in Hamburg, The Beatles' album *Sgt Pepper's Lonely-Hearts Club Band* was released. It had taken The Beatles more than 700 recording hours in the studio. Like a swift slap across the face, this was a wakeup call for all musicians. The rule book on composition, sound, instruments, themes, mixing, vocals and songwriting had all been changed overnight. Now anything could be achieved, it seemed. Concept albums could be created. Jon's mind must have been expanded, and a realisation of what he could potentially do hit home as he listened to this masterpiece.

Another offer came their way to record more material, free of charge, in the summer. The band spent the whole day in a TV studio in Frankfurt rehearsing and hanging out, before recording the show in the evening. The recording can now be seen on YouTube. Former P N Hit House DJ, Nikki Ragsdale, recalls the recording for the German TV show *Beat! Beat! Beat!* and her time with The Warriors:

> The Move were there too. They were on just before The Warriors, I recall. We were hanging out at the studio for some time. My memory is of us wearing rose-coloured glasses (yes, red) that day, like the ones Jon's sporting on stage in that video clip, and carrying lit joss sticks around. I can still remember the smell of the incense.

The popular *Beat! Beat! Beat!* TV show introduced the band as being from Manchester, and they were playing their own songs 'Mr Nobody Nothing' and 'Tango'. According to reports, Brian was stoned out of his head during the recording. The presenter did such a long introduction to the band that by the time the cameras zoomed in on Brian, his fingers wouldn't work properly. He was sweating, and his fingers were slipping off the keys. The rest of the band were more familiar with TV recordings, but Brian was new to it and was scared to death. In the video, Brian can be seen playing keyboards wearing a cape (in the style of Rick Wakeman). Apparently, Ian and Jon used to draw dragons onto it when they were stoned. Needless to say, it was exceptionally full of dragons!

On the 2nd February 2019, the missing song 'Tango' came to light for the first time in over fifty years, on the internet. It was the second of the two songs played live on *Beat! Beat! Beat!* It's a gem, with Jon (John 'soul man' - Anderson) in a flowery shirt and small shades singing in a deeper voice than we have become used to and screaming out the 'Tango' hook, 'yeah yeah yeah, do the Tango, feel alright, you gotta have soul, keep on dancing.'

The entire 3.45-minute song reportedly aired on the 19 June 1967. The tune is tightly backed by Ian Wallace and Dave Foster, with Rod Hill's rhythm guitar filling in well, while Brian Chatton plays a great keyboard solo. Together they come across as an extremely tight unit with solid backing vocals. It is upbeat, slightly frantic and rather like James Brown, with a bit of Sam and Dave's 'Soul Man' thrown in. You can see that the band are highly entertaining, with Jon swaying about and shuffling and he is clearly the focus of the band. With the benefit of hindsight, it appears strange, given what Jon went on to produce, but you can't deny the raw talent and stage presence he and the band had. The Warriors also show here that they could have 'made it' back in the UK too if they had chosen to come home.

It was noted by a fan that was following them, that there seemed some tension at this recording, with some discussions going on. There were still no specific changes, but clearly the end was nearing. Indeed, sex, drugs and rock 'n' roll were catching up on some of the band. Brian comments:

> When the band was coming to an end in Germany, I remember one night I had made arrangements but didn't realise it, to meet eleven girls in a club. There were loads of hookers and pimps and all sorts in Germany, looking after lots of the airbases. I got in with this girl, and they were all drop dead fucking gorgeous and about 16 -17. My arse looked like a dartboard: I use to get so many doses. The German doctors used to love us Brits going in because they could get their own back. We had been shagging all their daughters, and we would go in for a penicillin shot, and they would be so cruel sticking them needles in our arse like no tomorrow.
>
> I ended up at a girl's house for a time, but the band decided to go back home. Jon came over, pushed his way in, and said 'You're coming back with me'. The girl wanted me to stay and be her pimp! I said, 'Yeah. Yeah, sure, great idea'. The Warriors were falling apart and breaking up, so there was no reason to go back home. Anyway, Jon grabbed me and said 'I promised your mum that you would come back in the same state as you left', which of course couldn't possibly happen, as after the two or three years with The Warriors, I had done a lot of growing up. We had taken a lot of Acid. We had been all around Europe, and we had all changed drastically. Jon saved me really, by saying 'I've got to take you back to ya mum'.

Dissolution

On August 27th the manager of the Beatles, Brian Epstein, died. Perhaps this brought a realisation for The Warriors that time is short. Jon Anderson played his last show with The Warriors in late August 1967 at The Storyville Club in Frankfurt. Feelings were running high. The German dream was over for the band. Their excessive drinking and the taking of the easy-to-obtain-drugs, like LSD brought in from London in sugar cubes, had to stop. Although some crazy times would continue for Jon, his musical future would become more focussed.

By this time, Jon wanted more from his music. He had a mind full of ideas. So, by August 31st, The Warriors were finished in Frankfurt. For Jon, though, it was the new beginning. He reminisces:

> Like all the bands back then, you either made it on your first single or forget it. But I wanted to be a success at what I was doing. I was always happy when old friends used to tell me what a good group it was, even though we weren't making any money. It was nice to be able to turn around and say:
> 'I said I would do it and I'm damn well going to keep on trying my best until I really make it.'

Jon had ideas on his future beyond the band - he was becoming more driven all the time. Graham Evans, the drummer of the band the Big Sound, says:

> The Warriors were a good harmony band with a good ear, they played songs by The Beach Boys and some Tamla Motown material, because of Jon's voice. They were a kind of a 'Tremeloes' type sounding band, at that time when we were about nineteen to twenty years old, that's all, playing the American bases. It was good fun. It was in the Star Club that Jon told me he was going to leave The Warriors. He said he was going to London to do his own thing - he had many ideas.

Jon did sing once with The Big Sound according to Graham Evans, although this is not corroborated, and the performance was not recorded at all in any format. Around this time, Graham recalls seeing a picture of Jon in a Danish magazine called *Borge,* which hasn't been located. Apparently, it has Jon along with Rodney leaning out of a window watching people go by.

Jon recalls:

> I met Stevie Winwood from the Spencer Davis Group; he said what a great band we were and asked why we weren't playing in London. I remember that moment in time. It was becoming difficult as I had become a bit aggressive, trying to get guys in the band to rehearse more. I'd be hustling the guys, to wake up and practice. They would tell me to bugger off! It went on for about a week and then I said I was going. I packed my bags and went down to Munich and met Nikki and her friends. We went to Munich and Hamburg, and I took some acid because [my hero] Paul McCartney said he took some.

Right: Jon and Tony's first home - 13 Norfolk Street, Accrington. (*David Watkinson Collection*)

Left: Jon and Tony demonstrate how much they were influenced by film star James Dean by jokingly signing themselves as Johnny Dean and Tony Dean. This is a rare item that also includes signatures from Derek, Mike, Dave and Rod. (*David Watkinson Collection*)

BIG CHANCE '63

WITH just over a month to go before the grand final of Big Chance '63, the grand Northern talent contest organised by Mecca Dancing and sponsored by the "Lancashire Evening Telegraph," four of our six finalists have been chosen.

Last Saturday saw Ron and Donna from Wigan win with their vocal guitar duet "Ginny Come Lately."

Again on Monday the quality was very high but the judges, Mecca disc jockey, Mike Cameron, Alan Noble, and audience members Carol Simson (17), Gloria Pickup (16), and Bill Jenkinson (20) awarded first prize to The Warriors an Accrington rhythm group with a big future.

Other contestants on Saturday night were Mrs Barabara [illegible]tin, soprano, of Burnley, Mrs Agnes Charnley, [illegible]al singer, of Blackburn. [illegible]onday The All Stars [illegible] Preston, and Dean [illegible] and the Meteors from Blackburn, competed.

Quarter-finals winners — The Warriors, of Accrington

So good were competitors on Saturday night that Mr Bryan R. Gee General Manager of the Locarno, St Peter Street, Blackburn, is to offer them bookings at the ballroom on suitable dates.

Three more heats are left, before the last quarter final on October 14. Most dates are full, but if application is made to Mr Gee he may be able to fit a few last minute entrants in.

The wonderful prizes in the competition include recording tests and television auditions plus the "Lancashire Evening Telegraph" trophies (one for each section of the contest) and bookings, LP's, cash etc.

Above: A rare local paper cutting signed by all the band. It's possibly the earliest known. (*Ken Crabtree*)

Above & Below: The Warriors Rod, Dave, Mike, Derek, Jon and Tony. Both these photographs are clearly from the same photo shoot, and show the band looking very smart in their stage clothes. Note Jon's interesting hair! (*Garth Dawson -David Watkinson Collection*)

Above: Derek is teased while he appears to be getting the chop. In the end, he left of his own volition. (*Garth Dawson – David Watkinson Collection*)

Below: Rod, Mike, Dave, Derek, Tony and Jon. A happy photo shoot in Accrington. (*Garth Dawson – David Watkinson Collection*)

Left: A silver-suited Jon in the foreground playing to another packed house. (*David Watkinson Collection*)

Right: Rod and Mike with a parrot. Obviously. (*David Watkinson Collection*)

Below: The band point at Derek as if to say 'You're going soon.' Jon is on the far left. (*Garth Dawson – David Watkinson Collection*)

Right: The only officially released Warriors record, 'You Came Along'. This is the demonstration version. (*David Watkinson Collection*)

Left: The front cover of the music score for the single. Featuring Jon and Tony pictured in the centre of the photo, this item is very rare. (*David Watkinson Collection*)

Right: The inside page of the music score. (*David Watkinson Collection*)

Left: The official soundtrack album for the movie Just For You, released by Decca. The Warriors were featured. (*David Watkinson Collection*)

Right: A later VHS release for the film *Just For You* (*Network*)

Right: The Silver suited Warriors, performing the 'B' side of their single in the promotional movie *Just For You*.

Left: Tony Anderson with a captivated listener, as a happy band watch on.

Right: Another on-set picture of Tony and Jon Anderson in perfect harmony.

Left: The official press photo for the film release. (*Raymond – David Watkinson Collection*)

Below: A wonderful, full shot of the band at the movie premier. They are performing a few songs in The Empire cinema in Burnley. (*Raymond – David Watkinson Collection*)

Left: Back stage, signing autographs before the Burnley cinema gig. Jon is hiding at the back and there is a super grin from Ian Wallace in the mirror. (*Garth Dawson – David Watkinson Collection*)

Right: At Mary's record shop for the single launch. Rod, Ian, Mike, Dave, Jon and Tony. (*Garth Dawson – David Watkinson Collection*)

Left: The band are pictured at the TV and Radio Show in Earls Court with fan Ursula McCue from the Mullard factory in Accrington. Jon is seen on the far right, with cigarette, signing pad and pen in hand. Dave, Ian, Tony, Mike and Rod are also pictured. (*Wood Photography – David Watkinson Collection*)

Right: The pop star Lulu known for her hit single 'Shout' joins in the fun backstage with Jon holding one of the new Warriors postcards. Dave Foster is on the left with Ian Wallace on the right. (*David Watkinson Collection*)

Left: A later fan club postcard showing the new line up of Brian Chatton, Dave Foster, Ian Wallace, Rod Hill and Jon Anderson. (*David Watkinson Collection*)

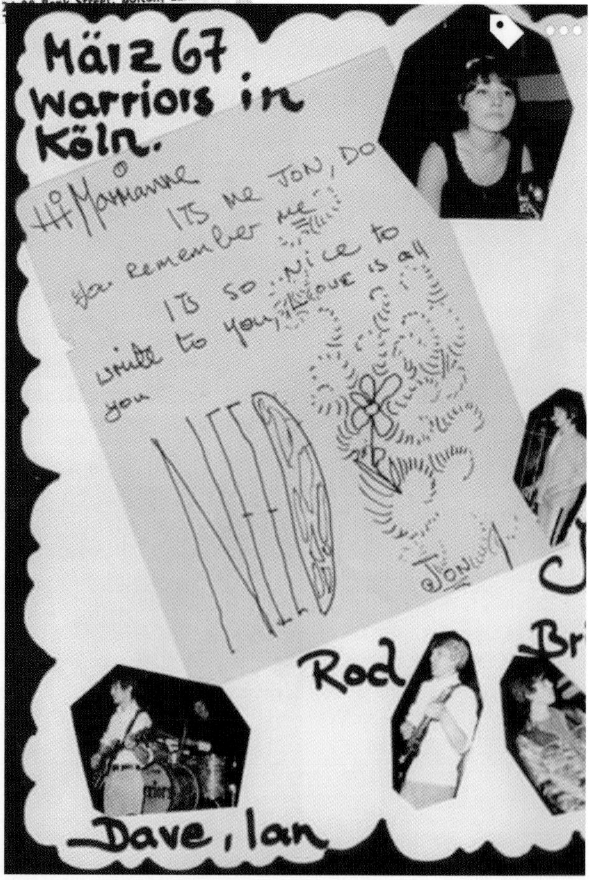

Right: A lovely letter from a creative Jon to long term friend and fan Marianne. It's signed 'Jon', showing that, even in 1967, he was already using this shortened version of his christian name. (*M. Evans*)

Right: The UK version of 'Never My Love' / 'All of The Time' by Hans Christian. Vinyl 7-Inch 45rpm standard release single. *(David Watkinson Collection)*

Left: The original EMI Records promotional photograph of Jon as Hans Christian, February 1968. (*EMI/Universal*)

Above: The 'early years' frame from the Yes exhibition seen at The London Palladium for Yes' 50th anniversary tour. (*David Watkinson Collection*)

Right: The very first drum head for Yes. The bubble logo followed until Roger Dean designed the classic Yes logo. *(Bill Bruford Archive)*

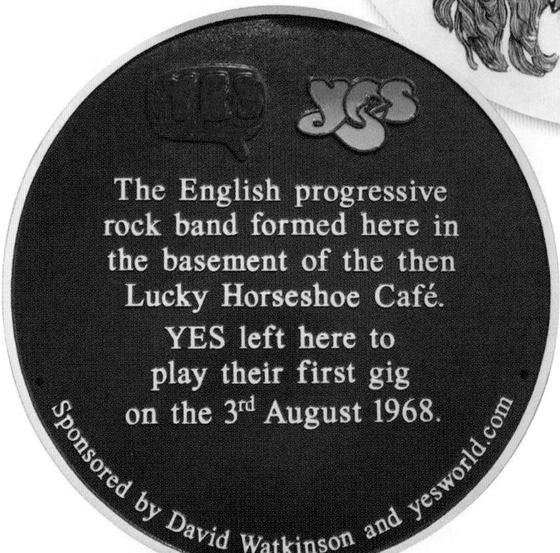

Left: The 50th Anniversary plaque in London. It is situated in the basement of 184 Shaftesbury Avenue, where, on the 3rd of August, they left to play their first gig in Essex. (*David Watkinson Collection*)

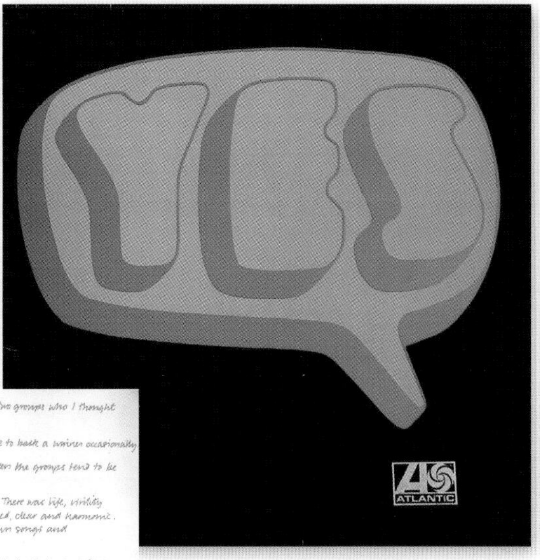

Right: The very first Yes album in the summer of 1969. This was a tentative start to a magnificent career. It has a wonderfully simple cover design that hasn't aged. *(Atlantic)*

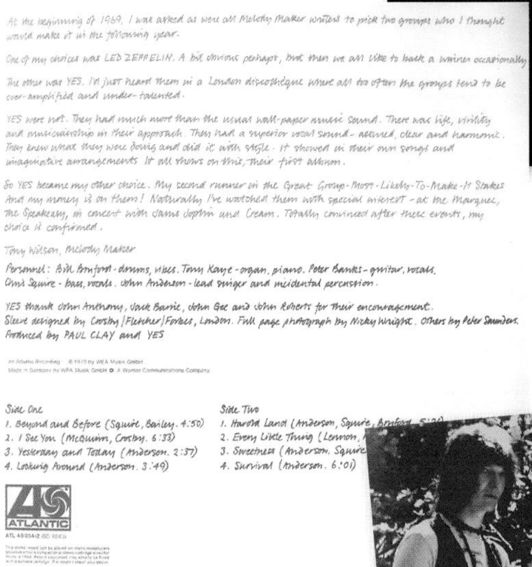

Left: Inside the gatefold cover, Tony Wilson said of Yes that they knew what they were doing and did it with style. *(Atlantic)*

Right: Yes images taken at the gig on Sunday 18 May 1969 at Parliament Hill, plus the main photo, taken around Hampstead Heath. *(Atlantic)*

Left: The USA-Canada release had a photo taken at the Fulham Architectural Centre, 120 Fulham Palace Road, London. It is now gone. However if you look hard enough, the two eagles can still found nearby in the Kings Road. *(Atlantic)*

Left: Marquee Club, London. 5 February 1969. Bill using a different drum head. (*David Watkinson Collection*)

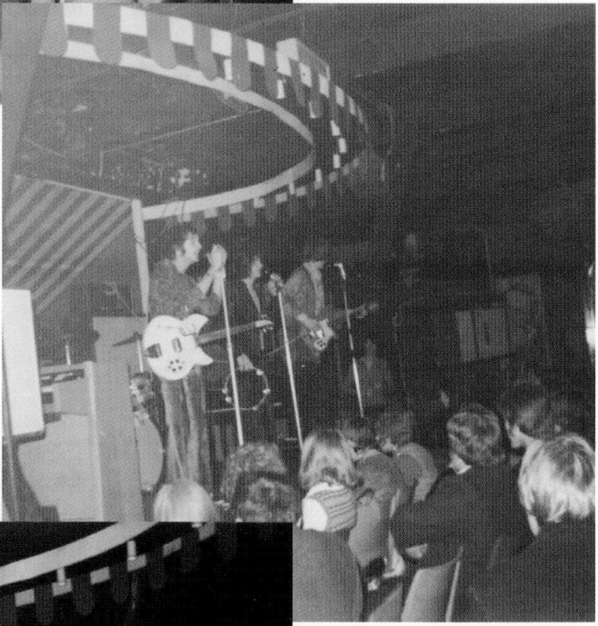

Right: Marquee Club, London. 5 February 1969. You can feel the atmosphere. (*David Watkinson Collection*)

Left: Marquee Club, London. 28 May 1969. It's almost like being on stage with the band. (*David Watkinson Collection*)

Right: Marquee Club, London. 28 May 1969. The Marquee design is clear in this shot. (*David Watkinson Collection*)

Left: Marquee Club, London. 28 May 1969. Vibrant close harmonies in action. (*David Watkinson Collection*)

Right: Marquee Club, London. 11 June 1969. Chris in the foreground, Peter far left. (*David Watkinson Collection*)

Left: Marquee Club, London. 2 July 1969. Peter Banks feeling the music. (*David Watkinson Collection*)

Right: Marquee Club, London. 2 July 1969. The Yes logo is back on the drum head. (*David Watkinson Collection*)

Left: Marquee Club, London. 2 July 1969. Bill giving it everything. (*David Watkinson Collection*)

Brian calls his first acid trip with Jon:

> After our first acid trip, we were completely fucking gone. Jon said to me 'when we are as high as can be and still be here, we will always be here'. We knew it was the acid talking, that's why we felt so good. Jon said 'we are never going to come down'. Despite coming down and off acid, whenever I see Jon now, we recall the taste of the acid from 50 years ago. Your saliva tastes come back, and we look at each other, and without sounding camp at all, we turn each other on to the acid trip we had. We always smile and laugh, and our eyes are watering; it's just a weird and wonderful thing that happens due to drugs.

DJ Nikki muses about Jon's time in Munich:

> Jon benefitted from our times of walking and talking together in Munich. It was an uncertain time for Jon, having made such a big change. I supposed I helped him to remain positive. In the letters I have, he extols my kindness and warmth at the time, my positivity. He just felt like expressing something positive back to me. On the back of one letter, where Jon says, 'Sorry I've no coloured pens', he drew some flowers, that refers to the fact that I often used to decorate my envelopes in all sorts of bright colours and 'psychedelic' designs.

The Aftermath

It was a hectic period for Jon after the breakup of the band. He wanted to take stock and move on, re-centre himself and create a new persona. One major change, for Jon, was the spelling change of his Christian name. He often toyed with such a change, and it was thought he began using it some years later, changing from John to Jon because he liked the spelling better. It is possible that he was inspired by his hero, the jazz singer John Hendricks - who was also known professionally as Jon.

Nikki, Jon's DJ friend, reflects: 'I don't know why he did it or where he got the idea. In any case, he signed his letter to me in September 1967 as 'Jon', emphasising that by underlining the 'on'. He wrote it on the envelope that way, too. He already had that notion then, that much is certain.' With the rise and success of Yes just three years later, Jon officially changed it legally in 1970 at a time when he was charging ahead with the developing young band Yes.

With everyone in the band now without work, they all went their separate ways, with Rodney Hill and Brian Chatton visiting Lancashire, before deciding to go to London. Jon had given out an address of some distant relations that could help in putting the guys up a while. Brian Chatton had changed a lot while away from Lancashire, and he announced to his parents that he needed to be in London.

With the band now home from Germany, Dave and Rodney stayed at 14A Gunter Grove in West London. Living on the first floor of that house, was the singer from the Moody Blues Denny Laine, - later Yes would also live there - and when Dave Foster moved out, Rodney moved in. Members of The Warriors used to stay in one of the many bed and breakfast places in Sussex Gardens, frequented by lots of travelling musicians, due to the low cost of the rent there.

The Big Sound also suffered a split as two members left the band - their bass player and drummer, who had joined together and left as a team. As the band had many gigs booked, Dave and Ian agreed to join them.

The Gentle Party Days

Having all left the band under amicable circumstances, everyone needed a rest or at least a change of scene. They were tired out - shattered and hungover - but still in need of work. Jon stayed on in Germany in a flat with friend Nora. Jon was seemingly a little lost in the party world the scene had now become. The kaftan-wearing Jon pondered his future, and he dreamed big. He smoked and drank a lot and waited for his next big chance to come along... soon.

He subsequently joined a Lancashire group he knew from Bolton. Jon said, 'I went off, but Brian called me and said come back to London. I said I wanted to do a couple of things before that. I joined a band of nice people called The Gentle Party - really lovely people.'

Jon had received a message from this other band just after The Warriors broke up and according to his friend Nikki, she received a letter which was postmarked 25 September 1967, from Jon in Giessen, Germany. This was just after Jon had received his invitation to join the Gentle Party.

She recalls that Jon seemed very excited about it.

> He didn't know what he was going to do next, Jon needed to regroup, get centred and decide what to do; he was a little lost but wanted to do something. Jon and I would meet up and hang out, talking about things, taking long walks in the country. It seems to me that Jon was delighted to have that opportunity and go on to a next phase with another band again.

Like most of the English bands of the time, the Gentle Party went to play in Germany. Not much is known about the band outside of their friends and family. The only known proof to be found so far of this elusive band was in Rodney Hill's diary entries. The band are shown as playing on 27 January 1967, but the venue is not noted.

The Star Club is also mentioned in the diary notes in between the 27 and 28 January as the Gentle Party, and Jon played at the most famous of all the clubs in Germany - arguably the scene's best venue at the time.

> Friday 27 January 1967
> JOHN - GENTLE PARTY

Then in between the 27th and 28th, it says:

> STAR CLUB
> Saturday 28 January 1967
> KAISER STR 95
> 15 KARLGKUHE

Two days later, we have an entry showing where Jon was staying:

JOHN ANDERSON
GASTHAUS
ST GEORGE, 8721
OBERWERRN
GERMANY

Playing the venues all over Germany, including the army bases, The Gentle Party seem to have done well. Jon was appreciated by the band who called Jon 'a great singer'. Jon remembers: 'I hadn't been treated like that before.'

It is thought that they played the classic songs of the time and altered versions of top twenty soul hits. However, they would have been just one of many English bands trying to make it big there and before long, like many of the bands at the time, The Gentle Party split. Although there is only this one firm diary account of Jon as their singer, it is clear from all the feedback that Jon sang more with them, or at least hung out with them straight after The Warriors' breakup. It seems that two of the lads in The Gentle Party band drove Brian Chatton and Rod back home to England with their gear, travelling on to Bolton later. Ian and Dave, however, chose to take the train back to Britain.

Jon began to relax a little and embraced their local hospitality even more. He was enjoying the care-free, musician's life of a lead singer. Massively influenced by The Beatles, Jon looked for other musical outlets and ways to enjoy himself.

> I lived in this place in Munich and was looked after by two beautiful groupies, mainly because we liked each other, and I was high on LSD for about a year. I think I was spaced out, really. I had this wonderful moment when Jimi Hendrix came to town and played in The Star Club or the P N Hit House. We went to see him play and he was amazing. They all came back to the apartment, and I was sitting quietly in my cupboard-bedroom, wearing my Kaftan and beads and bells, so spaced out I could hardly talk. Jimi looked over and then came and sat next to me. Yeah, it was a magical moment, I remember it well: we smoked a joint together! That's my claim to fame.

Things didn't work out quite the way Jon wanted with The Gentle Party, and he was ready for the next challenge. However, Jon recalls:

> In later years, when I was in Yes, and we became famous, and we were travelling a lot, I would keep bumping into the Gentle Party guys at concerts in Frankfurt. They all fell in love with German girls and continued to live over there - [they were] very sweet people.

Onwards and upwards

With Jon looking for the next challenge, England - and London - were calling him back. He picked up his trusty saxophone, which he had learned while on the German circuit, possibly with lessons from musicians from other groups. This was yet another sign that Jon needed to expand his musical ideas. Not that he could play too well, but at least it was a diversion and added another string to his bow.

By March of 1968, Jon was back in London searching for jobs, bands and stardom. However, about eight weeks after The Warriors had split up, Jon rang Rod up and suggested getting the band back together. Rod felt it would not work as Dave and Ian were in Denmark, and Brian was in London, so it really was the end of the band for good.

Arriving in London, Jon found a place to live and headed for the musical centre of the City, Soho. London's vibrant music scene could be found around the West End - this was where anyone who was anyone, was going to be. In an interview with *Neo Music Scene* (a US music news service), Jon was asked about where his drive and the spirit he has to be successful comes from. He explained:

> I think the fighting inside is possibly because I'm from a mill-town in Lancashire - whether poor or not doesn't make any difference. I think the energy comes from its being a working-class area. In Accrington, you work for a living; that mental attitude was really the norm: you did your hours. You learned a trade; you did an apprenticeship which could set you up for life. University places and further or higher education wasn't widely available. Being anything radical in life, such as a musician or a pop star would have seemed reckless or silly. Why would you want to jeopardise your whole future by not doing something steady, solid with a known life-long benefit?

Speaking with Klemen Breznikar in 2011 on *psychedelicbaby.blogspot.com*, Jon sums up his Warriors days:

> It was a crazy dream to be in music, to be in a band. We were travelling all around Europe, playing long, long shows in tiny smoky clubs. [There were] funny times and beautiful moments through the 60s, peace signs, drinking too much, waiting for the next Beatle song to be released. [There was] such amazing music in the 60s.

4. Beyond and Before Yes

Going their different ways

The mad, frenetic, colourful, psychedelic, German-lead drug and alcohol-infused heydays were over for The Warriors. Back in the UK, however, the likes of the Pink Floyd would carry this on, along with many other bands. It is crazy to think really, but many didn't get the Floyd in the beginning. They seemed too far out The Warriors, with Jon and Brian agreeing 'What's this lot - it's crap'. Ironically it gave Jon and Brian a boost, as they thought that if this band can make a success of it, then we can. Music was in their blood. Music had become such an integral part of society too, they needed to continue being part of this changing face of music, so excitedly they moved forward.

The individual Warriors would move on with other bands. Rod went to London and played in a band called The Attack, who played 'High Ho Silver Lining' before Jeff Beck did. Rod played with them for a few months. He had built up many contacts during his Warriors years, so he began to pick up gigs and got a job playing bass. He bought a Fender Mustang short-scale bass, which he later sold to a band called Grapefruit. He received a cheque for it signed by George Harrison and Paul McCartney, as it was bought by Apple, the same record company that was owned by The Beatles. He also went for an audition at the London Palladium for Sandy Shaw, got the gig, and then went on to tour Europe with the singer.

Rod also worked the London clubs, supporting bands at the Marquee, once even supporting Robert Plant with his new band. The Warriors knew Robert from an early band of his called Listen. He was preparing his new band for a tour of America - they were called Led Zeppelin. Rod said he wished him well with the band and hoped they did 'ok'. If there was ever an understatement, then that's it.

On one of his tours, Rod bumped into some Spanish guys from the band Los Bravos who were looking for a singer. He thought of Tony Anderson and so organised for Tony to come and do an audition in The Speakeasy Club (also known as The Speak, it was a club situated at 48 Margaret Street, in London). They loved Tony, but unfortunately, he was just too late. They had just signed on another singer, and went on to be quite successful with the single 'Black is Black'. The following Christmas (1969), two of Los Bravos turned up on Tony's doorstep in Accrington and asked him to join them. He accepted.

Dave Foster was waiting tables at the Marquee for a short time alongside Jon, when they returned from Germany. Dave did, however, reinvent himself and formed another band, with Rod Hill. On the advice of Mickie Most - their famous music producer - they named themselves Accrington Stanley, giving a footballing nod to the band's origins. The line-up was Rod Hill, Jim Payne, Brian Johnstone, David Foster and Dave Walmsley. The band was short-lived, however in their time together they did manage to play to large crowds at the very first Glastonbury Festival in England, which must have been a high point in their individual careers.

Dave went on to join the band Badger, who were a brilliant rock band with Yes connections. Indeed, Jon Anderson co-produced their first album, with Tony Kaye on keyboards and Roger Dean designing the cover. The band supported Yes at London's Rainbow Theatre in 1972.

Dave had been one of the few musicians in The Warriors who, at that time, could read music, so his skills as a writer, sight-reader, singer and bass player were in demand. He had been a tower of strength and a major figure in Badger, strongly influencing the quality of their musicianship. Badger ended too soon, and Dave was unable to stop the inevitable break-up of the band. Eventually, it all began to go wrong, or so Dave felt. There were personal life issues, the band didn't establish a settled line up, some problems with writing credits and recognition and issues with the business and management side of things. Drink and drugs hit him hard as he tried to cope with the rock and roll rollercoaster. He became more reclusive as time went on, but did remember with fondness his time with The Warriors at least. Speaking much later in life in his proposed book (with Ant Bee) about the early years in the music business, Dave explains how drugs affected his life:

> I've used practically every drug you can think of, and while I thought they were ok at the time, they have affected my life for the worse and have had a lot to do with the problems and break-ups of the bands that I was in.

Dave did go back to music, releasing a CD in 2004 called *Open Road*. On this album, he made a variation of the classic Yes track 'Time and a Word', which Dave had jointly written with Jon Anderson for Yes' second album.

Fortuitous serendipity and Hans Christian Anderson

Jon continued to hang out in and around the clubs and bars of London, looking for deals and a break. The narrow, bustling streets of London were an exciting place. 1960s London was a haven of hedonism - a far cry from the grimy, post-war London of their parents' generation. For Jon and friends, their days would consist of sleeping late, wandering down to the local bars for a chat over a pub lunch. A pub called the Ship was a favourite drinking hole and one that remains in the centre of the music and entertainment business in Wardour Street.

By now Rodney Hill had moved to London to stay with Jon's friends, but they lived a long way from the West End. Jon had called Rodney and asked if Brian Chatton could stay there too. The family said no, so Rodney went into town and spoke with Jack Barrie at the La Chasse Club, who suggested Rodney bring Brian in, and Jack would sort out his problem. A meeting was set up, and that's how both Brian Chatton and Jon met Jack, who would become a huge help in Jon's career, along with the likes of Terry Doran and Tony Stratton Smith, manager the Koobas at the time, amongst others.

Jon was working in the bars of Soho, serving and cleaning, waiting tables, sweeping the floors and hustling people to get noticed. Ending up in the La Chasse Club, just along from The Marquee Club in Wardour Street, he formed an association with Jack Barrie, who ran The Marquee. Barrie took Jon under his wing, along with his former bandmate Brian Chatton. La Chasse Club was a seedy little dive that was not much bigger than a front room. It was an off-shoot from The Marquee, which did not have an alcohol licence. It was Barrie's idea to open up the tiny club with a drinking licence. When it was crowded - with 30-odd people - the atmosphere would be smoky and intimate. It was definitely the place to hang out and be seen in the late 60s - 'the' place to be for those in the music industry. This was to be a period of flurried activity, leading to Jon's strange time as Hans Christian Anderson. A real solo singer's adventure in a time of flower-power eccentricity.

A piece of good fortune came along in the form of one of Jon's many revolving-door of flatmates, Paul Korda. Paul was in demand as a singer, writer and producer: a very talented man, with acting credentials in West End musicals in London, and offices in Denmark Street, London. He was also a record producer, who just happened to be looking for a singer to do a few demos for EMI. Jon's new recording career was started by Paul arriving home, having been offered the job at EMI. He immediately woke Jon up and offered him his first solo record deal, under the name of Hans Christian. Jon needed this break, so he happily did his bit and hoped for the best. Jon must have been praying that this was going to be the big time for him and feeling a bit of a star, he lapped up the attention. Self-confident and promoting himself far and wide, Jon's former local Lancashire newspaper picked up on the local-lad-done-well story. They covered the ex-Warriors' career, giving him a feature article as Hans Christian Anderson in the *Accrington Observer*, on the 12 March 1968. The article reads:

> Local pop singer, Jon Anderson, former lead singer with The Warriors, is to release his first single record next Friday. The record 'Never My Love' written by Don and Dick Addrissi, is produced by Tony Hall, one of the leading promotion managers in the country. It was recorded on the Parlophone label [a division of EMI], with vocal backing by The Breakaways. Although The Breakaways are featured on the record, Jon's backing group in the future is to be Gun.

That was perhaps the record company's plan, but the idea went sour after a few gigs were performed. Jon – at that point 23 – spoke about the exciting times he was going through in the northern press:

> It was a big decision to leave The Warriors, but I think I made the right one. The speed of the developments has amazed me. My flatmate had some recording time booked in the studios, and he asked me to sing along on his backing track. The record company liked it, so they promoted me as a pop singer, with a silly hair-do. I was never meant to be pop singer, thank god for that!

Record by local pop singer to be released this week

Local pop singer Johnny Anderson, former lead singer with the Warriors, is to release his first single record next Friday.

A Lancashire newspaper heralds the new venture for one Johnny Anderson, the ex Warrior. *(David Watkinson Collection)*

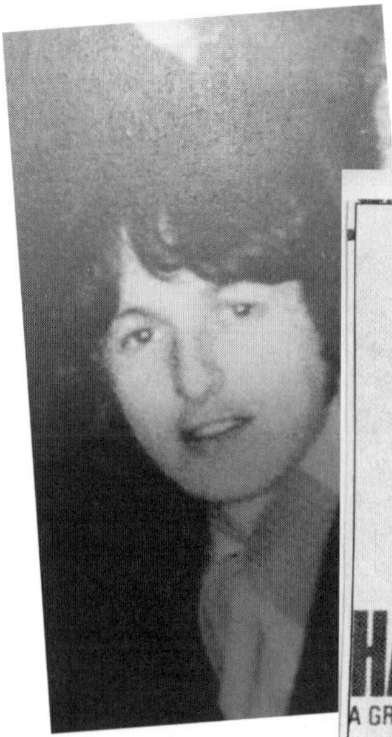

HANS CHRISTIAN: "Never My Love" (Parlophone). Leap into your Anderson shelters, here comes a blockbuster of a hit from a hip young fairytale teller with an emotion - packed voice.

The orchestral accompaniment builds up into a veritable frenzy with a gibbering vocal chorus and battering drums.

It's pretty exciting, and no doubt we shall all be seeing Mr Christian bringing mutiny to the good ship Top Of The Pops 'ere long.

Left: Jon pictured in London in 1968. *(Connie Biegler)*
Centre:. An advert in the *Melody Maker* music paper. *(David Watkinson Collection)*
Right: The original *Melody Maker* review of the new Hans Christian single by the legendary Chris Welch. Chris is a writer, journalist and was an all-round Yes supporter from the very beginning plus author of *Close To The Edge: The Story of Yes* in 2000. . *(David Watkinson Collection)*

The demos were turned into records, and Jon's first single 'Never My Love' was released on the 23rd March 1968. A very small promotional budget was spent on some photos in a studio, and two small reviews have been found in the music press. Jon's Hans Christian version of 'Never My Love' was nothing like the original version by The Association. Indeed, a radio DJ called 'The Baron' described the record as 'noise' and said that the B-side, 'All of the Time', sounded like a load of lunatics trying to break out of an asylum. Whether it was any good is subjective. Jon was trying to be different and to experiment a little with his career. The break would come soon, and he knew all he had to do was keep going.

Jon's friends Angelika and Marianne from Germany would join Jon when he played the Hans Christian single on the first floor of the Le Chasse Club, where 'Never My Love' rang out on the jukebox all the time. They loved his voice and have excitedly followed his career through 50 years and more. Jon became known at the club as the energetic northern chap who would speak to anyone in his funny, strong Lancashire accent.

Peter Banks recalled Jon working at the bar in the Marquee Club, and La Chasse Club:

One big reason I remember Jon was because they had a big jukebox in there which played his records, horrible records, one called 'Never My Love', a big kind of ballet thing. He had the single, Hans Christian Anderson in the jukebox, and he was always playing the bloody thing. And he'd be running around, this little guy, just helping and cleaning the tables, that kind of thing. He was a friend of Jack Barrie, who was running the club, and Jon was always very quick to tell everybody: 'It's my record on the jukebox'. We regarded him as a little bit eccentric only because the Soho scene was such a small scene, maybe a couple of hundred musicians and most of us at the time were from the suburbs of London. But Jon was totally Northern, from Accrington. He had this Northern accent, and he was a bit open and naive and enthusiastic in a way that we were far too cold to behave in. Because we'd been in Soho, we were used to the scene, whereas Jon, I guess, was more a newcomer to it. He would keep putting this damned record on, and we thought it was a bit of a pain that he would keep doing that.

Top: Jon as Mr Hans Christian as seen on Jon's *The Lost Tapes* box set. *(Voiceprint)*
Centre: The USA version of a Hans Christian single. *(David Watkinson Collection)*
Bottom: Jon in a reflective mood for the photo shoot around London. *(EMI-?)*

Jon came back to London from playing with The Gentle Party, for the promotional rounds of the first Hans single. They were released under the pseudonym of Hans Christian, without mentioning the 'Anderson' part of the name much in the press release. The record company press apparently had a grand marketing plan to match the rather grand name. The press advert campaign was in full swing in March 1968, with adverts in *The Melody Maker* music paper. Reviews and comments were scarce but publications that did find time to review it seemed to have given it fairly good comments. One young writer, Chris Welch, gave it a particularly glowing review. This was the first of many reviews by Chris Welch that Jon would get over the following years both as a solo artist and Yes singer. He wrote: 'Hans Christian Anderson. Leap into your Anderson shelters, here comes a blockbuster of a hit from a young fairy storyteller with an emotion-packed voice.'

However, the track sank without a trace selling just a few copies. EMI were not put off and released Jon's second single '(Autobiography of) a Mississippi Hobo'. This, too, did nothing much in sales, and apart from Jon playing the records to all and sundry, at all hours of the day and night, in the bars, not many got to hear the music and this distinctive singer. Clearly, the record company liked Jon's voice and wanted to make him a star - spending time on rehearsing and recording material with Jon. Sessions did produce many tracks, making up to three singles worth of material. Songs such as, 'Never My Love', 'All of The Time', 'Autobiography of A Mississippi Hobo', were backed by demo recordings of 'Sonata of Love', 'Out of my mind' and 'Someone in Heaven Knows'.

In 2016 new information came to light to say that Paul Korda (producer) and not Jon Anderson sang on the three unreleased Hans Christian single demo tracks. 'Sonata of Love', 'Out of My Mind' and 'Someone in Heaven Knows'. Though performed by producer Paul, the singing on the tracks does sound very similar to Jon's vocal style, with the slight differences being the lack of a northern accent and the power that Jon has is missing. Obviously, these tracks were prepared for Jon by Paul should the initial singles be successful. As it happens, they weren't, and so they remain Pauls demo's, - his voice and not Jon's.

A driven Jon Anderson may have not been the easiest person to deal with. Speaking in February 2018 to the author, Paul Korda made his thoughts clear on the whole relationship and short working time together with Jon at that time, along with his future projects with him in this way, 'Dave, I'm not keen on talking about Jon. I know how much you admire him, though, and I don't wish to spoil your belief in him, but I wish you well with your project.' It was a disappointing working relationship for Korda at that time, and not forgotten some 50 years later. That's Rock 'n Roll for you!

It must have been an exciting time for Jon in London, brushing up against so many famous musicians. Not only that, but he lived in shared accommodation, in which there were musicians living and breathing music day and night, both upstairs and downstairs. In 2014, summing up his brief experience as Hans Christian Anderson, Jon said: 'Yes, Hans Christian was my first single in England, and it was a flop. Not a very good record. But, Hans Christian Anderson, now I really liked the sound of that.'

With both the record company and Jon admitting defeat with the Hans Christian solo project, plan B went into action.

A sojourn in Holland

Not expecting too much from the EMI singles, Jon kept his options open. He was rumoured to have decided to join another band called Les Cruches, and he flew out to meet this band in Holland to play with them. Les Cruches was a band originating from Tilburg in Holland, where they played from 1965 to 1970. It's possible that Jon could have been joint lead-vocalist, as he had been in The Warriors and the Gentle Party. Nothing has been confirmed date-wise, so it is unknown if Jon replaced any members of the existing band or just joined in. The only - flimsy - reference for this speculation from Jon himself, is from a chat he had with a fan after the symphonic Yes concert in Antwerp (the day after the DVD recording in Amsterdam). Jon asked the fan where he came from, and when he said Limburg (a province in Belgium), Jon said, 'I played in a Limburg band once,' possibly mixing up the names Tilburg and Limburg. This seems to be referring either to one of those gigs, or other events that can't be confirmed.

Interviewing Jon in 2015, I asked him about this time period, and Jon said he doesn't recall anything. While that doesn't mean it didn't happen, at best it's vague. After all, this was a time when band members would often join in with others, checking each other out. The atmosphere was rife for stealing band members, enticing musicians to a better band or just to getting up and singing for a while with another band. Almost anything could have gone on, and the odd one-night stand, joining friends on stage wouldn't have meant much to them at the time - the musicians were just having fun, oh and probably smoking stuff too.

Bigger and better?

Not only did the top bands of the late 60s channel both a change in popular culture and in society, but they also began experimenting with how they presented the music to their audiences. The Beatles became the leaders in the development of new sounds - both standard and unconventional. Their album, *Sgt. Pepper's Lonely-Hearts Club Band,* is seen as a milestone. It was innovative, revolutionary and hugely influential in the history of music. It was also a representation of the counter-culture of the late 60s. It made everyone at the time sit up and listen - spellbound - whether involved in the making of, or just in love with, music. The device of this alter-ego 'band' gave them permission to experiment and go above and beyond what they or anyone else had been doing up to that point. Wikipedia cites the album as: 'An important work of British psychedelia, the album incorporates a range of stylistic influences, including vaudeville, circus, music-hall, avant-garde, Western and Indian classical music.'

Everyone sat up and took notice of this album, it shattered preconceptions in what could be achieved. Out of America came the Vanilla Fudge and their first album which was also hugely influential. Orchestrated works were becoming more mainstream. Music was becoming bigger, grander, cinematic, and for Jon, this was just the impetus he needed. It was becoming obvious that the next musical adventure for Jon was going to be more complex and larger in scale than his previous music. His taste in music was moving towards classical works. He'd listen to a piece long in form, or romantic one minute, something heavier the next, as his tastes changed and developed. He is reported to have said, that he would go through a 'dying routine' where he used to curl up into a ball and try to disappear into the music. Jon was becoming clearer on what he liked and didn't like in music. Heavily influenced by his constant reading of science fiction and listening to classical music, a grand vision played in Jon's head. He could visualise it, but he needed quality musicians around him that would understand his vision too.

Gunning for glory

Jack Barrie had always had a soft spot for Jon's voice and personality and he been constantly on the look-out for a band for Jon to team up with. When the band Gun had starting talking of a new line up, he immediately thought they would make a good band, or at least an excellent backing band, for Jon to use to promote his solo singles. Gun had made inroads into the scene already.

They had been featured on Granada TV's series *First Timers* and were booked to appear on the Radio One Sunday music programme *Top Gear*. They were also booked to tour as a support act with groups such as The Herd, David Garrick and Dave Dee, Dozy, Beaky, Mick and Tich.

Although only a short-lived venture, Gun at this stage, consisted of Jon Anderson, Adrian and Paul Gurvitz and Lewie Farrell. The band were run by the powerful and talented Gurvitz Brothers. Jon had seen them perform around London and had been impressed by them - they had a psychedelic pop-rocky feel to their music. Jon rehearsed with Gun for up to three weeks in London preparing for a series of gigs in March 1968, although the short run of gigs promoting both Jon Anderson and Gun ended with only two being performed. The first gig was on April 6th 1968 at the Marquee Club, on the same bill as the band Family. Their second gig was supporting The Who. The relationship wasn't destined to last, and a falling out between the brothers and Jon saw to that. Adrian and Paul Gurvitz did not want Gun to be a backing band for anyone, so with apparent financial issues and with the brothers not wanting to have any more to do with Jon, it spelt the end of that version of the band. This was bad news again for Jon, and yet another opportunity had gone.

Speaking in 2015, Paul Gurvitz said, 'Well, to be honest, it's a long time ago, all that and was probably 1967 before 'Race with the Devil'. I can remember Jon, he slept on my mother's couch for a while, but I don't remember much else from that time.' Gun would go on and have a major hit single called 'Race with the Devil' later in 1968 and have their album cover designed by Yes 'sixth member', Roger Dean.

Jon added his thoughts in an interview for the *Record Collector* Magazine:

> The Gun guys were really nice to me, and we got on well. But after the gigs, they said: 'Where's the money for the petrol'? Of course, there wasn't any. They got very uptight and, a week later, I saw they had advertised for a show, and they'd forgotten to tell me! We did two great shows, and I got the band a gig to play with The Who, just to get the exposure. But the guys in Gun hated me for that, and they fired me!

Early Yes fan Dermot Bassett saw Jon with the Gun as well as later with Yes:

> I'd seen him with Gun at The Marquee back on 6th April and they'd really impressed me, but completely dropped off my radar as instantly as they'd arrived. I discovered later that Jon's tenure with Gun was very brief and that the band was very different while he was with them, compared to the Gurvitz-Brothers-driven Gun and their chart success a few months on. At this point, they also had a keyboard player so had an identical format as his next band Yes. With hindsight, it appears Jon had used them as a Yes template. Jon and Gun were the first band on that night in April and were followed by Jethro Tull. This was the week before they were to start their weekly residency at The Middle Earth Club, and topping the bill were The Who.
>
> Gun opened with The Shangri-La's 'Remember (Walking in the Sand)', just Jon singing alone, with no accompaniment at all and then swirling

> organ bringing in the rest of the band. They also played something by The Byrds, which I'm fairly certain was 'Eight Miles High', and completely stunned everybody by taking on The Beatles' 'A Day in The Life'. I can't recall what else they played, but I'd never heard anything like them before and absolutely loved it. Then they were gone, and I had no idea how much better things would get towards the end of the year (October) with Yes.

There was a lot going on for Jon in March and April of 1968. The Hans Christian single appeared in the UK with a music paper review in the *Melody Maker* on the 9th March, and the fleeting collaboration with Gun. The band The Open Mind played the Marquee Club once or twice, and it is thought that Jon met them there for the first time. Was it this time that maybe Jon also met Chris Squire? April saw the band called Grapefruit put out a single called 'Yes', the advert for which has imagery that is very similar to how the first Yes logo would look. Did that sink into Peter Bank's mind? Mabel Greer's Toyshop gigged and appeared on the *Nightride* radio show, on 3 April courtesy of the BBC DJ John Peel, the night before band founder Clive's 18th birthday.

Be Open-Minded

With Jon now a free agent again, there is a suggestion that Jon now met the band The Open Mind. They came from London, where they carried their psychedelic sound around to all the usual cool, happening places. They had a minor hit record with 'Magic Potion' which later featured on their debut album in 1969 for the Philips label. This is currently a very rare and collectable album.

Tim Du Feu, from The Open Mind, speaking in the *Record Collector* magazine in August 2003, spoke about Jon and about his Marquee gigs:

> Jon was then Hans Christian Anderson. He joined us for a while at the suggestion of John Gee, who ran the Marquee. We used to go around to Jon's house in Bolton Gardens, have a smoke, chill out and listen to the Fifth Dimension. I'd have liked him to have joined the band permanently, but it would have meant a five-way split for wages rather than four

Adding more while speaking on the *Pooterland* website in 2001: 'We appreciated his input. Unfortunately, he left to form Yes, so I guess we lost out on a bit of fame there - we could have been Yes! In our dreams.'

The author interviewed Tim De Feu in 2018, and he added: 'It was suggested that Jon Anderson, being a great singer/performer, should be our singer, but like most bands, the money was a problem.' Tim came across Jon and Yes much later, meeting up in Kensington, while they hung around Gloucester Road, and played at the Blaises club. Tim added: 'By then Rick Wakeman and others were in the band, so we were socially all around the London scene the late 60s to early 70s'.

Interviewing Jon in 2015, we ran through these hazy days, and Jon does not recall meeting them or ever doing a gig, so if it did happen then, it seems likely that it was such a non-event in Jon's mind it has been forgotten long ago. Obviously for Tim, though, it would have been a more memorable occasion.

Bend me, Shape me. No thank you.

So once again, Jon returned to the bars and clubs, making contacts with everyone and knowing that it would all come good at some point. An important turning point was on the horizon. But in the interim, he went to see the management of the pop band Amen Corner, who had already had a chart hit record with 'Bend Me, Shape Me' - which reached number three in the UK charts. Jon attended an audition in South London for the band, and their manager said he was great, but that he should return the next week when they would do something with his image. Realising that he would have to comply with the pop-singer-in-a-band look, Jon was unimpressed and never went back.

Stumbling into the Toyshop

Around this time, the people and social scene of Soho contained an interesting mixing pot of drugs, criminals, overseas tourists, strippers, films, music, filth, eclectic food, awful cafes, loose women and artists. You name it, Soho had it all.

Jon kept busy, working on contacts, agents, bartenders and musicians, while sleeping in people's flats, cleaning tables, hustling and trying hard to get that break he so badly craved. Through a new friend called Chris Squire, he eventually stumbled on a band that he liked the sound of in Mabel Greer's Toyshop, an exciting group with a drug-influenced name, very much part of the 1960s.

marquee club
GERRARD 8923 | 90, WARDOUR STREET, LONDON W.1.
JAN. 1967 PROGRAMME

Sun. 1st — CLOSED
Mon. 2nd — THE HERD / The Nite People
Tues. 3rd — TONY RIVERS and the CASTAWAYS / Syn / Members 5/- Non Members 7/6
Wed. 4th — Folk Night / SANDY DENNY / RED SULLIVAN plus Special Guests
Thurs. 5th — THE PINK FLOYD / Eyes of Blue
Fri. 6th — HERBIE GOINS and the NIGHT-TIMERS / Wynder K. Frog
Sat. 7th — THE NEAT CHANGE / The Pyramid
Sun. 8th — BIG BAND WORKSHOP / The London Youth Jazz Orchestra / Pat Evans Orchestra / (Members 5/- Non-members 6/-)
Mon. 9th — THE HERD / The Bunch
Tues. 10th — THE CREAM / Catch '22 / (Members' Tickets 7/- in advance from Jan. 3rd)
Wed. 11th — Folk Night / DEREK BRIMSTONE, JILL DARBY, THE NATTERJACKS
Thurs. 12th — ARTWOODS / Mike Stuart Span
Fri. 13th — SANDS / and support group
Sat. 14th — THE NEAT CHANGE / The Ultimate
Sun. 15th — Theatrescope presents / CHAMPION JACK DUPREE / Savoy Brown Blues Band / (Members 6/- Non-members 8/6)
Mon. 16th — THE HERD / Richard Henry and the Time-Box
Tues. 17th — ZOOT MONEY'S BIG ROLL BAND / Syn / (Members' Tickets 7/- in advance from Jan. 10th)
Wed. 18th — Folk Night / FRUGAL SOUND, AL STEWART
Thurs. 19th — THE PINK FLOYD / Marmalade
Fri. 20th — SONNY CHILDE and the T.N.T. / The Nite People
Sat. 21st — THE NEAT CHANGE / The Bunch
Sun. 22nd — "SUNDAY SPECTACULAR" / AN EVENING with BEN WEBSTER and BLOSSOM DEARIE with the Ronnie Scott Quartet / (Members 10/- Non-members 12/6)
Mon. 23rd — THE HERD / The Ultimate
Tues. 24th — SPENCER DAVIS GROUP / Syn / (Members' Tickets 7/- in advance from Jan. 17th)
Wed. 25th — Folk Night / MARTIN WINSOR, RED WINSOR plus Special Guests
Thurs. 26th — HERBIE GOINS and the NIGHT-TIMERS / Jimmy Cliff and the Shakedown Sound
Fri. 27th — SANDS / Mark Barry
Sat. 28th — THE NEAT CHANGE / The Parking Lot
Sun. 29th — "SUNDAY SPECTACULAR": / ERIC BURDON / Sings the Blues with / THE NEW JAZZ ORCHESTRA / featuring Don Rendell, Ian Carr and other top jazzmen / (Members 6/-, Non-members 7/6)
Mon. 30th — JOHN MAYALL'S BLUES BREAKERS / featuring Pete Green / Stone's Masonry
Tues. 31st — JIMMY JAMES, COUNT PRINCE MILLER and the VAGABONDS / Syn / (Members' Tickets 7/- in advance from Jan. 24th)

COMING
FEBRUARY
Sat. 4th — Return of BERT JANSCH

(All Programmes are subject to alteration and the Management cannot be held responsible for non-appearance of artists.)

Printed by Hepworth and Co., (Tunbridge Wells) Ltd., Tunbridge Wells, Kent.

Left: The Syn featured at The Marquee club along with The Cream and The Pink Floyd. *(David Watkinson Collection)*
Right: A rare Syn poster from the Marquee. *(David Ridge)*

The sequence of events as Mabel Greer's Toyshop forms and gradually becomes Yes

- Bob Hagger buys a second-hand Premier drum kit in 1963, setting up in the attic at home
- He starts to visit London clubs and see many bands
- His first band is called So Rare, and his next is The Crash, featuring future 'Free' guitarist Paul Kossoff
- Meanwhile, Clive Bayley finds the bass player Paul Rutledge
- He places an advertisement in the Melody Maker music paper in 1966 for a drummer
- Bob Hagger sees the advertisement, and a meeting is arranged in a pub in Fleet Street
- Clive, Paul and Bob seem to get on well, so start to put some psychedelic material together
- All three live in Clive's house, in the attic
- After much hard work, they start to get regular work in London clubs and universities
- Clive has a vision, running the show creatively with Paul and Bob executing his dream
- Paul quits, so they need a new bass player
- Eventually, enter Chris Squire, previously of The Syn
- Chris energises their performances and focus
- Chris then asks Peter Banks to join in, also from the now-disbanded Syn
- Chris meets Jon and asks him to sing
- Shows billed as Hans Christian Anderson and Mable Greer's Toyshop attempted
- Peter Banks leaves and comes back
- Drummer Bob Hagger has other ideas and leaves
- A new band name is being thought of
- Bill Bruford joins
- The name is changed to Yes
- Clive also sees his band changing too much and leaves
- Tony Kaye is asked to join
- 3 August 68, Jon, Chris, Bill, Tony and Peter head out to play their first gig as Yes

For this new, exciting band and line up, things began to go well, with plenty of gigs. One night at a club called Middle Earth in Covent Garden, Jimi Hendrix and Chas Chandler came in while they were playing. After their set, Jimi was asked if he was there to see Mabel Greer. Typically, Jimi's response was 'Yeah, but I'm here to see everyone man!' As is often said, Jimi, was the most laid-back guy that ever existed, as well as being an incredible musician and showman on stage.

Bob reflects on the band's musical style:

> We were strongly influenced by The Pink Floyd and Jimi Hendrix at the time, but we were committed to creating our own music. We refused to play anything written by anyone else, and that was a trait that stayed with the band throughout [my time]. The only cover version that I can remember was of the classic 'Midnight Sleigh Ride' (otherwise called 'Troika', by Prokofiev). That was one of the most exciting pieces that we ever did, and we used the theme as a base for some stunning solos later in the band by Chris Squire and Peter Banks.

During this time, Mabel met and impressed the disc jockey John Peel at his house in Fulham, London. He invited the band to play on his BBC radio programme called *Nightride*. This appearance gave the band some much-needed publicity. The tapes were released many years later on a CD by Peter Banks called *Can I Play You Something*. The CD was a compilation of music that Peter was involved in prior to his days in Yes. It includes the original recording of 'Beyond and Before' that also featured on the first Yes album. The band also did a demo recording with the well-known producer Mike Leander for MCA records.

The key meetings that heralded the start of Yes are well known, but it's worth hearing Jon explain that famous initial meeting again,

> I was working in the Le Chasse club in Wardour Street. The Marquee is also there and some other clubs. That's where all the musicians would go to for a before and after drink. I was biding my time to see what came along. On that fateful afternoon, Chris Squire was at one end of the bar, and I was at the other end. We had never met. My friend, Jack Barrie, who ran The Marquee Club and Le Chasse Club said I had to come and meet this guy who was putting a band together. He said he thought we should get together, so he introduced us. We chatted for half an hour. I went around to his house, and we sang some songs together, and that's how we realised that there was every possibility that we should work together.

It was a good few months into 1968, and Chris told Clive about a guy he had met down at Le Chasse Club. Chris recounted that he was serving pints and

Above: The band that became Yes – the psychedelically named Mabel Greer's Toyshop. Pictured here are: Robert Hagger. (Drums), Peter Banks (Guitar), Clive Bayley (Vocals/Guitar) and Chris Squire (Bass/vocals) *(www.mabelgreerstoyshop.com)*

that he used to sing with the band The Warriors but had also done some solo stuff. Chris thought they should meet him. He mentioned that his name was Hans Christian Anderson. Bob Hagger recalls:

> Up until that point, Clive and I were not really interested. But that name? Right up our street, it was at Chris' attic flat in Fulham London that we all met up and found out his name was Jon! But that was fine, as I used to introduce myself as Alexander Belmont, a stage name I was using at the time.

Above: A Christmas thank you from Mabel Greer's agent in 1967. *(David Watkinson Collection)*

Jon's singing style was perfect for Mabel Greer's Toyshop because both Chris and Clive had been choir boys, and his higher register singing style fitted their voices. The addition of Jon's vocal gave Mabel Greer's Toyshop a Byrds-like harmonic vocal presentation. It all seemed to fit together perfectly as soon as Jon opened his mouth and sang. Remembering an early gig, Peter said: 'This little guy came up on stage and sang with us. It turns out that this guy was none other than

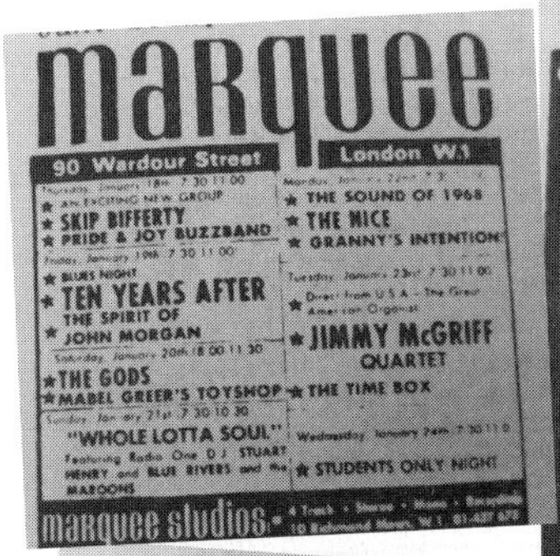

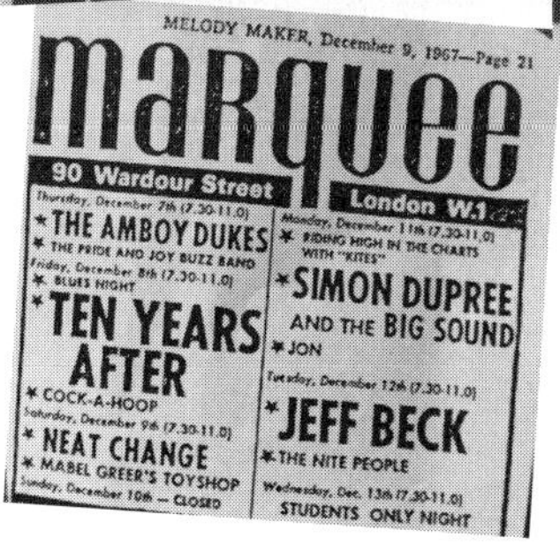

Above Left: The Marquee Club artist listings for January 1968. *(David Watkinson Collection)*
Above Right: The Happening 44 Club have the wrongly spelt Mabel Greer playing in September 1967. *(David Watkinson Collection)*
Left: The Marquee Club had a superb bill of artists in December 67. These include Neat Change – who would have Peter Banks as a member – Mabel Greer's Toyshop with Chris Squire and the mysterious JON on the same night as Simon Dupree and The Big Sound. *(David Watkinson Collection)*

Jon Anderson, I didn't know Jon then, but Chris did, so he must have invited him up to sing with the group.'

Bob Hagger wrote for the Yes release *The Word Is Live*, CD collection:

It was May 2, 1968, in Highgate, London. The line-up was Chris Squire, Jon Anderson, Peter Banks, Clive Bayley, and myself on drums. Bill Bruford replaced me in June, and Mable Greer's Toyshop changed its name to Yes two months later. The music and themes that were to become unique to Yes were already strongly in evidence from the beginning. They showed through in the excitement of the music we played that night in songs like 'Midnight Sleighride', 'Eight Miles High', 'Electric Funeral', 'Light My Fire', and 'Beyond and Before'. It was a fantastic night, and only a short time before the world discovered the magic of Yes.

Cracks begin to show

Up to this point, Clive had been the lead singer and rhythm guitarist for Mabel Greer's Toyshop, with the others all having a say on which musical direction the band would go in, but Jon was strong-minded. Jon had decided he was in the band and Mabel Greer's Toyshop had a new lead vocalist. It was now about what Jon wanted, and the others began to feel that their band was being taken away from them. Some had thought the band had started to spend much more time learning new material and not enough time looking for gigs. Indeed, Mabel Greer's Toyshop didn't really vote on what to do with Jon. Instead, Jon - with his work ethic from The Warriors' days - insisted on gruelling rehearsals every single day. Determined to be a success this time around, Jon was keen to work hard to get the band right. Cracks really started to show when they played a gig billed as Hans Christian Anderson and Mable Greer's Toyshop. Clive recalls it was worth trying out as they liked his vocals, but it just wasn't all working as well as it should have been.

The first song that Jon co-wrote with Clive and Chris was 'Sweetness'. In 2015 Clive recalled:

Jon was always very focussed on what music and construction he wanted. Playing with me couldn't have been easy as I hardly ever played the same thing twice note for note! I liked Jon, he was always ready to look on the positive side and had a similar intrigue towards and understanding of the mystical as I had. Although, at that time, I think we both kept that to ourselves. Years later listening to him on interviews or shows, I remembered that we had shared some similar views.

We worked hard when Mabel Greer was formed. The Lucky Horseshoe Cafe rehearsals were intense, and Jon was always keen on promoting the band. He is a few years older than me, so was a little more experienced. I found him to be good-natured, although at the time I was more creative than technical, so he was probably patient [with me] as well. We did create some great music though. I preferred the more psychedelic, flower power thing at the time and was always searching for new sounds and phrases.

One staple track they played live was their encore of 'In the Midnight Hour', which according to Peter Banks went on for about thirty minutes.

Transition

The transition of Mabel Greer's Toyshop began, and they started to become a different group. This represented progress and growth and marked the rise of Jon Anderson as a leader. By this time, Jon was focused and confident in his abilities as a singer-songwriter and bandleader. He could connect with an audience, and they could connect to Jon. This was his next important step to realising his dreams.

Throughout the evolution of Mabel Greer's Toyshop, with all its changes of style and approach, Bayley maintained his purity of vision in the band and its philosophy. Bob explains:

> Clive had this Brian Wilson-esque thing. He'd always be looking at songwriting, constructions, tweaking, and rearranging. When Jon chipped in to sing things like 'Beyond and Before', the harmonies were worked out. It sounded wonderful when Jon came in, and Clive would do backing vocals. To Clive, the art was the most important thing. The music was still all-important. He painted the pictures in his mind. But he was open to suggestions and how things were put together. At the same time, he had a clear picture of what he wanted. He lacked ego too.

Left: London and The Middle Earth Club in 1968. With Steve Howe's, Peter Banks' and Chris Squire's bands playing a night apart. Little did they know what the future held for them all.

Bob recalled his best moment with the band: 'The highlight for me, was when we played The Electric Garden in London. We were supported by Eire Apparent that night, and we had a visit from Jimi Hendrix - wow. I don't think he came to see us, though.'

Jon was a few years older than the other members of Mabel Greer's Toyshop which, at that age, is a big thing. Bob recalled:

> Jon was never bossy. Some people have said that, but Jon just has a strong mind. He was accommodating in his views, flexible. Jon would work with you quite easily. Peter, though, could rub people up the wrong way, he could be very dogmatic. Saying that, we all enjoyed working with both.

In the summer of 1968, Peter Banks suddenly said he wanted to leave the group. Working relations had become difficult, and part of that was having two guitarists in the band. He left to join the band Neat Change. Peter Banks stayed with that band for around six weeks, and then they disbanded soon after that. Bob remembers saying to Chris and Clive that they should raise their sights high and look for the best guitarist in town. They had recently played at the Middle Earth Club alongside a band called Tomorrow. 'I had been impressed by their lead guitarist Steve Howe and had suggested that we set off to find him for the band.'

Steve Howe wasn't available, so Peter Banks came back. But by mid-June of 1968, the spell had been broken, and it seems Mabel was broken too: some had had enough. Bob remembers the sequence of events:

> I left the group and I was replaced by Bill Bruford, and shortly after that they changed the name of the band to Yes. The day I quit was a sad one for me, and I was nervous about telling the guys, as there was a gig coming up in the next few days with nobody to replace me. We had been at Chris' flat going through the vocal lines. Later that afternoon, I called Chris to tell him that I had another offer. Chris was not pleased and said I was letting them down. It's true, I was, but felt that I just had to do it. Had I known the band would be supporting Cream at the Royal Albert Hall in November of the same year, I'm not sure I would have made the same decision, but a lot happened for between June and November 1968. It was the start of something big and we are all proud of that.

Clive Bayley was also gradually losing grip of his beloved band and perhaps never felt he got the credit that he deserved for founding the group. Was it time to leave the band for Clive, and to leave it to the others? Bob says:

> Clive's original ideas, his music and his influence were the very beginning of the group. I give Clive full credit for Yes because I was there and participated in the birth of this great band. My last gig with Mabel was in Highgate, North London in May 1968. The line-up was Jon Anderson, Chris Squire, Peter Banks and myself.
>
> In terms of the changing personnel, some music fans see line-up changes and think 'tabloid'. They see betrayal, treason, knives stabbing in backs. With

a band like The Warriors, Mabel Greer's Toyshop and later, Yes, there was a whole host of changes in personnel, largely because of clashes in personality or different visions on how the band should perform. During the 60s, though, this sort of behaviour was rife. Everyone was at it.

Above: Yes at the Marquee Club in London on the 27 November 1968. Still under four months old, this is one of the very earliest photos of Yes. A 7.30 – 11.00pm show along with Van De Graff Generator. Notice the early drum head and a Syn member in the audience. *(David Watkinson Collection)*

5. Yesterdays

Plans for bigger and better

The somewhat bumpy ride from the band called Mabel Greer's Toyshop to one called Yes would be of those career-defining moments. Change they must and change they did as this unique music - Yes music - began to be gradually made. According to Clive Bayley, they had rehearsed at a big concrete warehouse in Shepherds Bush for a couple of weeks, the 'Mabel - Yes', songs such as 'Carpetman', 'Beyond and Before', 'Sweetness', 'Jeanetta', 'Electric Funeral', 'Get Yourself together' and 'Images of You and Me'.

Jon spoke about creating new music and where the ideas came from in an interview by the *RABD Music station*,

> I just became more and more amazed at how music was being created. In those early days, I would listen to Elgar and wondered how he created that. When I was 20-21, The Beatles were happening. Their inventiveness confused me, how could they come up with such great music? I used to listen to the popular classics, Holst's, The Planets Suite, The New World Symphony by Dvořák and to Tchaikovsky. And then suddenly I started to listen to Stravinsky, and that was when I started to think if I was going to be in a band, I wanted to do things like this, crazy, wild, wonderful music.

Metamorphosing out of Mabel Greer's Toyshop after losing one of the founding members to musical differences, the strong new partnership of Jon Anderson and Chris Squire started taking hold. With Jon's confidence in his ability growing, he knew what he wanted - and what he didn't want - in his next band. Having fronted the Little John Skiffle Group, The Warriors, Gun, The Gentle Party, Hans Christian and Mabel Greer's Toyshop, meant he had the right instincts - not to mention the experience - to build the next band. It needed to have the right members and ones who would have time to practice. Jon recalled: 'Too many of my bands didn't [practice enough] or there were too many drugs, not enough fun.'

The music of Yes would be founded on some basics: great musicianship, solid professionalism, wonderful harmony vocals, a sense that anything could be possible and a great instinct for live performance. There would be less pop chart material, and the music would be more symphonic in structure. Yes' aim from the beginning was to be different. Chopping and changing song arrangements, they also wanted the best equipment on stage and in the studio. Just sounding good was not an option, they also had a keen eye for any emerging technologies. However, they still admitted that they would be happy to get a recording deal and maybe last five years as a band. That was 'success' to a band in those days. Yes, they would have been happy with that. But most of all, both Jon and Chris were just eager to be in a successful band and by then both had enough experience to choose their future band members wisely.

At this stage, Jon lived in the London suburb of Fulham, a vibrant and cosmopolitan area where many of the London musicians and artists hung out. In their rented flats there was a huge number of illicit comings and goings.

Friends and band members would often be smuggled in. Brian Chatton, Dave Foster and Jon had remained friends after The Warriors had split up and spent much time together rotating around Wardour Street, Blaises Club and La Chasse Club. After these clubs closed 'early' at about 11 o'clock, everyone would drag themselves up to The Speakeasy Club - a short walk to Margaret Street - to continue the chat, take various substances and listen to the music.

Finding a new name for the band

Jon and Dave Foster still hung out together, and on a visit to the cinema to watch the film *Yellow Submarine* by the Beatles, released 17 July 1968, they spotted that at one point in the movie some cartoon graphics were shown with a bubble-speech saying YES. Dave recalled that Jon had a light-bulb-moment where he said: 'That's it, that's a great name for a band!'

Jon, speaking about the naming of Yes with Ray Shasho of *Examiner*, said: 'I said to Chris, listen, we've got to shorten the [band's] name.' This simple change in the band's name has always been credited to Peter Banks, who it seems had the foresight and wherewithal to get the band noticed. He was apparently inspired by the three letters of The Who on advertising posters. However, Jon remembers it slightly differently. He remembers a moment when all the names they had discussed went into a hat. The one that got pulled out was Yes, and so they became Yes, which was the name that had been put in by Peter Banks.

Jon added, 'I came up with Life, and Chris came up with World. Then Peter suggested we call ourselves Yes. We thought of The Yes. But Peter wanted it to be just Yes. We all agreed that Yes was great. Yeah, those were wild and beautiful times.' Apparently, the name was a temporary one to see how Yes would go down. Clearly there were no issues there then.

Into the first week of June a new band was up and running. Was it Yes at that point? We're not sure. The soon-to-be-Yes rehearsed any place they could, with the affordable basement of the Lucky Horseshoe Cafe in Shaftsbury Avenue being a favourite.

New members arrive

Kent-born Bill Bruford was an ambitious man. He was creative and extremely driven. He had acquired some drum brushes from his sister – who had been given them by a boyfriend - but then he needed drums to continue this new interest. Rhythm was in Bill's blood. He heard it everywhere above the mundane drone of life. At fourteen, Bill played his first gig on a holiday trip. He enjoyed the applause and so worked hard at learning more. Jazz was perhaps his first love, but the young Bill was inspired by all kinds of music and by the time he had four more years of living and breathing music and drumming, he felt that the time had come to turn professional, which he did on 1 January 1968. By June 1968 Bill had played in a few bands and felt confident enough to put out feelers for a more ambitious band. His advert in the musician's weekly paper *The Melody Maker*: 'Named drummer seeks work' was seen by Jon and Chris. Hoping this Yes band was a jazz outfit, Bill enthusiastically joined up. Although Bill had exaggerated the make and model of his drum kit at the time, this didn't matter, as the guys in the band liked Bill, and were genuinely excited about him joining them.

The band members had known Tony Kaye for a while, going back to when he played in the Midlands and the North West of England, at the same time as The Warriors. Tony's previous band, The Federals, had crossed paths with all the other bands during their gigs across the country. He came highly recommended, and after a chance meeting at the La Chasse Club one night, it was Chris Squire who asked Tony to join the band.

Tony Kaye and Brian Chatton had become friends over the years, in and around the circuit. Brian recalls:

> I first met Tony in South Kensington for the first Yes rehearsals. He's been a friend since then. I lived in a hotel called De Europe, which was across the road from Blaise's. This later became the Cromwellian Club, and that's where the very first rehearsals for Yes were held. It's often been asked why I wasn't a keyboard player for Yes, as I had been Jon's mate for all those years. I honestly believe it was because my family and I were so close to Jon that he didn't want to tempt providence. So often when you work with someone close, it becomes a whole different relationship which can sour a friendship - a true friendship.

Recalling those hot days in the basement of the Café in an interview conducted in 2018, Bill Bruford remembers: 'It was dark and dingy, and a lot smaller than you think. But it worked, it was enough to start off with.'

Over those eight weeks in June and July of 1968, some of the exact days and dates of events have become blended together, with reports saying that Bill did play with Mabel. Bill has always denied this. Reportedly at a later stage in Jon's career when Clive Bayley popped in to visit Yes backstage, Jon introduced Clive to the members of a slightly bemused Yes, as 'our first guitarist in the band', thus, giving Clive some unofficial credit for his part in Yes. The truth remains hidden in and around those smoky basements. The cross-over happened, and a new band had risen. Jon, Chris, Peter, Tony and Bill were ready. But was the world?

It was only a matter of time before a bit of luck came Jon's way. They say you make your own luck, but Jon really worked for his. Jon comments:

Above: Tony Kaye, 31 May 1969. Lewes College in East Sussex. *(David Watkinson Collection)*

> I was in the club one day, and suddenly the person next to me said 'You must be from Accrington with an accent like that.' I asked him how he knew, and he said he was from Skipton, which was around 25 miles away from Accrington. He told me that at one stage he had been thinking of putting some money into a band from

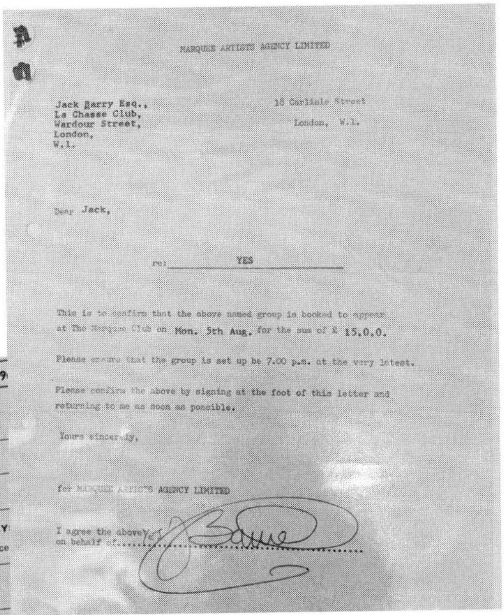

MARQUEE ARTISTS AGENCY LIMITED

Jack Barry Esq.,
La Chasse Club,
Wardour Street,
London,
W.1.

18 Carlisle Street
London, W.1.

Dear Jack,

re: YES

This is to confirm that the above named group is booked to appear at The Marquee Club on Mon. 5th Aug. for the sum of £ 15.0.0.

Please ensure that the group is set up by 7.00 p.m. at the very latest.

Please confirm the above by signing at the foot of this letter and returning to me as soon as possible.

Yours sincerely,

for MARQUEE ARTISTS AGENCY LIMITED

I agree the above Yes
on behalf of..........

Right: The Jack Barry contract for the first real gig by Yes after their warm up in Essex. The Marquee Club would become their home for quite some time. They were paid £15.00. *(David Ridge)*

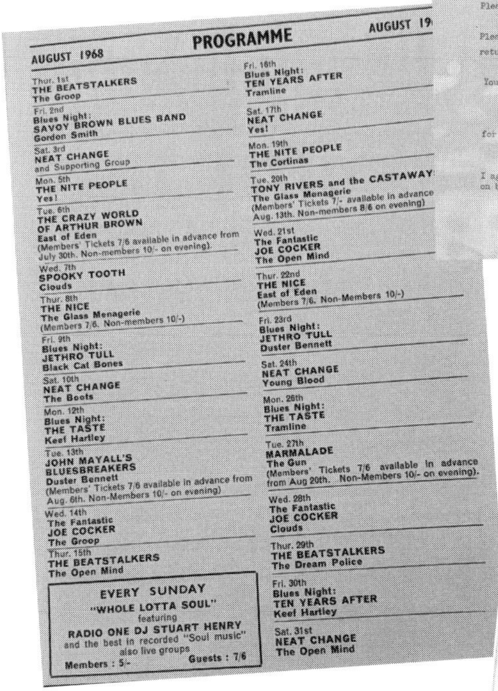

PROGRAMME

AUGUST 1968

Thur. 1st
THE BEATSTALKERS
The Groop

Fri. 2nd
Blues Night:
SAVOY BROWN BLUES BAND
Gordon Smith

Sat. 3rd
NEAT CHANGE
and Supporting Group

Mon. 5th
THE NITE PEOPLE
Yes!

Tue. 6th
THE CRAZY WORLD OF ARTHUR BROWN
East of Eden
(Members' Tickets 7/6 available in advance from July 30th. Non-members 10/- on evening).

Wed. 7th
SPOOKY TOOTH
Clouds

Thur. 8th
THE NICE
The Glass Menagerie
(Members 7/6. Non-members 10/-)

Fri. 9th
Blues Night:
JETHRO TULL
Black Cat Bones

Sat. 10th
NEAT CHANGE
The Boots

Mon. 12th
Blues Night:
THE TASTE
Keef Hartley

Tue. 13th
JOHN MAYALL'S BLUESBREAKERS
Duster Bennett
(Members' Tickets 7/6 available in advance from Aug. 6th. Non-Members 10/- on evening)

Wed. 14th
The Fantastic
JOE COCKER
The Groop

Thur. 15th
THE BEATSTALKERS
The Open Mind

EVERY SUNDAY
"WHOLE LOTTA SOUL"
featuring
RADIO ONE DJ STUART HENRY
and the best in recorded "Soul music"
also live groups
Members : 5/- Guests : 7/6

AUGUST 19

Fri. 16th
Blues Night:
TEN YEARS AFTER
Tramline

Sat. 17th
NEAT CHANGE
Yes!

Mon. 19th
THE NITE PEOPLE
The Cortinas

Tue. 20th
TONY RIVERS and the CASTAWAYS
The Glass Menagerie
(Members' Tickets 7/- available in advance Aug. 13th. Non-members 8/6 on evening)

Wed. 21st
The Fantastic
JOE COCKER
The Open Mind

Thur. 22nd
THE NICE
East of Eden
(Members 7/6. Non-Members 10/-)

Fri. 23rd
Blues Night:
JETHRO TULL
Duster Bennett

Sat. 24th
NEAT CHANGE
Young Blood

Mon. 26th
Blues Night:
THE TASTE
Tramline

Tue. 27th
MARMALADE
The Gun
(Members' Tickets 7/6 available in advance from Aug 20th. Non-Members 10/- on evening).

Wed. 28th
The Fantastic
JOE COCKER
Clouds

Thur. 29th
THE BEATSTALKERS
The Dream Police

Fri. 30th
Blues Night:
TEN YEARS AFTER
Keef Hartley

Sat. 31st
NEAT CHANGE
The Open Mind

Above: Marquee Club flyer with Yes showing on the 5th August, supporting the band Nite People. *(David Watkinson Collection)*

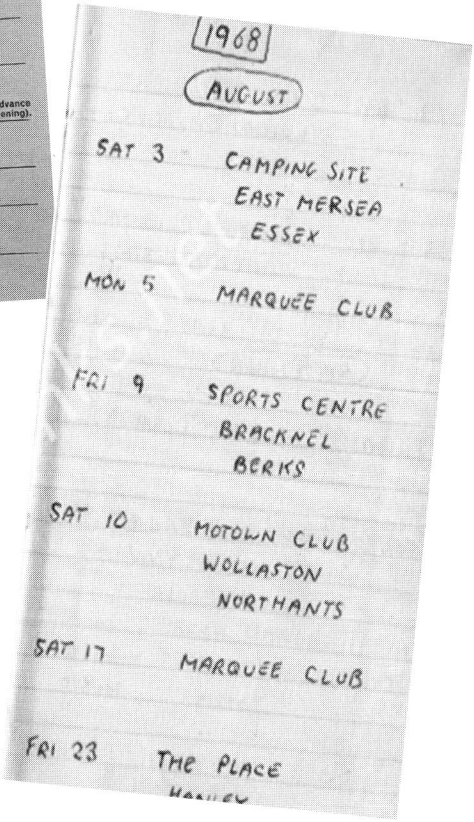

1968

AUGUST

SAT 3 CAMPING SITE
EAST MERSEA
ESSEX

MON 5 MARQUEE CLUB

FRI 9 SPORTS CENTRE
BRACKNEL
BERKS

SAT 10 MOTOWN CLUB
WOLLASTON
NORTHANTS

SAT 17 MARQUEE CLUB

FRI 23 THE PLACE

Right: Peter Bank's diary entry for the very start of Yes. *(Peter Banks Collection)*

Accrington called The Warriors. I couldn't believe it, and neither could he, when I told him I used to sing with them. His name was John Roberts, and when I told him I was in town trying to raise cash for a new band, he loaned me £500.

Yes, as rhythm raced inside, the ship came alive

The night of the 2 August faded away, and the sun rose on the 3 August, so did Yes: this has become the agreed date of the beginning of the band. For their first outing later that day they went off in their van to their very first Yes gig - out of town to Essex, playing at the East Mersey Youth Camp.

Chris Squire reflected: 'I always think the first gig was in Basingstoke, but it could've been in Essex. [We played] little-known clubs out of town, for very little money.' No records exist of any reviews for this gig, and one can only imagine how well it went down with the few who were there that day. This, of course, was a warm-up for their first big show in London on the 5 August at The Marquee Club. Indeed, in these early days, the club managers were not too sure about this new band and went on to advertise them in various ways as Yes – YES – The Yes - Yes!

The Marquee Club really was the start of their career. It was the best gig in town, where everyone played, including the biggest artists of the day. Yes

Right: Part of the first promotional pack for Yes. Notice the miss-spelt Bruford and that John is still being used, rather than Jon. A rare item nowadays, the sales pack came with other cuttings and reviews. *(David Ridge)*

supported The Nite People on their first gig in central London at one of the most important venues for them, where they played 38 times.

Very much like The Warriors, Yes were a cover band in the beginning, but with their sights set on something much bigger. Early setlists could have included any of the following:

'I'm Only Sleeping' (Beatles)
'Eleanor Rigby' (Beatles)
'Every Little Thing' (Beatles)
'Paper Cup' (The Fifth Dimension)
'Heaven on Your Mind' (Traffic)
'I See You' (The Byrds)

Jon Anderson explained in an interview with *Prog* Magazine in 2015:

> The band's early gigs were, by necessity, heavy on cover versions. We'd play [the Wilson Pickett soul classic] 'The Midnight Hour' for an hour, and then because we only had half a dozen songs, we'd do a couple of 5th Dimension songs, even a Supremes' song at one point, but we slowed things down. [We] changed the music around, [we] didn't stick to copying, like in The Warriors. That's what helped the band develop. We became a live band, a good band. Later to go into a studio and record, that was an amazing feeling - the cherry on top.

Sweet dreams can solve the future, sweet dreams provide the past...

Yes were settled in London but old friends hadn't been forgotten as the band charged ahead. Jon kept in contact with his ex-bandmates from The Warriors and often tried to help them get a foot in the London scene. Rod remembers:

> Jon helped me and Brian out in London, [finding us] somewhere to stay ... at Jack's house... in 5 Drayton Gardens, in London. Everyone gathered there; the place was buzzing with musicians, [who were] smoking stuff, drinking stuff, lots of it, at all hours of the day. I was even a Yes driver and roadie a few times right at the beginning, driving them to Stoke (23 August 1969), to a club called The Golden Torch in Kings Lynn. I drove to Ely near Cambridge (Tuesday, 25 February 1969) and various other places while Peter Banks was with them.

All of Yes, right from the start, were mini veterans of the music business, having had years being in various bands, even Bill Bruford, who was just eighteen. As a result, rehearsing in basements was just the norm. Late nights and running equipment up and down the stairs from the van after a gig at three in the morning was what you did.

The Blaises Club was an important place for Yes as many of their first rehearsals were there. Jimi Hendrix, The Pink Floyd and The Byrds also played there. On 15 September 1968, Sly and The Family Stone didn't show up for a gig as they were detained at the airport with visa issues. For Yes, this became their first break. At the last minute, they were asked to fill in.

Rod remembers the event well as he was around at the time:

> Thanks to Jon, I moved into 5 Drayton Gardens. I took a room on the first floor. Chris Squire was in the basement and Jon and Tony were in rooms above. Our band Sleepy (with Dave Foster, Ian Wallace, Geoff Peach and me) was used as a stand-in band for any last-minute gigs at the Marquee and Blaises Clubs when artists couldn't do the gigs. On the night 15 September we got a call, Jon was there and he said that all our lads were there and we could do it. So that's what happened, I helped out, and the rest is history.

That evening, Roy Flynn saw Yes perform, and he liked what he saw. This led to Roy becoming the band's manager that evening. Although as Chris Squire once hinted, it probably wasn't necessarily the smartest of moves, as Roy had no experience in the business at all. Loving the Yes sound, he backed them and got them known in their early years. In January 1967, Roy Flynn managed the newly-opened Speakeasy Club, which went on to become one of the most popular meeting and drinking clubs for the music industry. At the time of meeting Flynn, Yes only had two gigs booked at £15 each. However, Flynn's influence and confidence in the band changed their fortunes, getting them a residency at The Marquee Club, tours, radio and TV appearances, and securing for them – what seemed at the time – a great multi-record deal with Atlantic Records.

Seeing the things in different lights, [their] life was redeemed

Chris Squire remembered: 'At one point we managed to get a roadie, Michael Tait. And armed with Michael and a couple of lights, we started to progress.'

It was Roy Flynn who introduced Mike Tait, an Australian who moved to London in the 60s, to Yes. Roy asked Mike if he could drive the lads to a gig. Mike had worked in the club The Speakeasy, and like Jon Anderson, he was a bartender in the beginning. Mike drove to the Leeds University gig (16 November 1968) and he picked up the members of the band from all over London. Mike drove the van and carried stuff into the gig. Fitting in well with the band, he started working as a van driver and roadie for Yes.

In the beginning stage equipment for Yes was limited: they had a three-channel vocal mixer, with three round knobs to turn (just for Jon on stage, and these were the days before instruments were mic'd up), and a couple of extra guitar speakers, no monitors. Back in the early days Yes struggled with a lot of equipment breaking, especially Peter Banks'. He had a couple of pedals, a volume, a wah-wah pedal and a fuzz box. In an interview with the author, Mike Tait chuckled as he remembered:

> [Peter] kept stamping on them and breaking them and the cables. After a few gigs, I thought I'd better do something about that, so I set about building [what was], I believe was the first pedalboard ever.

Above: Mike Tait, taken on 11 June 1969 at the Marquee Club London. *(David Watkinson Collection)*

Yes knew they had someone special, but life on the road was always tough. Mike Tait had been Yes' driver, roadie, electrical genius and general dogsbody for about a year when he decided he had had enough and said he wanted to return to Australia. Jon pleaded with Mike not go to and convinced him to stay and become their main lighting engineer. Mike discussed his wonderful ideas he had for lighting the band, which would become known as 'Genie towers'. He was so enthusiastic that the band arranged some finance for him to get the towers built. This was the unleashing of Mike's inventiveness. He became an integral member of the Yes experience that lasted for many years.

With Mike's background in electrical engineering, it seemed a logical progression that he became Yes' lighting engineer. He would go on to build the first pedalboards and early moving lights. He invented the rotating stage, the Genie towers for lights, the Swing-wing Truss and the first pin-matrix lighting board. Mike has left a lasting legacy for modern live-event design. He became an extraordinary lighting designer and technician, both a visionary and an engineer for Yes. He helped Yes become world leaders in stage and sound presentation. Mike Tait has been compared to Leonardo da Vinci - an artist, an engineer, a sculptor - a true genius. His remarkable career helped pioneer a new industry, and his incredible work ethic and creativity has left a lasting impression on his contemporaries.

Necessity is the mother of invention, and Mike's attitude that 'anything-is-possible', helped the band strive for consistency in playing live. But even at this very early stage, Mike said, 'Peter and Chris would have volume battles. It never stopped. And I do mean the battle between them two NEVER stopped.'

Tony couldn't compete on a sound level with Chris and Peter and only had a basic organ at first. He later rented a Hammond C3 organ, which by then was THE keyboard to have. It's clear from my interview with Mike that he was a positive element for the band - he was always building things. No one had lights, so Mike started gathering items, he collected some coffee cans and light bulbs together for their first lights. Always looking for more, they tried to come up with lighting ideas. The first ones they used were modified car fog lamps. Jon was always the one pushing for more. He would say that he couldn't hear the bass drum or something. It all started from there.

Survival, survival ... we're all going somewhere!

At this time, gigging was just like the early Warriors days for Yes. The band would drive to wherever the gig was and then drive back to London. Yes never used to stay in hotels in those days, but when they began to perform shows up north, they would stay in dingy bed and breakfasts. Yes lived all over London. Chris lived out in the East End, and Peter Banks lived in Barnet initially. Apparently, the band always got back to the Speakeasy Club, as it didn't close till 4 in the morning.

Yes would usually compose when they rehearsed, rather than when they were on the move in the van. They rehearsed in some pretty dodgy basements, which were often damp, dark, poorly decorated and cold, but it seems that it was this environment that gave Jon ideas. Chris would join in, and then everyone else added to it. Mike Tait recalled:

> Jon drove the band on and on, but Chris was very important too. It would be like The Beatles and McCartney - he couldn't do it on his own, he really needed Lennon. He would call me in the middle of the night, saying, 'Micky can you get me some cassettes.' Jon had two cassette players, and he would record one to the other to double-track. He was always coming up with new ideas, the whole time, he NEVER stopped, he was totally driven.

Making music was hard. Technically, in the beginning, Jon wasn't up to speed, but he constantly wanted to make new music. Mike chuckles: 'And some of it sounded shit.' However, Jon would persevere, and he played those basic tape ideas in rehearsals back to the band. With his very 'Italian' style of gesturing, creating sound paintings in their minds, Jon would put across what he saw and heard within his head. Hanging out in each other's flats and basements was a daily occurrence, as was sitting around on the floor of Roy Flynn's basement to write. The Warriors' Dave Foster would also join in some of these writing sessions.

Above: The Marquee bands for late 1968.

Yes sometimes rehearsed in the Marquee Club through the day and soon earned themselves a residency there every Wednesday night. The Yes lighting in those days involved switching the red and blue lights off and on, to flash in time to the music. Yes were rather broke at this time and Mike remembers one night when Yes were playing at The Marquee Club with The Who. 'The Who were throwing drums and shit all over the place, and all the Yes guys were at the back trying to save them and catch stuff because no one had any money and none of us could afford anything.'

Some of the very first Yes rehearsals were in the basement of the Blaises club in Harrington Gardens, London. Brian Chatton of The Warriors recalls:

> I used to see them all the time from their very first rehearsals and just about every other gig, I met them all and thought, 'Fucking hell! What a band'. I lived right across the road from where they rehearsed. Soon as Yes got a name, it just spurred me on because I would get a mention having been part of The Warriors band with Jon. It helped me get a ton of gigs.

Driving around London was the normal way to get to gigs and to socialise. The Edwards Hotel, Paddington is where a long-term friend of Jon and the band, Marianne used to stay. From the early days of Yes, Jon would pick her up and drive around London. She said, 'Jon used to look good wearing those white, flowing shirts with a string of bells around his neck. He once gave me [a string of bells] which I still own.'

Brian and Jon were close friends and chatting up the girls was all part of those days in a band. It appears Jon had just about one joke in his chat-up lines and according to Brian Chatton would come up with a few lines that always worked, but if Brian used the same lines, he ended up getting nowhere. The lead singer usually got the girls and the attention.

Yes were working hard, and while things were looking good for the band, theirs was basic life and they were living without much money. A feverish musical atmosphere and a determined band were not all it seemed, and it was not enough for everyone. Bill - after a few months in which he'd played about nineteen gigs - was not happy. He was fed up with the music business and the striving for a professional career. Pushed by parents, he felt the security of his long-term future needed further study. Bill decided to quit the band around 28 September 1968 to go to University. A shocked Yes were really thrown by Bill's move, espccially Chris Squire, but with gigs booked and bills to pay, they had to keep going.

Looking for a new drummer

The hunt for a replacement drummer started. Finding the right replacement was not going to be an easy task. Yes tried out a few drummers, who remain unknown. Dave Potts was drumming in the band Skip Bifferty from October to November 1968, and he explains:

> I was with Yes for about a week. They were looking for a drummer, and I lived with Jon Anderson. I rehearsed with them for about a week. At the end of the

Left: The only photo of this very short-lived line-up of Yes featuring drummer Tony O'Reilly (far right). Also included are Jon Anderson, Peter Banks, Chris Squire, Tony Kaye. *(Laurence Sackman)*

week, they had to decide which drummer to keep. Jack Barrie tells me that he suggested they keep this other drummer on trial. He was called Tony O'Reilly and came recommended by the manager [Tony Stratton Smith] who later in life managed Genesis. Tony had played with the band the Koobas. Although nobody knows much about him being in the band - or me, for that matter - it was apparently between the two of us. He was 22, and I was 18. Jack Barrie said he suggested keeping Tony in the band because he was more level headed - as if a 22-year-old can be more level headed! So that was a little kick [in the teeth]!

Tony O'Reilly, KOOBAS, The Official Fan Club Release. October 1965
Name: Antony Richard Thomas O'Reilly
D.O.B: April 19 1947
Place of Birth: Liverpool
Height: 5ft.10ins
Weight: 10st.5lbs
Eyes: Blue
Hair: Black
Where educated: Liverpool Art School, College of art
Favourite film stars: Sophia Loren, Bugs Bunny
Favourite Recording Stars: Beatles, Dave Brubeck, Count Basie
Hobbies: Horse-riding, Drawing Caricatures
Likes: Christmas, Girls, Eiffel Tower
Favourite Colours: Turquoise, Black
Favourite Drink: Milk, Tea
Favourite Food: Mixed Grills, Steak
First Public Appearance: Labour Club in Liverpool aged 12
Ambition: To be a top - rated drummer and travel all over the world
Odds and Ends: Tony at first appears to be the quiet one of the group, but he has amicable humour, that creeps into conversations when it's least expected, he certainly has no reserve when playing drums!
The youngest KOOBA, Tony is also a modern Jazz fan.

Tony won the new drummer spot, and it worked for a little while. He was a good-looking young man, clean-shaven and fit, looking a little like Peter Banks. He was probably informed about joining the band at The Ship Pub at 116 Wardour Street, Soho, as most business deals were finalised there. However, challenging drink issues affected his playing and commitment, but beyond those issues, people liked him.

In what has to be one of the most unusual Yes band photoshoots ever, the young Yes lads are captured staring out in all different directions, resembling the Yes *Tormato* cover of 1978. This line-up was photographed just this once, it would seem, for this official Yes band photo by the photographer, Laurence Sackman, who also photographed the band for the *Time and a Word* album cover. He went on to become a hugely respected photographer. In this photoshoot, Yes are captured shirtless, chests out and posing for this black and white image, in a spartan room in the basement at the Blaises Club. The photo was taken at this famous venue on the 13 October 1968, situated at the Imperial Hotel at 121 Queen's Gate, SW7. Yes not only practised there but went on to play around nine times at the venue. According to Melody Maker journalist, Chris Welch, Blaises Club was a venue, 'Where musicians, agents, managers and writers allowed themselves to be deafened, whilst imbibing quantities of alcohol.'

Mike Tate recalled the early Yes and their stand-in drummer Tony O'Reilly:

He was in the drum seat for Yes when I first started, and he had a big drinking problem. I remember him well, it was on the first pick up with the Yes boys in the Ford Transit van, and we went to get Tony from a pub in Camden Lock in London, and they told me where to find him. We drove over there and pulled up. I walked into the pub, and there he was with a half a pint left in his glass. I said, 'We are all here and ready to rock and get out of here.' And he just said, 'No, I have to finish my pint.' Meanwhile, the boys in the band were left sitting in the van.

Yes lived here at No 50A Munster Road, Fulham, London, for the first year of the band's existence before moving out into their own accommodation. Jon occupied the top floor with Chris Squire in the basement along with Bill Bruford. *(David Watkinson Collection)*

The short-lived life of the drummer Tony O'Reilly has not been covered much in the history of Yes because of the tragic circumstances that befell him. Tony had a lively personality, though, and was well-liked. It is suggested that during one of his drinking bouts, he had an accident which left him injured and unable to play the drums, missing a show and leaving Yes – once again – looking for a drummer.

Ian Wallace, the ex-Warriors' drummer,

was brought in for one show. Jon always had great praise for Ian's work, and he could have been the full-time drummer for Yes if different circumstances had arisen. Ian Wallace explained:

> Yes, I did play with Yes. At some point, Bill decided to give up drumming and go back to university. Yes had recruited another drummer for a short while. One-day Jon came knocking on my door in a panic. The drummer had had an incident and was in hospital. They had a gig that night and desperately needed a substitute drummer. So, I was the guy!
>
> I remember really enjoying the gig, and at one point, Chris Squire turned to me in the middle of a song and shouted out, 'Do you want to join the band?' I thought long and hard about it. Two weeks later they were due to open for Cream's farewell concert at the Albert Hall. I had dinner with Yes' manager, Roy Flynn, who almost persuaded me to join. But I felt too loyal to quit the band I was in and turned them down.

Prodigal Bill returns

Ironically though, both Ian and Bill went on to drum for King Crimson, probably the key rivals of Yes. Also, in that turbulent time, another candidate for the drummer post was Phil Collins. He didn't get the job after trying out for the band, although they liked Phil a lot. He went on to be the drums and voice of Genesis and had a hugely successful solo career.

It has been intimated that Yes had no shortage of eager potentially good drummers to pick from, and this assisted Bill Bruford's decision to come back to the band. On a trip to an earlier gig Mike Tate and Bill Bruford travelled in Mike's Volkswagen van, where they discussed whether Bill should stay in the band or go to university full time. Over that lengthy journey, they talked about the options and pros and cons, and by the time they arrived, Mike had apparently convinced Bill to come back to the band. Chris Squire had been deeply affected by Bill leaving, to the extent that Chris had thought long and hard about his own role in the band and the future of Yes without Bill. Chris had seriously considered moving on. According to Dave Foster, there were negotiations regarding Dave joining and playing bass in Yes. Dave immediately turned this offer down, dismissing it as a nonsensical idea saying, 'It was only

Inset Left: A ticket from Royal Albert Hall concert, supporting Cream.
Above: On 26 November 1968, The Royal Albert Hall saw the super group Cream play their final gig. Yes were one of the support acts, on for half an hour. This was one of the most important gigs in their history.

Chris who played that way, and he was impossible to replicate and replace.'

Bill thankfully returned to the band after seeing them play live in Leeds. Bill's perception of the gig is that stand-in drummer Tony was poor and a beat behind the rest of the band, and so proved to himself that they needed and missed his unique drumming style. That said, there are conflicting reports on this gig as Tony Anderson was there and thought it was terrific.

A few months later, young Tony O'Reilly, who was rumoured to have been playing with a band called Bakerloo, sadly passed away. Brian Chatton says of him: 'He was a nice guy and a good drummer. But I suppose it was his time. He was very young, though, maybe twenty-two years old or younger.'

With no success just yet and still very little money, flat-sharing was the name of the game. A friend of Jon's, Jim Payne of the Accrington Stanley band, ended up sharing a flat with Ian Wallace in Drayton Gardens for quite a while. It was a hectic place to live. Many musicians would come around, including Robert Fripp (King Crimson), Boz Burrell (King Crimson and Bad Company) Keith Emerson (Nice, Emerson, Lake and Palmer) and Graham Bell (Skip Bifferty). Jim Payne described the scene:

> Most who came around used to get seriously wrecked. You could hear them trying to get down the stairs at 5 in the morning, falling and laughing. On one occasion, I tried to match Ian [Wallace] drug for drug, as it were. We started at 11 a.m. with lots of coke, followed by more joints than I can remember. Then Jon arrived with some Mescaline (the hallucinogenic drug), which we took, then we went down to the Drayton Arms (153 Old Brompton Road, London SW5 0L) for many more pints of beer. That night I played at the Marquee Club with the band Jonesy, and the next night it was Ian's turn with King Crimson. Two drummers from Accrington playing at the best gigs in London, one on Friday, one on Saturday, it was crazy.

A fan's view

Yes were just three months old, and a Yes fan, Dermot Bassett had attended both gigs by Gun and some early Yes performances. In an interview, he gave his account of seeing Yes.

> It was 1968, Friday 15 November - well actually Saturday 16th as it was now five or six o'clock in the morning, at an all-nighter at The Roundhouse, North London. [The gig was] headlined by The Who and The Small Faces, with Yes as supporting act. The Who had just finished their set and people were drifting away, but there were still quite a few there, as it was too early for the trains to start running. [It was] time for the 'warm down' band. The DJ for just about anything significant at the time, Jeff Dexter, said, 'It's not often a band plays the Middle Earth Club for the very first time (26 October) and completely blows us away, but this is one, Yes!' I was half asleep and not desperately interested, to tell the truth, but as the band walked on, I thought 'Blimey, it's that little bloke I saw from Gun.' Anyway, Yes played their set, and I thought they were very good, especially when they closed with 'Something's Coming', which was very impressive!

The big break - crème de la crème

Cream's farewell concert was on the horizon in London on 26 November 1968 at the Royal Albert Hall. After much work by Roy Flynn, confirmation of Yes as the support spot for the band came through. This would be their biggest and most important gig up to that point. Approximately 50 gigs into their first-ever tour and Yes were due to play a dream support slot to that legendary rock supergroup, Cream. Made up of Eric Clapton, Ginger Baker and Jack Bruce, the band had been riding high for years but decided to bow out at the top, leaving the way open for the likes of Yes.

Yes played their short half-hour slot to a superstar audience. They were nervous yet confident. We get a quick idea on how they went down with this review in the *Melody Maker* music paper which describes their performance as follows:

> Opening the Tuesday night concert were Yes, a highly impressive group featuring nice harmonies, good lead vocals, a balanced sound and clever arrangements. Their music was intelligent and tasteful. They played a selection from West Side Story that went on a trifle too long but featured some fine drumming. Some of their stop-timing and use of dynamics was electrifying.

Yes had finally arrived. With enthusiasm, talent, dogged determination and belief in their craft, Yes were going to be the proud banner-waver for the progressive rock movement. However, the band had always been on the hunt for new small improvements in sound and technology, as this was still on a basic level in 1968. The Cream gig was important for the band, not only for the great publicity they received but also because Cream had the best American PA system. Mike Tate says:

> That's the gig that broke Yes. That's when we would see the PA systems with horns and large sound boxes and other things. Cream had something better than the WEM [Watkins Electric Music] equipment of the time. In those days the Royal Albert Hall was full of echoes - it was a horrible sounding room. Yes played there a couple of times, once with Janis Joplin, but with Cream, Yes would have a half-hour set, three songs. I think one was 'America'. Once we got a front-of-house WEM low-impedance mixer, and some microphones, with a Charles Watkins mixer, a five-channel thing. It became better. I did mix the sound in the beginning but wasn't very good at it.

Jon Anderson spoke with *Seconds* magazine about the famous gig:

> It was the first time we played in front of so many people. I tell you, it was amazing to see because Cream were the best of the musicians in London at the time. There was another guy on the bill, Rory Gallagher [the Irish blues and rock instrumentalist]. We just went on stage and probably sounded like a little band because emotionally we were a little band. After that, we thought all we've got to do now is go out to the sticks and play clubs and get some university gigs. That's all you think about.

Rod Hill recalls the important evening: 'I was lucky to have been a part of it all also. To be at the Cream farewell concert at the Albert hall was magical. I saw the show from a box to the left of the stage and had backstage access, as a roadie.

Dermot Bassett was in awe of the fledging band at the concert at the Royal Albert Hall:

> From the opening chords of 'Carpet Man' I was hooked. The sound, the look, the movement, the songs: everything! Eleven days after Yes at The Roundhouse, and again I was completely blown away! As a support act at Cream's farewell concert, my friend who was with me felt the same way, and we came away with Cream long forgotten. Yes was the only topic of conversation.

Jon Anderson's brother Tony reflects about the end of The Warriors and Yes finding a place on the map:

> We could never have imagined that Jon was going to soar to such unimaginable stardom. One of the main things Jon took from The Warriors to Yes was the harmonies we did, Jon loved doing them. I was so amazed when I first heard him with Yes: I honestly couldn't believe how brilliant he was when we went to see them at Leeds University. Then Jon told me that Yes had been asked to support Cream at the Royal Albert Hall in a couple of weeks, and the rest, as they say, is history.

The time has come to talk of many things: of managers, and recording studios and possible dirty deals

Talking with Jack Barrie about the early Yes days, it was clear he was proud of his involvement with Yes and with the important work he did in setting up Yes in the formative years:

> I never knew The Warriors as a group but only ever knew them as individual musicians when eventually they drifted down to London following in the footsteps of Brian Chatton. It was he who introduced me to Jon Anderson when he first returned from Germany after the break-up of The Warriors. As Jon Anderson's first manager and the first manager of Yes from the inception, it was I who introduced Jon to Chris Squire, and it was to me they looked for the initial finance of rehearsal rooms hiring costs. In addition to giving them their first gigs at The Marquee and me finding them their first agent, it was I who arranged their initial management deal with Roy Flynn as I was too tied up managing The Marquee to be able to give them the full time and attention they required and deserved.

A somewhat forthright and proud response to Yes' beginnings!

January 1969 saw Yes gigging in London mostly with the odd trip further afield. Surprisingly, they were invited to the BBC music show *Top Gear* for a recording session, at the Maida Vale studios in North London, with the famous BBC DJ, John Peel. Tuesday 7 January saw the band spending all day laying down the tracks that would give them a good plug on nationwide radio. These were songs heading for their first new album, and they played tracks such as 'Something's Coming', 'Everydays', 'Sweetness', 'Dear Father', 'Every Little Thing' and 'Sweet Dreams'. The latter song would become the one the band would play live for a decade or more, with Jon Anderson playing the track over 50 years later on a solo tour in 2019.

In March, an excited Yes manager, Roy Flynn, spoke with Atlantic Record's managing director Frank Fenter. He arranged an audition with Ahmet Ertegun, head of the company, at the Speakeasy Club in London. Ahmet was the man to impress, as he was looking to sign on bands who were going to make the big time. Yes signed with him the same month that Led Zeppelin did. They began working on their first recorded album in the Advision Studios at the Bond Street site, as well as at Trident Studios - only minutes' walk between the two studios - thanks to the good negotiating by Roy Flynn.

The first album, inventively called *Yes*, was released in July 1969. It was a mixture of songs from the Mabel Greer era, the Beatles and the Byrds, as well as some self-penned material. They mixed things up here and there, 'borrowing' from wherever they could. Everyone seemed to be somewhat challenged being in the studio. For many in the band, this was their first real experience in a studio situation. Paul Clay and his engineers were chosen to work on the production. The producer pulled the first Yes record together in a matter of weeks, which nowadays would be unheard of, but in those days, time was money, and the record companies needed a swift return on their investment when the band was so unknown.

Peter Banks later voiced his thoughts on the producer Mr Clay, which weren't flattering, but at the time all in the band were fresh and young, and so were the production crew. There was much to learn all round but in spite of this, Yes put in a good effort and created a work that still resonates with listeners and stands up strongly today.

With little money thrown at Yes or any serious push on the marketing front given by the record company, it was going to be down to a lot of touring to get the band and the album noticed. In those days, most of the bands

Left: A rare advert for Yes' single 'Sweetness' on the cover of the popular *New Musical Express* in July 1969. *(David Watkinson Collection)*

had terrible deals and, in the end, like most bands, Yes were in debt to the record company. In those early days, the record companies had all the power because the bands had little understanding of the business.

Yes' press release – 1st album, July 1969

YES were a year old and these are comments that were made about their music:
'Hits of the show were quite definitely YES they stole the show in the same way that 'Jethro Tull' did last year.'
Melody Maker at the Plumpton Festival.
'YES were greeted with the only second standing ovation in the history of the club – the first was 'Nice'.'
Western Evening Harold at the Van Dyke Club
'Every time I see them, I am amazed'
International Times at the Janis Joplin concert, Royal Albert Hall.
'Success! Who and YES triumph!'
Top Pops at the Plumpton Festival.
'YES' are going to be Giants. They deserve nothing less.'
Cash Box

AGENCY
MARQUEE MARTIN AGENCY LIMITED
41/43 Wardour Street, London, W.1
PUBLISHER
YESSONGS LIMITED
80 Hanover Square, London, W,1
RECORDING
ATLANTIC RECORDING CORPORATION
1841 Broadway
New York, 10023, N.Y. USA
MANAGER
ROY FLYNN
40 Carlton Drive,
London S.W.15

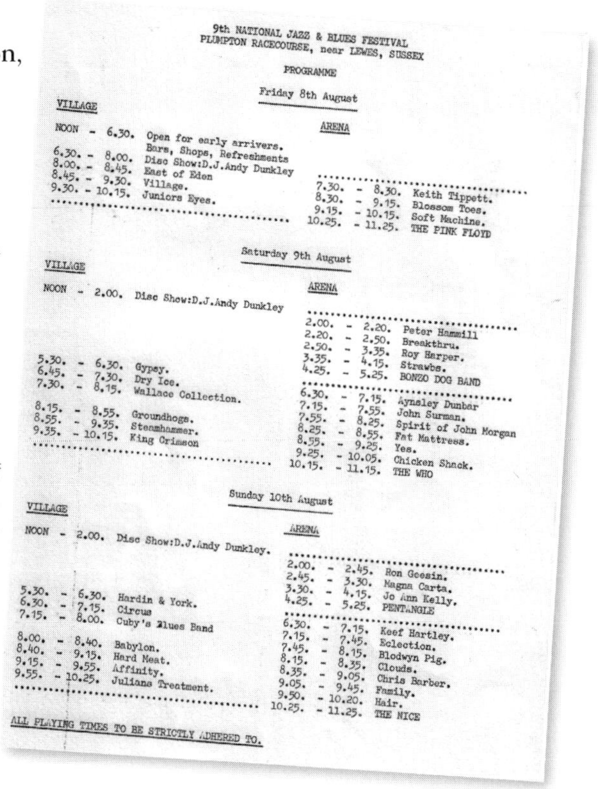

9th NATIONAL JAZZ & BLUES FESTIVAL
PLUMPTON RACECOURSE, near LEWES, SUSSEX

PROGRAMME

Friday 8th August

VILLAGE

NOON - 6.30. Open for early arrivers.
Bars, Shops, Refreshments
6.30. - 8.00. Disc Show:D.J.Andy Dunkley
8.00. - 8.45. East of Eden
8.45. - 9.30. Village.
9.30. - 10.15. Juniors Eyes.

ARENA

7.30. - 8.30. Keith Tippett.
8.30. - 9.15. Blossom Toes.
9.15. - 10.15. Soft Machine.
10.25. - 11.25. THE PINK FLOYD

Saturday 9th August

VILLAGE

NOON - 2.00. Disc Show:D.J.Andy Dunkley

5.30. - 6.30. Gypsy.
6.45. - 7.30. Dry Ice.
7.30. - 8.15. Wallace Collection.

8.15. - 8.55. Groundhogs.
8.55. - 9.35. Steamhammer.
9.35. - 10.15. King Crimson

ARENA

2.00. - 2.20. Peter Hammill
2.20. - 2.50. Breakthru.
2.50. - 3.35. Roy Harper.
3.35. - 4.15. Strawbs.
4.25. - 5.25. BONZO DOG BAND

6.30. - 7.15. Aynsley Dunbar
7.15. - 7.55. John Surman.
7.55. - 8.25. Spirit of John Morgan
8.25. - 8.55. Fat Mattress.
8.55. - 9.25. Yes.
9.25. - 10.05. Chicken Shack.
10.15. - 11.15. THE WHO

Sunday 10th August

VILLAGE

NOON - 2.00. Disc Show:D.J.Andy Dunkley.

5.30. - 6.30. Hardin & York.
6.30. - 7.15. Circus
7.15. - 8.00. Cuby's Blues Band

8.00. - 8.40. Babylon.
8.40. - 9.15. Hard Meat.
9.15. - 9.55. Affinity.
9.55. - 10.25. Julians Treatment.

ARENA

2.00. - 2.45. Ron Geesin.
2.45. - 3.30. Magna Carta.
3.30. - 4.15. Jo Ann Kelly.
4.25. - 5.25. PENTANGLE

6.30. - 7.15. Keef Hartley.
7.15. - 7.45. Eclection.
7.45. - 8.15. Blodwyn Pig.
8.15. - 8.35. Clouds.
8.35. - 9.05. Chris Barber.
9.05. - 9.45. Family.
9.50. - 10.20. Hair.
10.25. - 11.25. THE NICE

ALL PLAYING TIMES TO BE STRICTLY ADHERED TO.

Right: The small town of Lewes in Sussex had a wonderful line up for the festival in 1969. On Friday, you could have seen Pink Floyd, on Saturday Yes, King Crimson and The Who, with Sunday offering The Nice. *(David Watkinson Collection)*

Yes Manager Roy Flynn Letter

This is an example of correspondence from the band's original manager Roy Flynn, to promoters and agents. The letter was on two sides of a single piece of Speakeasy-headed notepaper:

> Dear Geroed,
> Re Yes tour of Switzerland which was cancelled. I enclose contract and correspondence. The deal was done by my agent, Marquee/Martin with the Swiss Agent's representatives in London The London City Agency (JCD) Ltd. Perhaps it would be easier to take action against them in London?
> The fact is though I did not have it confirmed finally that the tour was off until Monday 7 April – just a couple of days before we were due to go. Also, as a direct result of this, we lost a further £180 from a German promoter which we had hoped to tie in with this tour. Making a total of £360 + £180 = £540. Incidentally, I just heard, that the same Swiss Agent 'Sound Package' has just done the same to another English Group. Let me know what you think of our chances.
>
> Best Wishes
> Roy Flynn

Above: A business card from Roy Flynn – Yes' manager – from 1968.
(David Watkinson Collection)

Meanwhile...

Future prog-rock giants and hugely influential rival band King Crimson made their debut at the London Speakeasy on 9 April 1969, and on July 5th played to 650,000 people at the Rolling Stones' free Hyde Park concert. King Crimson were creating quite a stir from day one. Their musicianship and songwriting seemed to be on another level to the then-embryonic Yes.

Yes returned to the London Royal Albert Hall on 21 April supporting Janis Joplin. On 24 April at the Golden Rose Festival in Montreux, they bumped into Patrick Moraz, who would be the future Yes keyboard player. During May and June Yes carried on with gigs all over the country, including favourites: The Marquee Club, Blaises, Ronnie Scotts, and the Roundhouse. In July, they ventured to Holland and Belfast and had more studio time. Yes released their first single from the album Yes, 'Sweetness/Something's Coming' on 4 July 1969.

Although the first album released 25 July 1969 did get a few good reviews, it was otherwise pretty much ignored by the press. The positive, bright and striking cover was well designed: the inside images and front logo, and the gatefold sleeve made it a good package. This was a naive Yes, and although the band did have many issues with the production of the record, it was a lively start for the band with music different enough to gain a small fan base early on in their career. Looking back at the album, I like this madcap-mixture of talents, all vying for position in the mix as the band tried to figure out a Yes style and sound.

Bill Bruford made the following comment regarding recording other artists' material and playing cover versions: 'I'm a keen believer in starting with covers, but then 're-imagining' them when you are beginning to find your stylistic feet.' In an interview in 2001, Bill was asked how he felt about Yes at that time and what his favourite memory of those days was. He answered:

> Sitting around with Jennifer [the future Mrs Anderson], Carolyn [the future Mrs Bruford] and Jon - listening to a test pressing of 'Every Little Thing' from our first album in a Fulham Road restaurant after closing time.

In October King Crimson released the startling *In the Court of the Crimson King* album. It was endorsed by Pete Townshend of The Who as 'an uncanny masterpiece.' Crimson would go on to celebrate 50 years in the business, led by Robert Fripp, their long career a seemingly endless series of personnel changes, not unlike those that Yes would go through.

In October 1969, just after the King Crimson's album came out, Jon and Brian Chatton met Greg Lake of King Crimson and later Emerson, Lake and Palmer. Greg had heard about Brian's band Flaming Youth, so they all had much to talk about. Jon and Brian, clutching a copy of the first Yes album, went around to Greg's flat and got progressively more and more drunk. They put on the King Crimson album first, while they were still relatively conscious. Even in that hazy, half-world they were in, Brian recalled:

> We were knocked out; Jon and I were really fucking impressed. I tell you I wasn't looking forward to putting our album on, coming after those two albums. Ours was very 'poppy' in comparison. And then we put the Yes album on, and at that point, we were just about losing it. But the Yes album sounded great as well. Greg was very impressed. King Crimson were a great band.

Friends

Although not a member of Yes, Brian Chatton's friendship with Jon was still strong. Brian followed every single Yes gig for the first two years. Then he saw King Crimson for the first time - what a shock! Brian relates this:

> Jon and I went to the Lyceum Club in London [to see them]. We stood at the gig with our mouths wide open and left in a complete dream. We came out of the gig, shaking our heads. Typical for Jon, he said, 'Brian, we haven't even begun yet, we have a hell of a lot to do. We have so much work to do: we can't sit on our laurels. We need to get this shit done.'

Future Prog legends The Pink Floyd were playing London at the Speakeasy Club. *Dark Side of The Moon* was still a long way off, but in those early days, Brian and Jon saw them. Not the only ones to be confused at seeing the band, Brian remembers those early days of Floyd:

> We were scratching our heads. It was a pile of crap, a load of shit! We came out and asked each other how these guys could make a name for themselves because at the time everyone was talking about them. We couldn't see it at all; we just didn't get it. I think if you were stoned, then you got the Floyd.

Marianne, Jon's friend, hung about with Tony Kaye and Peter Banks of Yes and used to drive them to and from the studio. By then, Peter lived in Lots Road, Chelsea, and the rest stayed around the Fulham area. Both Marianne and DJ Nikki followed the band, helping out and having a good time. Most of the members of Yes lived in a house at 5 Drayton Gardens until 1970, just as their star was beginning to rise. Soon after this, they moved out of the Drayton Gardens house to their own places. Marianne remembers fondly: 'I saw Yes in 1969 in Germany, and Jon bought me a fish gift, which I still have! I remember Yes playing on the same bill as Pink Floyd, who had a crazy light show at the time. Yes were fantastic and a step above The Warriors.' [This may very well have been 11 October 1969 at The Pop and Blues Festival, Essen. Other bands on the bill were Fleetwood Mac, The Nice and Deep Purple with Floyd playing the last night of the three-day festival].

Jon's life changed in late 1968 when he met Jennifer Baker, his soon-to-be girlfriend. She worked in a London hotel as a chambermaid. She was friends with a girl called Karan, who knew long-time fan Marianne and it was Marianne who introduced Jennifer to Jon. Jennifer would become Jon's first wife on 22 December 1969, in London. Marianne made clothes for Jon and Jennifer, as they used to have a clothing shop in the Kensington Market. Jennifer was also in the music business, singing with her two sisters in a group called Shades of Blue. As Jon says of Hans Christian and Jennifer's band, 'they both flopped'.

I'm with Yes…who?

Being in a new band was not easy, and not everyone was fortunate enough to get the break that Led Zeppelin did with their first album. Sometimes, it took years or even decades to become famous. And for others, it never happened. Atlantic was a large organisation, and even if a band had been signed up as Yes had, it did not imply that their label knew anything about them. At one point, Mike Tait realised that the record company had no idea about Yes. He had gone on a trip to Australia and on his way back called into the record companies offices in New York. He told them that he worked with Yes in England and they hadn't even heard of the band! Really *no idea* who I was talking about, it was crazy: we were nothing to them.'

But Yes were quietly grabbing those fans who were prepared to give them a chance. Yes were a thinking person's rock band, one to 'get into'. Yet they were a long way from reaching their potential, even though all the signs were there at the beginning. But Jon was no Mick Jagger and Yes had a serious image, leaving the strutting to others who did it so much better. Could Yes have been bigger earlier in their career? It appears that it was a slog for them to achieve fame. Maybe that was how it was for most bands, but personnel changes would be the key to Yes' success.

Mike Tait, reflecting on the success of Yes said:

The biggest problem with Yes and why its success was limited in a way, was that Jon was not sexy enough. The more successful bands had more sex appeal and Yes didn't really have it. Yes never had enough of the sex, drugs and Rock 'n' Roll to be bigger than they were. In those days, Jon was married and was relatively clean living. Chris was always mucking about, and then he got married. But Chris was always all over the place. He was doing drugs, some serious drugs and was a mess. The band did low profile drugs, Jon didn't do the hard stuff. He would just sit around and get stoned a bit, have a beer and some crazy mushrooms. Chris would be out partying all night long. Bill Bruford was clean - not into anything. Tony Kaye liked to party a bit. Peter Banks didn't do much. In fact, I'd pick him up and drop him off, and that would be that.

The Warriors' guys were off doing other things by now but did keep in touch with Jon. David Foster recalled those the early days of Yes:

I have known Jon for a long time, and we were good writing together. In the early days with Yes, Bill Bruford and Peter Banks couldn't understand Jon and I because of our northern accents! They couldn't understand the lyrics we wrote either. On the second Yes album *Time and a Word*, we had no idea either what the lyrics meant, they just fitted in and sounded right. Sometimes we just needed a lyric there and then and it didn't matter what it meant. The rest of the band never questioned us on the lyrics; they thought we knew what we were doing. We didn't understand them either, but we didn't say so. Jon and I wrote the song 'Time and a Word'. We played it before Yes with a group called Head Hands and Feet. We did all the backing vocals for it, and they are still there to hear. Jon and I did all the orchestration together. We did all the writing in the cellar of Roy Flynn's house in Putney, London. I remember Jon and I doing 'No Opportunity' in a Park Lane hotel in London with Jon Hendrix [John Carl Hendricks, known professionally as Jon Hendricks, was an American jazz lyricist and singer], we played it to him. [Yes played 'No Opportunity' in 2019 on tour to celebrate their 50th anniversary].

Jon was always pushing for bigger sound, better playing, more diversity and advancement in all areas for Yes. He was always looking for better musicians. If he felt one of the band was not suitable, he made changes. He liked being in control. Dave Foster explained:

I remember the fateful day that Jon made his mind up about Peter Banks. It was at the London gig at the Royal Festival Hall. I remember to this day the expression on Jon's face at the end of the gig when Peter did his Pete Townsend impression with his arm swinging around. Jon was not happy or impressed; it wasn't long after that he went. The thing is once Jon realised, he could write a good song, he was away, and nothing could hold him back. He couldn't talk about the intricacies of the key or the chord, but once he knew he had a gift for writing a great tune and people liked it, he felt he was in control and could contribute.

Even though Peter Banks left Yes under a cloud, many years later, when he spoke about Yes on The *Marquee Days* website, he was unequivocal in his recognition of Jon's role in Yes:

If anyone had the grand vision of what Yes was all about, it [was] Jon. There is no question Jon Anderson was and will always be the driving force behind Yes. Also, there's no doubt that his voice is the most identifiable characteristic of Yes.

The basic concept for Yes by Jon and Chris had been quite a simple one, as Jon explained in my interview with him in 2015:

It was to put on a good show, never ever to try and make a hit record. I thought we were a bit old to be pop stars, so I just wanted to make great music for the stage. I'd seen such great bands over the years when we travelled, and in Frankfurt where they had really great artists where you could spend an hour watching someone perform without knowing any of their songs, but because they were that good, it didn't matter. I realised that was what I wanted to do: to be in a band that puts on a good show.

By the time I got to London, there were some good bands. Ones I thought who were particularly good were Family and Vanilla Fudge. They slowed songs down. I thought about how we could do that, slow [songs] down and make [them] better. Modification and change [were needed]. So, working with Chris in a whole new realm of playing, without overthinking we rehearsed our first shows. We met some people like King Crimson, who were [also] doing something different. In the same year, there were about five other bands, playing similar experimental rock music.

Asked in 2000 why he thought Yes was such an enduring band, Bill said:

Jon never knew when to quit, an enduring quality. And, even if he had, Chris would have been late for the occasion.

How Time Flies

Now, all these years later, with Jon and Yes having celebrated their 50th anniversary in 2018, and Jon Anderson boasting a lifetime in the music business, those early days of learning their trade and becoming rounded professional musicians - albeit forgotten for the most part - are a reminder to us of what an effort, a journey, it was for them to become the legends that they are now in progressive rock. Jon Anderson reflects:

The Warriors was a special [time] for me. We became such a great band and even though we were a bit reckless here and there, and probably nearly died a few times, we were still a good band - we survived. It was a great learning time for me. I was just a singer in the band who couldn't play an instrument.

> I had to carry all the gear, but still, I was happy, a happy guy. All that time with The Warriors means I can do anything I want now, instead of having to do the latest hits all day long. When I met Chris Squire, my life changed.

Speaking in February 2019, about his *1000 Hands* album and tour (original titled Uzlot, a Lancashire slang for saying 'all of us'), Jon remembered how his project all started some thirty years ago. Working once again with his old Warriors' bandmate Brian Chatton, Jon recalled after receiving a tape from him, 'I've known Brian from when he was just a wee lad of sixteen, he had joined my first band The Warriors way back in 1966, playing a Vox keyboard.... wow! How time flies.'

Tempus Fugit indeed. The Yes story began on the 3 August 1968 with a small out of town practice gig at the East Mersea Youth Camp, but really took flight for Jon, Chris, Bill, Tony and Peter after the Royal Albert Hall gig a few months later. Atlantic Records gave them a solid base to work from and Yes' non-stop musical adventure just kept on rolling. Fans have been amazingly lucky to have seen this incredible musical story played out before them.

Let's not forget though how it all came about in the 1960s as both Jon Anderson and the band Yes - in all its forms - propels itself beyond 50 years. It looks like Yes music is here to stay in one form or another, and as for a musician of Jon's eminence - it's hard to see such another artist like him coming along again anytime soon.

The journey has taken Jon from Lancashire to Los Angeles, but his music, unique voice, spirituality, words, positivity, lyrics and love has reached the world, and it's a better place for it.

Left: Marquee Club London 5 February 1969 and velvet is most definitely in vogue. *(David Watkinson Collection)*

Right: Marquee Club London 28 May 1969. It must have been electrifying. *(David Watkinson Collection)*

Left: Lewes College nr Brighton 31 May 1969. Yes would return on the 9 August for the Jazz and Blues Festival on at Plumpton Racecourse East Sussex. *(David Watkinson Collection)*

Left: Lewes College nr Brighton, 31 May 1969. *(David Watkinson Collection)*

Right: Lewes College nr Brighton, 31 May 1969. *(David Watkinson Collection)*

Left: Marquee Club London 11 June 1969. It looks like Chris's floor pedal has been hit with a hammer!. *(David Watkinson Collection)*

Right: Marquee Club London 11 June 1969. Chris Squire sports some interesting 1960s fashion. *(David Watkinson Collection)*

Left: Marquee Club London 11 June 1969. Yes are supported by Sweet Marriage. *(David Watkinson Collection)*

Right: Marquee Club London 11 June 1969. . *(David Watkinson Collection)*

Left: Marquee Club London 2 July 1969. Chris and Bill rocking, as Mike Tait watches on. *(David Watkinson Collection)*

Right: Marquee Club London 2 July 1969. Bank's soloing to a long-haired and seated crowd. *(David Watkinson Collection)*

Left: Marquee Club London 2 July 1969. Yes are supported by Andromeda. *(David Watkinson Collection)*

Above: No! Performing 'No Opportunity Necessary, No Experience Needed' on *Beat Club* in 1969.

Left: Chris Squire with his 'Survival' face on, from *Beat Club*.

Right: A studious Bill 'Tubs' Bruford, just 'Looking Around'.

Left: An animated Tony Kaye from the *Beat Club* set.

Right: Jon Anderson caught up in the music during 'Survival'.

Left: Peter Banks in full flight with his famous Yes logo'd Rickenbacker.

Appendix 1 After The Warriors

The band contributed a great deal to the music scene over their seven-year history. This next section gives the reader an insight into what came next for each of the band members, and a few other key musicians. As you will see, everyone seems to have led colourful and varied lives.

Jon Anderson (Vocals)

With more than 50 years in the music business, Jon has constantly been busy with collaborations, solo works and Yes. Now officially an American citizen, he lives and creates music in California.

From 1968 through to 1980 Jon was the frontman for Yes, where he played a major role in creating the classic Yes music and legendary albums. He also appeared on the album *Lizard* for Yes rivals King Crimson and had his first collaboration with the keyboard artist Vangelis on his album *Heaven and Hell*.

He released his first solo album, the stunning *Olias of Sunhillow* in 1976. He left Yes along with Rick Wakeman after the *Tormato* LP and tour in 1979. Both were tired after touring solidly for ten years, and musical differences meant it was time for a change for both musicians, Jon going on to a solo career, touring regularly.

He produced songs and collaborations with Vangelis and Mike Oldfield amongst others. He was involved with movie soundtracks, one with electronic music giants Tangerine Dream, for the movie *Legend*, Led Zeppelin's John Paul Jones for the movie *Scream*, the re-release of the Fritz Lang film *Metropolis*, plus songs for movies *St. Elmo's Fire* and *Biggles: Adventures in Time*.

He re-joined Chris Squire, Alan White, Tony Kaye and Trevor Rabin in 1983 for a proposed new band called Cinema. This swiftly turned into the new line-up of Yes. They went on to produce the biggest selling Yes album called *90125* and had an American number one single 'Owner of a Lonely Heart'. They toured around the world to great acclaim – a new sounding Yes for the new decade – surprising many by their choice of musical direction. Jon once again left Yes in 1988, following the *Big Generator* album.

He formed the band ABWH (Anderson – Bruford – Wakeman – Howe), which was, in essence, Yes without officially being so, producing a successful album and world tour. This all changed again when the band morphed into the eight-man Yes line-up in 1990.

Yes toured with an 'in the round' circular centre stage as they had done in 1978. The live shows touring spectacle for Yes fans came to an end with more changes in personnel which lead to the classic line up regrouping to play in 1996, via a brief return to the *90125* line up for the *Talk* album. Jon, Chris, Alan, Steve and Rick would delight fans with some exclusive gigs in America. Further line-up changes kept Yes and Jon together up to their 30th anniversary in 1998.

Along the way, Jon produced various solo albums but left Yes again, this time due to a life-threatening illness. Jon was looked after by his devoted wife Jane (Janee), and he continued to grow in strength and confidence, working on music and projects with young people, both around the world and with locally home-based musicians in California. Jon also toured with his long-term friend and ex-Yes man, Rick Wakeman. There were various other musical adventures which included working with an orchestra, and 'The School of Rock', while Jon built up both his strength and voice, leading to a joint venture with violinist Jean Luc Ponty in 2015. They recorded and toured under the title of Anderson Ponty Band, creating the album *Better Late Than Never*, which sold well. With this project, Jon again engaged in longer tours, the first since his illness.

In 2015 the legendary joint founding member of Yes, Chris Squire, sadly passed away. Unquestionably one of the best bass players who ever lived, Chris' passing understandably had a profound impact on Jon and on other Yes musicians. 2016 saw Jon working with Roine Stolt of The Flower Kings and Transatlantic, on an album called *The Invention of Knowledge*. With music in the style of *Olias of Sunhillow* and *Tales from Topographic Oceans*, the double album did very well for them both with future collaborations planned.

A surprising collaboration came together in 2016. After a gap of some 25 years, three ex-Yes members formed a new band to play Yes music under the name of ARW. Featuring Jon Anderson, Trevor Rabin and Rick Wakeman, they would aim to recapture Yes' music and add to the musical legacy they had all jointly created. Under the banner of 'Anderson, Rabin and Wakeman – An Evening of Yes Music and More', ARW carried on touring through 2016 up until the name of the band was changed in 2017. Finally, Yes was inducted into the *Rock and Roll Hall of Fame* in the USA, after a long battle by their fans to get them there. For this event, Jon teamed up with Steve Howe, Alan White and Geddy Lee of the band Rush, showcasing 'Owner of a Lonely Heart' and the Yes classic 'Roundabout'. Also in attendance were Rick Wakeman, Bill Bruford, Trevor Rabin and members of Chris Squire's family.

ARW changed its name to Yes featuring Anderson, Rabin and Wakeman. This meant there were now two versions of Yes in existence in 2017 and 2018, both playing live and celebrating Yes' 50 years in the music business. From April 2018, Jon's Yes toured under the name *Quintessentially Yes 50th Anniversary Tour*. A new track called 'Fragile' was premiered by Yes featuring Anderson, Rabin and Wakeman in 2018 and a live recording of the Manchester show in England was released on various formats called *Live at The Apollo*. In 2019, the official Yes (Steve Howe, Alan White, Geoff Downes, Jon Davison, Billy Sherwood, with Jay Schellen) carried the Yes flag into the future with Jon's Yes resting for the year. It was rumoured that Jon's Yes would return and record an album and tour in 2020. Jon's *1000 Hands* album project was released in mid-2019. Thirty years in the making, the album was made up of a vast array of musicians and would be a highlight of his solo career, according to Jon. The Warriors connection came around again as this project was started by Jon and Brian Chatton. In March 2019, Jon went on a solo USA tour with his band, the setlist featuring music from the new album along with selections from Yes, his solo music and his collaborations. In his promotional video for the song 'Makes Me Happy', Jon can be seen acting out being at an Accrington Stanley football match waving a scarf. It is thought that Jon will continue to tour and make music way into the 2020s.

Prolific in his workload, Jon's solo career has been extensive and hugely varied. Here I give a brief list of Jon's work. I cannot give much detail here, as Jon's fifty-year career is one that would need a detailed book written about it. This is an overview of his key releases to search out. I have not included all of his collaborations, compilation or bootleg albums, videos, DVDs or singles.

Jon's solo albums and collaborations: *Olias of Sunhillow* (1976), *Song of Seven* (1980), Jon and Vangelis – *Short Stories* (1980), Jon and Vangelis – *The Friends of Mr Cairo* (1981), *Animation* (1982), Jon and Vangelis – *Private Collection* (1983), *3 Ships* (1985), *In the City of Angels* (1988), *Anderson Bruford Wakeman Howe* (1989), Jon and Vangelis – *Page of Life* (1991), *Deseo* (1994), *Change We Must* (1994), *Angels Embrace* (1995), *The Deseo remixes* (1995), *Toltec* (1996), *Lost Tapes of Opio* (1996), *The Promise Ring* (1997), *Earth Mother Earth* (1997), *The More You Know* (1998), Anderson / Wakeman – *The Living Tree* (2010), *Survival & Other Stories* (2011), AndersonPonty Band – *Better Late Than Never* (2015), Anderson/Stolt – *Invention of Knowledge* (2016), *1000 Hands: Chapter One* (2019)

For Jon's full work in Yes, the amount of space required for a detailed listing is best shown in books on Yes, such as *Yes: Perpetual Change* (Plexus Publishing, David Watkinson, 2001) *Yes: Every Album, Every Song* (Sonicbond Publishing Ltd, Stephen Lambe, 2018), *Solid Mental Grace – Listening to the Music of Yes* (Cultured Llama Publishing, Simon Barrow, 2018). A fuller picture of Yes and Jon's output in all areas can be seen at the web site run by Henry Potts. This is a wonderful, up-to-date resource. *www.bondegezou.co.uk*

This is a list of Yes studio albums released featuring Jon, with just one live album covering the Yes featuring ARW era:
Yes (1969), *Time and a Word* (1970), *The Yes Album* (1971), *Fragile* (1971), *Close to the Edge* (1972), *Tales from Topographic Oceans* (1973), *Relayer* (1974), *Going for the One* (1977), *Tormato* (1978), *90125* (1983), *Big Generator* (1987), *Anderson, Bruford, Wakeman, Howe* (1989), *Union* (1990), *Talk (1994), Keys to Ascension* (live/studio) (1996), *Keys to Ascension 2* (live/studio) (1997), *Open Your Eyes* (1997), *The Ladder* (1999), *Magnification* (2001), *Live at The Apollo* (2018) Yes featuring Jon Anderson, Trevor Rabin, Rick Wakeman (ARW).

Yes did proceed at various times without Jon in place on studio albums such as *Drama* (1980) with Trevor Horn, *Fly from Here* (2011), Benoit David, *Heaven and Earth* (2014), Jon Davison and *Fly from Here – Return Trip* (2018), Trevor Horn.

Jon's official website shows current projects and tour details:
www.JonAnderson.com

Tony Anderson (Vocals)

A short time after leaving The Warriors, Tony joined Los Bravos, a band in Spain who had some hit records notably 'Black is Black'. Later in life, Tony moved away from Lancashire and became a pastor at the Elim Pentecostal

Church on the beautiful Isle of Wight, located off the south coast of the British mainland. He continues his love of music through his band 'STOP', releasing the CD *Signs* in 2012. Tony is now retired and lives with his wife on the Isle of Wight. He still loves his guitar and riding his motorbike.

Brian Chatton (Keyboards)

After the Warriors, Brian worked with Phil Collins in the band Flaming Youth. He moved to America in 1989, and had a hit record all over the world with the single 'I Wanna be a Cowboy' by Boys Don't Cry. Brian wrote for Dick James Music and was also a producer. Some of Brian's bands and collaborations include: John Walker Band, Hickory, Flaming Youth 1969-1970, Eclection, Jackson Heights, Snafu (whose album had a Roger Dean cover) in 1974, Rock Follies, Michael Chapman Band, Brian Parrish Band, The Eric Burdon Band in 1976, The John Miles Band, The All-Star Rock Band, The Pat Travers Band, The Hollies, The Meat Loaf Band, The Mystic Orchestra. He played with BB King on the *Tonight* show. Brian's biography *Rolling with Rock Royalty* was published in 2018. Deborah Anderson (Jon's eldest daughter) supplied photos of Brian for the book, which takes the reader on a humour-filled ride through his 50-year career. Brian's work on the UZLOT project eventually saw the light of day, metamorphosing into the Jon Anderson album *1000 Hands* in 2019, which features the two Warriors members once again working together. In April 2019 Brian met up with Rodney from The Warriors in Lancashire, on the promotion tour for Brian's book, the first meeting in about 50 or so years. A further tour was planned for Brian in 2019 -2020. He isn't going to stop; he loves what he does, and so do his fans.
www.brianchatton.com

Dave Foster (Bass Guitar/Vocals)

Following The Warriors, David played in the band Accrington Stanley. He continued to collaborate with Jon, helping to write the future Yes classic songs, 'Sweet Dreams', 'Time and a Word' and contributing some lyrics for 'Yours is No Disgrace'. Dave continued the Yes link with the band Badger, with Jon Anderson helping out on production of the album. With Tony Kaye providing keyboards, the album sported a Roger Dean cover. After moving to Ardross on the Scottish Moors, he ran his own recording studio and label called Rowen Records. In the late 80s to mid-90s, Dave produced modern Celtic music for several local bands. He recorded with his own band Wolfstone, for his own record label. Although Dave suffered from some health issues later in life, he did continue in music, making a solo album called *Open Road*. Retiring to Scotland, David passed away in November 2017, aged 71.

Rodney Hill (Guitar)

Once the band finished, Rod worked with Gordon Kenyon of The Warriors in his hairdressing salon. Rod carried on with music in between many other adventures. These are some of them: Sleepy, Sandy Shaw, Lou Christi, Marbles with Graham Bonnett, Jackie Lomax. Rod ran a clothing fashion shop, became a guitar tutor, worked in a local music shop at weekends (*Mary's Music)* and during the week laboured for a local builder. He played regularly in different bands in Lancashire. He studied classical guitar and achieved Royal Schools of Music Grade Eight within fifteen months, studying under a Bolton Guitar player, Neil Smith. Rod played in many Country bands, even playing at Wembley and most of the Country festivals in England. He taught BTEC music, delivered brickwork, became an internal verifier and was a quality control assessor for Blackburn college. Rod has now slowed down in life and has effectively retired, but keeps his hand in playing now and again. He currently gigs once or twice a month. Rod smiles contentedly: 'I have a small studio in my garden and my wife Julie and I have four grandchildren. Life is good here in Lancashire.' Rodney still plays guitar in working men's clubs, as he did in The Warriors' days, which has been witnessed by the author. Speaking in 2019 Rod added, 'It's important to us Warriors that there were no extra members after Brian joined. We were all stepping stones for Jon. One of us deserved to get there. Good for Johnny Electric Boy.'

Ian Wallace (Drums)

Ian Russell Wallace moved on from the band to play for Big Sound, but performed most visibly and successfully as a member of the progressive rock band, King Crimson. He appeared on the album, *Islands* in 1971, and on the live album, *Earthbound* in 1972, as well as many archival releases later. An extensive career path followed, so here are a few key contributions: Sandie Shaw, Don Henley, Bob Dylan, Foreigner, Traveling Wilburys, Eric Clapton, Jon Anderson, Alvin Lee, Crosby, Stills and Nash, Brian Eno, Stevie Nicks, Lindsey Buckingham, Steve Marriott, Al Kooper, Tim Buckley and Procol Harum. Ian's main project later in life, was the 21st Century Schizoid Band, a tribute to King Crimson. He also released solo albums, *Happiness with Minimal Side Effects* and *Take a Train*.

In 2005 he formed the Crimson Jazz Trio, performing jazzier versions of some classic Crimson songs. For a short while in the 1980s, Ian was in a curious gigging Los Angeles band called The Teabags. This band featured Peter Banks (ex-Yes), Jackie Lomax (ex-Badger, Undertakers), David Mansfield, Kim Gardner (ex-Creation). However, in 2006, Ian Wallace was diagnosed with cancer.He chronicled his illness in his online blog in the hope his story would encourage others with similar symptoms to pursue treatment. He died, aged 60, on 22 February 2007.

Tony Alveston (Vocals)

Tony worked as a self-employed business development consultant for many years. Later in life, he became involved in local football clubs, in and around Lancashire. He also became a Master of Ceremonies (MC). He still lives and works in Lancashire.

Ian Alveston (Guitar)

Leaving the band at the same time as his brother Tony, Ian continued his love for music by being involved locally with bands, playing the Lancashire

Colne Blues Festival every year and, later in life, making his own personal recordings. Ian passed away in January 2020, aged 72.

Fletcher Richardson (Spiritual Advisor)

Fletcher was a minister at the Antley Methodist church when he became The Warriors' unofficial spiritual advisor. He was there for them in all manner of ways and helped them greatly on their rise to pop stardom. After being a minister, he went to work for the BBC in the 1960s. His hippy look (for a man of the cloth) of long hair, earned him the title of 'The Beatnik Vicar' and his strong Newcastle accent gave him a clear identity on the airways of Lancashire Radio. Fletcher died in 2014 at the age of 73.

John Howarth (Guitar)

John has been difficult to track down, and little is known as to where he may have gone. It appears that following The Warriors he continued to live and work in Lancashire and leaving the band in about 1961 he became a draughtsman. Perhaps more will be uncovered about John in time, but for now it seems that he has passed away, and the date is unknown.

Derek Thornhill (Drums)

Following his departure from the band, Derek dedicated himself to study and eventually became a successful accountant. He is now retired and still lives in Lancashire.

Gordon Kenyon (Vocals)

Gordon left the band with one real aim, to become a full-time hairdresser with his own business. Fulfilling his dream, Gordon continues to run a very successful salon in Accrington today. Gordon Kenyon and Rodney Hill of The Warriors did meet with Jon Anderson at a Yes concert on the 2003 UK tour. The three members of The Warriors band came together to catch up at the Liverpool venue, situated at Liverpool's Kings Dock, where the Yes concert took place as part of the city's 'Summer Pops' series of gigs. (The author also attended the concert but was unaware of the meeting at the time). Gordon still lives and works in Lancashire.

Kenneth Borwick (Guitar)

Kenneth became a pub club singer but also qualified as an engineer. Kenneth has now passed away, although the date is unknown.

Pete Hibbert (Vocals)

Peter performed hundreds of gigs in the 50s and 60s, some with his band Lennie and The Teenbeats who shared the stage with the likes of Billy Fury. Pete, then of the band Mark Day and The Knights, sang a couple of times for The Warriors and played on the same bill as them, but he was never a full member. He continued performing with bands including the Dappers, Blue Star Combo and later the Accy Rockers. Over the later part of his life, he developed Alzheimer's disease. He died aged 69 in 2010.

Mike Brereton (Guitar)

In 1969, Mike began working for the Accrington Corporation Highways Department. He is no longer involved with live music, but is still living in Lancashire, and loves his classic cars.

Mabel Greer's Toyshop (Pre-Yes band)

Mabel Greer's Toyshop founders Clive Bayley and Bob Hagger reformed the band in 2014 after Bayley met Hagger again after a 45-year gap, prompted by the untimely death of the first Yes guitarist Peter Banks. They recorded a new album with ex-Mabel and Yes member Tony Kaye, Yes bass player Billy Sherwood and jazz-fusion bass player Hugo Barré. They released the album, entitled New Way of Life, on 9 March 2015.

The music is a combination of psychedelia, blues and internationally influenced arrangements with poetic lyrics. Their second album The Secret was released on 8 December 2017. The introduction and history in the CD booklet were written by David Watkinson, who has championed their comeback since the beginning. David also recommended Max Hunt as a keyboard player for the band, who went on to join them as a full-time member. Max had decades of experience in the business, including the Yes tribute band Fragile. The key highlight of the album, however, was the special title track 'The Secret', which featured the original Mabel and Yes guitarist Peter Banks. This was created by using newly-found historical material by Banks. Clive Bayley then wrote a song around Peter's work, which was a celebration of both Peter and Chris Squire, who had also recently passed away. Mabel have plans to tour and possibly make more music.
www.mabelgreerstoyshop.com

Roy Flynn (Early Yes manager)

A fine first manager for Yes, Roy moved on from the band – and the whole industry – a few years later. After experiencing some difficulties within the music business, a new life within the hospitality world opened up in the 1970s. He became a very successful manager of numerous pubs and was voted 'Host of the Year' by Egon Ronay in 1997.

Mike Tait (Sound and Lighting)

From being the Yes driver and roadie, Mike moved on to become the owner of the biggest company in the world, supplying live concert stages and lighting. He continued his relationships with Yes members after taking a back seat in his immensely successful business. He worked with both Yes Official and Yes with Anderson Rabin and Wakeman, on preparations for tours – and the tours themselves – up to and including their 50th year. The company is now called 'Tait' and can be found at www.taittowers.com

Accrington Stanley Football Club

The town's famous association is with Accrington Stanley F.C. the butt of many largely affectionate jokes, they try hard but most often don't get to the top. However, if you were born there then you would have an affinity with the club and probably keep an eye on how they do, even if you live far away. Jon has had a love of football since he was a small boy and his love for Accrington Stanley has not waned. All his life he has followed them through thick and thin. Jon also has an interest in Manchester United, another Lancashire team and a growing admiration for the great Lionel Andrés 'Leo' Messi of Barcelona. Interviewed in 2015, Jon mentioned he was following Messi's career and thought he was amazing.

In 1994, Jon along with his wife Jane, visited his home town and was filmed during the trip. The short programme showed Jon walking the path he had trod all those years ago onto the Peel Park football pitch, clearly loving the experience as the memories came flooding back. He has mentioned the importance of the club to him on many occasions throughout his life.

In 2005, when Jon played Bridgewater Hall in Manchester, he told the audience that his highlight of that last year was watching Accrington Stanley live on Fox TV. 'I was ringing my brother Stuart, who was behind the goal and then ringing my friends to tell them Accrington Stanley were on TV. They were saying rather unexcitedly "alright love, calm down".'

Jon played a show in Manchester, UK in 2013. The day before the show, Stuart had taken Jon around their old haunts in Accrington. They visited Norfolk Street, St John's School and the farm on which Jon had worked. Further visits seem likely.

Appendix 2 Other Key Locations and Events

The Cavern Club – a Brick in the Wall

The UK music industry has had many great venues, and The Cavern Club in Liverpool is one of the best and most iconic of all. It had been the location of almost 300 gigs by The Beatles, as well as countless other major musical acts, including The Warriors. The venue found itself fighting for its life in the 1970s and almost left us for good.

Rodney from The Warriors explains:

> The Warriors guys joined the fight to save the club, which lead to one of the national papers giving a half-page of coverage on it. I remember it being a broad-sheet newspaper – possibly one of the Sunday's – and it showed all the people on it, either bands who had played or were playing there, and all the fans waiting to get in. Ian Wallace, Mike Brereton and I are in the photograph close to the front, and the rest of [the band] are there somewhere, Jon is probably chatting some girl up! It was originally taken on Mathew Street, Liverpool outside the Cavern.

The Liverpool Wall of Fame, Mathew Street, Liverpool, Merseyside, L2 6RE, was commissioned for the 40th anniversary of the Cavern Club in January 1997. The Wall of Fame spans the entire front wall of the Cavern Pub. Painstakingly constructed by a local stonemason, it features 1,801 bricks engraved with the names of all the artists who appeared at the original club from 1957 to 1973. A must-visit for music fanatics and historians, the wall makes fascinating viewing as it features pop, funk, soul and rock icons alongside local and national acts that have disappeared into obscurity. There are too many artists to mention them all, but The Warriors sit along-side such greats as Queen, Rolling Stones, The Hollies, The Temptations, Little Stevie Wonder, Yes and The Beatles! The wall also features 54 Liverpool Number one chart hits since 1952.

Yes / The Warriors Exhibitions London 2004 and 2018

For the 35th Anniversary of Yes, along with Jon Andersons 60th birthday, Yes author David Watkinson ran a Yes exhibition called *Yes – 35 Years of Wondrous Music*. This ran from the 16 October to 14 November 2004 at the Haworth Art Gallery in Jon Anderson's home town of Accrington, England. The Edwardian house is set in the local park, and it houses an internationally renowned collection of Tiffany glass. The Yes memorabilia exhibition featured the history of Yes, including pre-Yes bands such as Tomorrow, The Syn and The Warriors. Displayed in frames, the memorabilia spanned many rooms and was opened by the town's Mayor.

Rodney Hill, The Warriors band member, attended the exhibition along with the local press, who covered the opening, tours, and the exhibition. Fans from all around the country travelled to see the show, as well as friends and family of Jon Anderson. At the event, a local musician played Yes classics on the piano in one room with various Yes videos and music playing in others. Guided tours were given by the author throughout the day. Hundreds of pieces of collectables were shown, along with the Yes book *Perpetual Change*, which was on sale. At the end of the exhibition, many of the Yes collection pieces could be bought. It was the most successful exhibition ever held at the gallery and remains one of the very few Yes exhibitions ever held. It was planned to take the exhibition on the Yes tour of the USA around that time, but logistically it proved to be too big a challenge, and unfortunately, it didn't make it through the costing process.

The *Rock and Roll Hall of Fame* in the USA displayed a small exhibition case for some Yes memorabilia material at the time of their induction into the hall in 2018. Within that case was the flyer for the UK 2004 *Yes exhibition* and named on that was Rod Hill of The Warriors as a guest along with the author as curator of the event.

In 2018, a second Yes exhibition took place on the 24 and 25 March at the London Palladium. This ran alongside the last Yes gigs in the UK on their 50th-anniversary tour. Over 50 individual frames and 400 separate pieces of memorabilia covered the history of Yes, along with more showing the history before Yes, which included The Warriors, and The Syn. This ran alongside an exhibition by Roger Dean, arranged through the progressive rock live venue Trading Boundaries. It was one of the many Yes Fan Day Celebrations organised by the author and Brain Neeson of the Scottish YES Network. The author was hoping to stage a small Warriors exhibition around the book publication date, possibly somewhere in Lancashire in 2020.

The Jon Anderson Plaque in Accrington

In 2019 in Jon's hometown of Accrington, a number of granite information boards showcasing Accrington's heritage were installed on the square in front of the town hall. The six boards include text and images about the Accrington Pals, famous celebrities from the town such as David Lloyd, Ron Hill MBE and Jon Anderson. The simple wording which acknowledges along with well-known locals Jon is JON ANDERSON MUSICIAN.

The Jon Anderson Celebration Wall

The Wetherspoons pub, The Commercial in Accrington, in Jon's home town centre, where The Warriors played many gigs, has a section of a wall dedicated to Jon Anderson. It has a permanent display of three different black frames showing photographs of Jon on stage with Yes in 1977, one with a Yes logo, and a closer image of Jon taken in the last few years live on tour.

Jon Anderson's Yes Harp on Display

In the Hard Rock Café, 150 Old Park Lane, London, W1K 1QZ, England, there is a harp owned by Jon Anderson. The large wooden harp is decoratively carved, and it is housed in a glass case where it has been on display for many years. It is believed to be from Yes' Relayer tour.

The 50th Anniversary Yes Plaque in London

On the 3 August, 2018 in London, a 50th-anniversary commemorative Yes plaque was unveiled by Yes' original drummer Bill Bruford. Also attending the opening day were Chris Squire's brother Tony, Chris' sister and journalist and long-time Yes supporter Chris Welch. Organised by the author David Watkinson and *Yesworld*, the plaque featured both the original red bubble Yes logo and the classic Roger Deans design from the 1970s. The event was filmed by Yes Music Podcast's Kevin Mulryne and can now be viewed online via www.yesmusicpodcast.com. Bill, Tony and Chris made entertaining speeches about their experiences in and around Yes in the early days.

The location was the original basement area of the Lucky Horseshoe Café on Shaftsbury Avenue. The was the very place that Yes rehearsed, changed its name, and became Yes – the band – for the first time. The venue is still a restaurant and can be visited by Yes fans where they can take in the atmosphere of what it must have been like to be in that rehearsal space, just as the band had done. The original windows in the upper part of the restaurant are the same as they were in 1968, offering visitors the same view out that Yes would have had in 1968. The address is 184 Shaftesbury Avenue, Covent Garden, London WC2H 8JB. For a visit to the downstairs restaurant please book through their website:

https://wildwoodrestaurants.co.uk/restaurant/london-shaftesbury-avenue/

The Meetings 1978 and 2018

The photograph overleaf shows my first meeting with Jon Anderson. It was taken inside the entrance of R.A.K recording studios, in St John's Wood, London in 1978. Jon and I met while he was taking time out from recording the new Yes album, *Tormato*. I visited with my brother John. I witnessed different mixes of the song 'Money' being worked on, and Chris Squire's amazing bass introduction for 'Don't Kill the Whale', which was never used. This was the post-punk era and Yes knew that they were out of favour with the British music press. Yes had their say, because on the wall of the studio, they had a hand-made poster that pronounced 'Never Mind the Bollocks: Here's Yes'. Steve Howe, Chris Squire and Alan White were there along with Nigel Luby, the recording engineer. Sitting with Chris and Steve by the mixing desk, listening to them discuss these tracks, was a little mind-blowing as a fan and now more than ever, I realise how privileged I was to have had that opportunity. Chris Squire turned up in his Bentley with the registration number CS1 and Steve drove the short journey down from Hampstead in his rare, blue English Bristol car. A small number of photos were taken on the day, and this is one of only two ever to be published.

In Yes' 50th year I once again met up with Jon Anderson at the London O2 Arena gig for Yes – featuring Anderson, Rabin and Wakeman. Forty years on from the *Tormato* sessions photo above shows both of us still immersed in all things Yes.

Left: Jon and David Watkinson meet up for the first time in May/June 1978 at the R.A.K recording studios in London. The *Tormato* sessions where in progress. *(John Watkinson – David Watkinson Collection)*

Above: Meeting up many years later at the London ARW concert. Even after forty years we still have Yes music in common. *(David Watkinson Collection)*

Jon Anderson Exhibition 2020

From 27 April to 30 May 2020, a Jon Anderson and The Warriors display was shown in the Accrington Library, St James Steet, Accrington, which was Jon's home library. It featured original photographs, records and memorabilia from this book and the limited edition vinyl EP by Jon and The Warriors called The Lost Demos. The author attended on 27 April and 30 May - the opening and closing days.

Jon Anderson was celebrated in the Accrington town by being included into the 2019 historic stone plaques in the town centre. There is also a wall dedicated to Jon Anderson in a local pub showing various images of Jon throughout his long career.

Appendix 3 Local Comments and Memories

On the journey to finish this book, the author spoke with many people to find out what they thought of Jon, The Warriors and those fun times in the 1960s. I came across some wonderful comments that I hope will make the reader smile. They come from meetings with the band members, my signed Yes Exhibition wall poster from Accrington, plus Lancashire-based web sites such as *accringtonweb.com* and the author's cuttings collection. They range from funny through humorously abusive to excited. I hope you enjoy them. Some comments are anonymous, but where known, names or nicknames have been added.

> I lived on the corner of Norfolk Street next-door-but-one to Jon Anderson. My late father used to tell Jon to park The Warriors' van further along the street, so my dad could park his car in front of our house.

> I saw The Warriors at the Conservative Club during a private function. They were very young at the time and, although good, they fluffed some of the guitar sequences. When I saw them some months later at Great Harwood's Mercer Hall, they were terrific.

A teenage fan at the time, Bob Mitchell, recalled:

> I have been reminiscing about the old 'Jazz Club'. I remember The Warriors rehearsing on Saturday mornings for a while in the old church hall at St Augustine's on Bolton Avenue in Huncoat. This would be when about 1963/64. I think the Anderson brothers lived near Peel Park school and worked for a while delivering milk for 'Walt' from Huncoat Hall. I remember the milk having to be delivered by 'Sledge' in the long, snowy winter of 1963! There were very few cars on the estate in the fifties, and most people kept tidy gardens. Then it all changed in the late sixties.

Accrington Memories from a young local called Mari:

> Joy (Jon's sister) went out with my brother Colin for a while. She really liked him – Jon came to our house too sometimes. I remember my dad telling Jon that he wouldn't make any money at the music game.
>
> I remember when Anderson was with The Warriors, and their studio was an old shop on Henry Street up near a church hall. The kids used to go in and watch them.

Two sides of the same coin:

> We used to write stuff on their van with lipstick. Other people did too, and it was plastered with it all over.

> I used to go to Jon's house after school with my friends. We'd clean all the lipstick messages off the van for them. We'd also watch them rehearse at St Augustine's church hall in Huncoat.

General comments about The Warriors:

Tony was actually a much better singer than Jon.

When he lived on Norfolk Street, my friend used to idolise him [Jon] but would never speak to him – we had to walk past the house (by going on a detour) just in case he might be sitting on the garden wall, and she could see him. WillowTheWhisp.

I remember they used to park the yellow van with horns outside Rodney's house on Pilot St. It could be seen from the High School. WillowTheWhisp.

They used to practice at the Springhill Car Club at the Mount Carmel. They had to get special permission to play as they were all still at school then.

I used to have the autograph book with their signatures in it. I think I was probably about ten or eleven years of age. One of The Warriors' band lived in a house close to my old junior school, and a group of over-enthusiastic kids went in one day to have a look round at what we saw as a rock star's home (it was a very old terraced house which was demolished a few years later). I also remember there being trouble in school. I was 14, and at secondary school. For some reason, their van would drive past the school, or we would sometimes see it parked outside one of the houses opposite. On this day they were seen getting out of the van, and all the girls rushed to the windows – some standing on the window sills to get a better look – really quite dangerous in a four-storey building. Wow, we got a telling off I can tell you, and all for a pop star.

Group rivalry on each half of the revolving stage at the Bolton Palais led some artists to sabotage the opposition by unplugging each other's amps at the start of their performance, leaving them literally powerless in front of the audience.

Jon, remember the St. John's Pantomime in 1954-ish? Love Linda Kemp and Eileen Knowles.

Jon you used to deliver my milk; I fell in love with you when you were a Warrior. Diana x.

Wasn't Jon Anderson also a milkman with the nick-name the 'singing milkman'? Kestrel.

I remember booking The Warriors at St John's Youth Club in the early sixties. We charged 2 shillings a ticket – well worth it. Linda Wilkinson.

Jon ya bastard ... you owe me a pint! Jimi.

Ian is probably one of the best local guitarists I've ever seen. He used to use lots of Jazz cords – brilliant. Jaysey.

My claim to fame is that a friend and I got on stage and played with Jon Anderson – well the Warriors, actually. They invited two people to join them, one to play maracas and the other a tambourine; I think we did 'Not Fade Away.'

Jon, you owe me a wine gum xx. Mavis from St John's School.

Jon – do you remember Butlins? Steve Coulsdon of Bold Street.

Appendix 4 The Warriors' Tribute Song

Jon's Warriors' tribute song was sung on his solo tours from about 2009 onwards. It is an autobiographical, historical look at his fun, early days with brother Tony, called 'Tony and Me'. This tribute song about Tony and the band is a light-hearted piece, which fondly recalls those times that still had meaning for Jon, some fifty years later. Although the song's basic theme remained the same, the stories and words evolved slightly as the tours progressed.

'Tony and Me'

Tony and me
we had a real good time in a rock and roll band back in sixty-three
we had it going strong
we made music all night long

Tony and me
we worked hard on the farm
we didn't have a care
we would sing all day
and chase the blues away
we just wanted to go to Liverpool and...

All those Beatles' songs
she loves you yeahhhh yeah yeah yeah
and those Everly Brothers' Wake Up Little Susie wake up
wake up little Susie wake ...

Tony and me
we had a real good time in a rock and roll band back in sixty-three
we used to go crazy and drink and drive too much
and just wanted to be in a rock and roll band...

Tony and me
we worked hard on the farm
we didn't have a care
we would sing all day
and chase the blues away
we just wanted to go and sing in the cavern...
all those Beatles' songs
she loves you yeahhhh yeah yeah yeah
and those Beach Boys' songs
Help me, Rhonda, help, help me, Rhonda
Help me, Rhonda, help, help me, Rhonda...

Tony and me
we had a real good time in a rock and roll band back in sixty-three
Tony, he lives in the Isle of Wight
he's a preacher
I've always looked up to him
he was taller than me...

Appendix 5 Author's sources, interviews and media contributions

Yes Music – *An Evening with Jon Anderson LP* Atlantic Recording Co. 1977
Elephant Talk newsletter – Ian Wallace interview DMME.net April 2003
Paul Rigby – Jon Anderson interview 1 September 2016
Prog magazine Mark Blake – UK 1 September 2016
Billboard Magazine – Michael Tate – November 2003
Rolling with Rock Royalty – book by Brian Chatton 2018
RABD music – Suzanne Chancellor – Jon Anderson interview 31 May 2014
Yours is No Disgrace – a Rock and Roll Memoir – book by Dave Foster and Andrew Blake
Record Collector magazine – Tim Jones
Seconds Magazine – Jon Anderson interview Steven Blush 1994
Beyond and Before – The Formative Years of Yes – book by Peter Banks and Billy James – Golden Treasures Publishing 2001
Vagas Rocks magazine – Jon Anderson interview – Sally Steele – 2012
Examiner – Ray Shasho interview – 16 August 2011
psychedelicbaby.blogspot.com Klemen Breznikar – Jon Anderson interview 2011
accringtonweb.com various – 'Vox Pop' quotes
Greg Drugan at *Neo Music Scene* – Jon Anderson interview – January 2017
Yesmusicpodcast.com (Kevin Mulryne and Mark Anthony K)
forgotten-yesterdays.com (Steve Sullivan)
Bondegezou.co.uk (Henry Potts)
The David Foster Archive. (David Watkinson)

Interviews by David Watkinson

Jon Anderson 5 August 2015
Tony Anderson 20 April, 19 March 2015, 17 October 2016
Stuart Anderson 2000
Mike Brereton 7 March 2015
Rodney Hill & Mike Brereton 13 March 2015
Garth Dawson 27 March 2015
Derek Thornhill 18 July 2015, 6 May 2015, 14 April 2015
Franny Franks 29 July 2016
Geoff Peach 2 December 2015 and 26 November 2015
Marianne Evans 30 January 2016
Angelika Granaht 18 February 2016
Kevin Parrott 11 November 2015
Graham Evans 18 November 2015
Brain Chatton 24 October 2015
Robert Kelly 25 July 2015
Brian Parrish 17 March 2015
Gordon Kenyon 4 March 2015
James Payne 3 March 2015
Nikki Ragsdale 17 March 2015
Tony Alveston 7 March 2015
Ian Alveston 29 February 2015
David Foster 2000
Mark Day 16 October 2004
Martyn Adelman 29 November 2016
Steve Nardelli 15 September 2016
Bill Bruford 2000 and March 2018
Dave 'Wammy' Walmsley 15 March 2015

Paul Korda 9 June 2016
Mog Stevenson 26 May 2016
Clive Bayley 12 January 2017
Dermot Bassett 19 April 2017
Bob William Hagger 22 June 2016 + 2000
Jack Barrie 15 November 2015
Paul Gurvitz 18 March 2015
Tim De Feu 29 January 2019

Contributions to Yes (and related) Books, TV, Radio and CD Booklets by the author

Jon Anderson: The Warriors' Bolton Club 65 CD promo booklet for Voice Print 2012
Asia: Supplied photographs for The Authorised Biography book 2001
Yes: 'The Collector' No 5-page feature on Yes collection, *Record Collector* magazine
Yes: *Record Collector* magazine, supplying memorabilia, history, various years
Yes: Price guide details *Record Collector* 2000
Yes: 'The Tours' *Record Collector*, with Tim Jones, photos and memorabilia, May 2000
Yes: Convention 1980s Blackpool 1980s
Yes: Official biography *Perpetual Change* 2001/2
Yes: Photos for *In A Word* CD insert official Yes release 2002
Yes: Photos for *The Word is Live* official Yes release 2005
Yes: Collectables for *Close to The Edge – The Story of Yes* by Chris Welch 2000
Yes: Imagery for the Aymeric Leroy Yes book 2017
Yes: Fanzines, *Relayer*, *Close to Yes*, *Going for The Two*, *Yes Music*, 1980s
Yes: BBC TV *The Summer of 1977* TV program 2002
Rick Wakeman: *Record Collector* 'Myths' article images, December 2003
Mable Greer's Toyshop: CD insert and Video 2015
Mabel Greer's Toyshop: CD liner notes for the album *The Secret* in 2017
Yes: Imagery for the official 50th tour programme 2018
Yes Music Podcast contributor various years
Yes: *Yesworld.com* contributor, sections from Perpetual Change book, 2018
Yes: Researched and created the *London Historic Yes Bus Tour (Tor)* which the *www.londonrocktour.com* ran for Yes' 50th anniversary weekend in 2018
Yes: Curated the Yes memorabilia exhibition for Yes' 50th anniversary at the London Palladium 2018
Yes: Collaborated with Yes management (QEDG) and Brian Neeson to organise the Yes 50th Anniversary Fan Day at The London Palladium. Nominated for the 'The Event of The Year' by Prog magazine, eventually coming a very healthy 7th overall in 2018.
Jon Anderson and The Warriors: Wrote the history, provided collectables and photos for *the Record Collector* article August 2018
Jon Anderson: Providing images for the *1000 Hands* video project 2019
A.B.W.H. Memorabilia for a feature in *Prog* magazine UK 2019
Peter Banks: Memorabilia on the band Flash for his web page 2019
Yes: Created and funded along with *Yesworld.com* the Yes 50th Anniversary blue plaque. Sited in the basement of what was the Lucky Horseshoe Café in London in 1968. Now the Wildwood restaurant at 184 Shaftsbury Avenue, Covent Garden, London WC2H, where Yes began, 2018

Appendix 6 Gig Dates and Diary Entries

Left: Rod and Dave ran the gig personal diaries, which cover 1963 to 1967. *(Rod Hill – David Watkinson Collection)*

The following concert venues, gig dates, events and general happenings have been created from various sources, including The Warriors guitar player Rod Hill's Diaries, a Dave Foster diary, Derek Thornhill's memories, adverts, my archive and cuttings from Lancashire local papers at the time, internet searches, reference books, my own collection of Warriors' memorabilia, the *Yes: Perpetual Change* book and interviews with the band members. It represents the most up to date concert listings for The Warriors. However, it should be noted that even the band don't recall everything they did, and never wrote it all down at the time. It isn't complete as such, and it may never be so, but a later edition could be updated if further information comes to light. However, for now at least, this is the best gig listing for the band and Jon Anderson's early years.

These are the main sources for each section:

1950 – December 1962

Local newspapers, old friends of Jon such as Mog, interviews with original member Derek, interview with Jon Anderson, some internet searches, cuttings from my collection, *accyontheweb*, Rod Hill's diary, library searches.

January 1963 – December 1963

Rod Hill's diaries, poster, cuttings, interviews with Derek, Gordon Kenyon, Tony Alveston, Rod and Mike.

January 1964 – December 1964

Dave Foster and Rod Hill diaries, cuttings from my collection, library searches.

January 1965 – December 1965

Rod Hill's diary, library searches, interviews with Tony Alveston, Ian Alveston, David Foster, Mark Day, internet searches, cuttings from my collection, *manchesterbeat.com*, *accyontheweb*, Yes exhibition signed board comments.

January 1966 – December 1966

Rod's diaries, *accyontheweb*, *Perpetual Change* book, *Bolton Evening News*, vinyl records, interviews with Dave 'Wammy', Geoff Peach, Marianne Evans, Angelika Granaht, Kevin Parrott, Graham Evans, Brain Chatton, Robert Kelly, Brian Parrish, James Payne, Nikki Ragsdale, Yes exhibition comments board, cuttings from my collection.

January 1967 – December 1967

Diaries, internet, cuttings from my collection, Perpetual Change book, Steven Sullivan's *forgotten-yesterdays.com*, interviews with Martyn Adelman, Steve Nardelli, Clive Bayley.

January 1968 – December 1968

Interviews with Clive Bayley, Dermot Bassett, Bob William Hagger, Internet search, David Watkinson's cuttings collection, Bill Bruford diaries, accyontheweb, Steven Sullivan's forgotten –yesterdays.com, cross-referenced with Yes books by Chris Welch, Peter Banks, Bill Bruford and Watkinson's books, Marquee flyers, NME, Sounds and the Melody Maker adverts.

Notes on the diaries

As I worked through his diaries, there were an increasing number of notations added to the pages from Rodney Hill. I have transcribed most of them, as it's interesting material, and has never previously been seen. It shows people, places the band went to and a load of other bits and pieces, including phone numbers and addresses. I'm not aware of all the connections or relevance of the names or dates. Some are obvious, but most are not. They include friends, managers, contacts, and other personal links, both familiar and completely obscure out of the context of the time they were written. I do hope, though, that some will bring back a memory or two for those who were there should they see their names again after all these years:

> Eilegn Beck, Linda Dean, Pixie, Manni and Mickie in Germany, Mick and Tony at the Rum Runner Club Birmingham, Jennie in Leeds, Issy from Scotland, Marion in Cheadle, Gillian in Bury, Colin Ward, Liz Mc Alister from Liverpool, Hassy Hansen, Annette Eyhr, Lone Thorson, Elly Glockner, Garen, John Bull all in Germany. Dana London, Gail – The Creation, Sushi.

1950s

Johnny (Jon) makes his first appearance in a school play at St John's school. He then moves onto St Christopher's Secondary Modern School. School friend Mog remembers, 'Jon and I used to play football at St Christopher's School at dinner time in the yard. We would throw our school jackets down as goalposts.' Jon loved walking his dog to the Coppice Hill

11 April 1955

Jon makes his first public appearance as a ball boy for the Accrington Stanley football team. Aged 11 he would dream of being a football star

December 1959

The Warriors begin life as The Strangers group before Jon joined, they played a few times at the Accrington Spring Hill Methodist Dance

December 1960

Jon leaves school aged 15. He is needed straight away to make money to help the struggling family. Driving trucks for the local brickyard, delivering milk with Tony plus dreaming and singing was the way forward for a year or so.

1960-1

The Warriors – performance locations

Accrington – Spring Hill Methodist dance
Accrington – St Mary's RC Youth Club
Rishton – Harmonic WMC (2 – 3 times)
Accrington – Whalley Road Methodist youth club dance (6 – 7 times)
Accrington – St Oswald's, Knuzden a few times
Accrington – Marlborough WMC (working men's club) (4 – 5 times)
Great Harwood – Mercer Hall. Nero & the Gladiators ('In the Hall of the Mountain King' Decca 1961) Derek: 'They were at the top and we were at the bottom of the bill.'
Accrington – Conservative Club?

1962

January 1962

The Beatles audition for Decca Records but are turned down, as 'guitar bands are on the way out'. They sign for Parlophone later that year. Dick Rowe will be forever be remembered as the man who turned The Beatles down after their audition, saying 'we don't like their sound'. He did however make up for this slight oversight by signing the Rolling Stones.

The Warriors – performance locations

Accrington – practiced at the Springhill Car Club and Christ Church School
Accrington – Marlborough WMC (working men's club) practised here (4 – 5 times)
Nelson – Imperial Ballroom
Accrington – Conservative Club
Bolton – Casino
Blackrod – St Oswald's C.O.E. Primary School, 5/6 times
Accrington – The Arts (ARCS)
Blackburn – Joe Mortimer's Dance Hall
Manchester – Piccadilly Plaza
Manchester – Devonshire Sporting Club (THE DEV)
Manchester – Southern Sporting Club
Levenshulme – Sporting Club
Accrington – practice in Henry Street, The Warriors used a room above one of the shops there
Accrington – practice at Downham Drive, Fern Gore, they practised in a wooden hut
Harpurhey – Northern Sporting Club
Sale – Locarno Club

August 1962

The Beachcomber Coffee Club opens in Bank Street, Bolton
Jon remembers the early days well:

> My brother drove the milk van, and I used to hang on the side, and we'd sing Everly Brothers songs together as we did the round. We were always singing. That was a very happy time. It was the beginning of rock 'n' roll with Buddy Holly and Elvis and all the skiffle music. That was the beginning of everything.

October 1962

The Beatles release their first single 'Love Me Do' backed by the B – Side 'P.S. I Love You'. The music world would never be the same again. The Beatles' manager Brian Epstein reportedly buys 10,000 copies to ensure it a place in the top twenty.
Jon: 'We went and saw The Beatles when they just released 'Love Me Do' and life changed for everybody! The 60s were an amazing time you [also] had R&B and Motown.'

December 1962

Accrington, Town Hall, this was probably to have been guitarist Jon Howarth's last gig as it was cancelled due to his illness. From this point, the band had to find another guitar player. Mike Brereton was recruited.

1963

January 1963

1. Accrington – Canine Club
5. Manchester – ARCS
6. Accrington – practice at Georges (The local pub on Blackburn Road)
9. Went to cinema to see *Corridors of Blood*
10. Accrington – practice at Georges
11. Accrington – practice
12. Accrington – ARCS (Arcadium Building, also called The Arts, a local hall, holding about 100-150)
13. Blackburn – Mecca (with Ian and Bob)
16. Harry's
17. Accrington – practice at Georges
18. Accrington – practice at Georges and night school
19. Accrington – ARCS
20. Blackburn – Mecca with Ian, Roger and Les
22. Accrington – practice at Georges
26. Accrington – Globe Club
27. Blackburn – Mecca with Roger, Ian, Les
29. Jon joins the Warriors
31. Accrington – Practice at Derek's

February 1963

1. Accrington – practice at Derek's
2. Accrington – Marlboro practice Dave's
3. Accrington – practice at Mick's
4. Accrington – practice at Marlboro
7. Accrington – practice at Marlboro
8. Accrington – practice Rodney's house
9. Accrington – practice/play at Marlboro (paid £1.00 / got new guitar today)
10. Accrington – practice Rodney's house
11. Accrington – practice Marbro
11. *Please Please Me*, the Beatles first album is recorded in a 10-hour session
12. Accrington – practice Rodney's house
13. Accrington – practice in Hut
14. Accrington – audition James Street Club
15. Accrington – St Augustine's School Dance, Maudsley Street
16. Accrington – Marlboro Club
17. Accrington – practice at Rods House – Photos with Duke
18. Accrington – practice Marlboro
19. Accrington – practice
20. Accrington – Night School (Rod)
21. Accrington – practice Rodney's house and Marlboro
22. Accrington – Beatnik Evening and dance at the Town Hall…'A good doo'
23. Accrington – Marlboro Club Notes – cinema – *How to Make a Monster* (1958 Movie)
24. Accrington – practice Rodney's house (Pat)
25. Accrington – practice at Marlboro (Chinney & Tony). It is at The Marlboro Club that Tony Anderson was auditioned for the lead singer's position. In the diary, both are mentioned together, so this is likely the handover day when Chinney left the band and Tony agreed to join. Tony sang 'A Fool Such as I' by Elvis Presley.
26. Accrington – practice Rodney's house
27. Accrington – Night school (Rod)
28. Accrington – practice at Marlboro

March 1963

1. Accrington – went up Conservative Club with Pat and Wendy
2. Accrington – Marlboro Club paid £1.00
3. Accrington – practice Rodney's house. The Sundowners played ARCS
4. Accrington – practice

5. Accrington – practice
7. Accrington – practice Marlboro
8. Accrington – play St John's School
9. Accrington – ARCS with Pat
10. Accrington – ARCS
11. Accrington – practice Marlboro
12. Accrington – practice Rodney's house
14. Accrington – practice Marlboro
15. WBS (Pat, Gally, Bob, Ian)
16. Blackburn – St Pauls...'Good eve'
17. Accrington – ARCS (Pat) ARCADIAN DANCE HALL
18. Accrington – practice Marlboro
19. Accrington – practice Rodney's house eve. Johnny Anderson went to the Cavern Club in Liverpool in the afternoon to watch a band called The Big Three. This gave him 'the bug' and he realised that music was what he wanted to do for the rest of his life.
20. Accrington – night school (Rod)
21. Accrington – practice Marlboro
22. Marsden Park, The Lido with Pat at 7.00
22. *Please Please Me*. The Beatles first album is released
23. Accrington – Hargreaves 21st party
24. Blackburn – Longshaw Club Auditions evening
25. Accrington – practice Marlboro
26. Accrington – meeting
27. Accrington – Night School, Odeon, Woolworths
28. Accrington – practice Marlboro
29. Accrington – St John's with a New Amp & Drums
30. Accrington – Chapel Street
31. Accrington – ARCS

April 1963

1. Accrington – practice Marlboro
2. Accrington – practice Rodney's house
6. Accrington – Marlboro – was paid £1
7. Oswaldtwistle – St Mary's – was paid 10 shillings
10. Blackburn – Longshaw Club, apparently the band played the national anthem there
13. Accrington – Willow Club – paid £1
14. Blackburn – Regency – paid £1
15. Accrington – Conservative Club
16. Accrington – practice Rodney's house
17. Bolton – Casino
18. *Girls Girls Girls!* (Elvis Presley movie)
19. Accrington – St Tennyson's (? – not legible writing)
20. Accrington – Marlboro – paid £17
27. Great Harwood – Lomax Arms (cancelled)
28. Accrington – ARCS

May 1963

Accrington – Marlborough WMC. The band auditioned both Tony and Jon Anderson here.

4. Accrington – Marlboro
11. Burnley Padiham Working Men's Club, JOHN ANDERSON'S FIRST GIG
17. Nelson – Imperial?
18. Accrington – Marlboro
19. Accrington – Regency Bar (Commercial Hotel)
20. Blackburn – King George's Hall (contest?)
22. Clayton – Middle School
24. Blackburn – King George's Hall (contest?)
31. Accrington – YMCA

    Rodney remembers:

    'We would be deadly serious about the band and practice a lot. [We were] picked up at 10.00 in the morning and then onto St Augustine's RC Church in Runcorn for a practice. We practised all over the place at our house also. We have these reels of tape with it on. They had [the band's] Saturday shows and lots of material on them'.

June 1963

1. Accrington – YMCA (cancelled)
2. Accrington – ARCS
7. St Tennyson's (? – not legible writing)
21. Blackburn – YMCA

July 1963

7. Swiped all Les's bedding and Tony slept in our bath!
29. Birthday

August 1963

26. Blackburn – Mecca with Pat
29. Manchester – Sale – Mecca
30. Manchester – Devonshire
31. Manchester – Southern Sporting Club

September 1963

1. Manchester – Southern Sporting Club
7. Manchester – Plaza (Mecca)
8. Accrington – Regency
13. Accrington – YMCA This would be at the Ambulance Drill hall.
14. Accrington – St Paul's Youth Club
15. Burnley – Mecca
16. Blackburn – Mecca
19. Sale – Mecca
20. Runcorn – St Joseph's RC Church
21. East Lancashire Club
23. Accrington – Conservative Club
26. Burnley – Mecca
27. Manchester – Devonshire
28. Southern Club
29. Burnley – Miners Club played 1.00 and 7.30

October 1963

4. Manchester – Southern Sporting Club (situated behind Belle Vue Speedway track) Representatives of Decca records visited to see the band play live. A meeting was arranged by Jonnie Moore for Phil Solomon and Dick Rowe the head of Decca Records to check out the band.
5. Levenshulme Club – Another of these so-called Sporting clubs in Levenshulme. We worked here with Sid and Eddie (Little and Large, Karl Denver etc)
6. Manchester – Plaza Club
8. Manchester – Church / Abbey (with Fletcher Richardson)
11. Manchester – Devonshire Club (Rod added, 'this was where they had the wrestling and Jimmy Saville one night, strippers regularly did their thing')
12. Southern Club
13. Levenshulme Club
16. Nelson – Imperial 8.00 pm
18. Southern Club
19. Manchester – Devonshire Club
20. Southern Club
22. Blackpool – North Pier. The Warriors play in a talent competition and come second. Strangely, the winning band didn't want to go any further and pulled out, so The Warriors made it to the final.
24. Blackburn – Mecca – The final. The *Lancashire Evening Telegraph's* The Big Chance

Competition. Winners – The Warriors.
25. Manchester – Devonshire Club
26. Accrington – Liberal Club
27. Blackpool – South Pier
31. Blackburn. The *Lancashire Evening Telegraph* has The Warriors on the front cover. It shows them accepting a cake from the 'M' block workforce at the Mullards factory, for winning The *Lancashire Evening Telegraph's* Big Chance contest. 'Girls go crazy for the guys,' it reports. Jon Anderson is shown on the front cover with the band.
31. Accrington – Conservative Club

November 1963

1. Southern Club
2. Nelson – Imperial supporting Billy J. Kramer
3. Burnley – Mecca
7. Accrington – Con Club
8. Manchester – Devonshire
   Rod took some time off work due to illness but still played in the band in the evenings. On one occasion, he played at a factory through the lunch break for fans and was seen by his employer on the front page of the local newspaper. He was in trouble as a result of that. The company confronted Rod and said, it's your music or your job – you choose. Without a moment's thought, Rod said 'music' and left English Electric, where he had worked for some years.
9. Manchester – Southern Sporting Club. Rod saw the Beatles here and got their autographs, the place probably held about 150 people
11. Blackburn – Mecca
15. Blackburn – YMCA (King St)
16. Accrington – Methodist Church (with Fletcher Richardson)
17. Blackburn – Mecca
20. Burnley – Bank Hall Miners Club (Paid £9.00, Rod said, 'Probably a Sunday and a Cracking gig')
22. Nelson – Imperial Ballroom (Every Saturday night. Rod said, 'Everyone played here. We did it with Bill Haley, Gene Vincent Swinging Blue Jeans, Little Richard, everyone who was anyone in the charts.')
22. Blackburn – Mecca
   The band had serious rehearsals of up to six hours a day which kept them busy as they worked hard on their performances to win the competitions and get more gigs. Later they went on to enter the finals, but as they refused to sign management contracts if they did well, they were never going to get far in the competition. The band of the day was Joe Brown and his Bruvvers.
23. East Lancashire Club
24. Burnley – Miners Club (£12-10)
28. Burnley – Mecca (cancelled?)
29. Manchester – Southern Sporting Club
30. Manchester – Southern Sporting Club

December 1963

1. London – Maybe at the Tiles Club
6. Manchester – Devonshire
7. Southern
13. Southern
14. Southern
20. Accrington or Blackburn YMCA
   Manchester Southern Sporting Club, representatives of Decca records visited to see the band play live. A meeting was arranged by Jonnie Moore for Phil Solomon and Dick Rowe the head of Decca Records to check out the band.
27. Southern
28. Southern

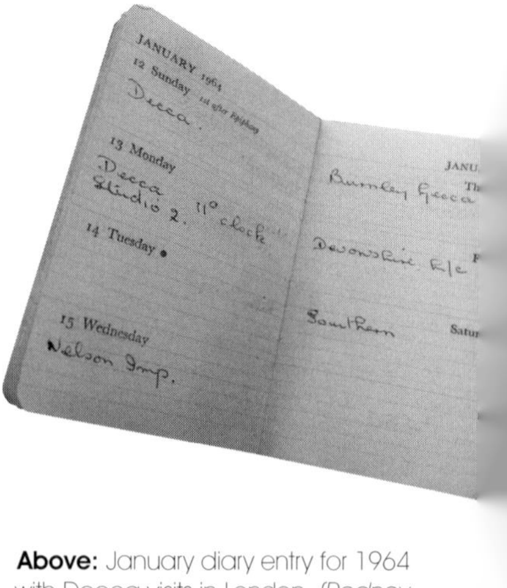

Above: January diary entry for 1964 with Decca visits in London. *(Rodney Hill – David Watkinson Collection)*

29. Burnley – Mecca
    Bolton – The Dungeon Club. The Beachcomber Dungeon Club opens up for the first time for the Christmas festivities, changing from the Coffee Club. The young owners Eric Eckersley, Eddie Grindrod and Norman Clements said at the time, 'We felt Bolton needed a club like this. We will serve meals in an upstairs room; pop music and dancing will be confined to the cellars.' The club had dangling swords and rattling chains for added atmosphere.
31 Burnley – Miners Club (£17-10)

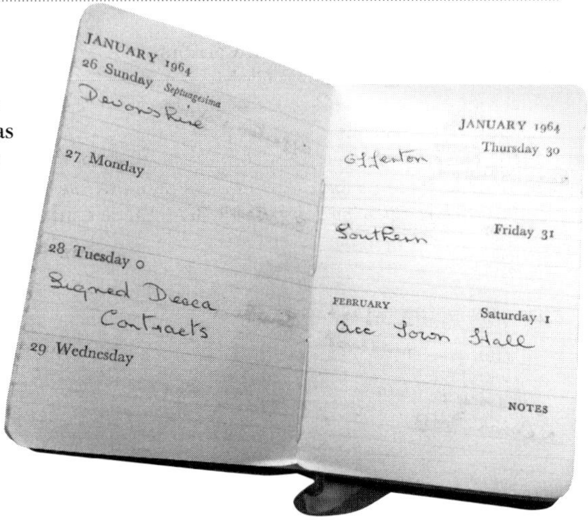

Above: The entry covering signing for Decca Records. *(Rodney Hill – David Watkinson Collection)*

1964

January 1964

The church gig in Accrington goes ahead with great crowds. Fans turned away as too many turn up

1. Manchester – Southern Sporting Club – Decca visit the band to see their show. On the back of this visit, auditions were arranged for them to record the same month on the 13th
3. Manchester – Devonshire
4. Nelson Imperial / Ricky Fenton & The Sonic Shotguns
5. Levenshulme
6. Blackburn – Mecca
9. Blackburn – Mecca – Mullards company dance
10. Nelson – Imperial with singer Kathy Kirby
11. Manchester – Plaza
12. London – Decca Records. Travel down to London
13. London – Decca Records Audition. Recording sessions in studio 2, at 11 o'clock with Derek playing the drums
15. Nelson – Imperial
    Dance on Saturday night at DP with Chinney – Burnley Road
16. Burnley – Mecca
17. Manchester – Devonshire
18. Manchester – Southern Sporting Club
19. Manchester – Devonshire
20. Accrington – Holbrook 5 Queens Road
21. Accrington – Downham Drive
    A local fan commented on the band,
    'What made them special and different was they had two lead singers.'
22. Bury – Palais
23. Stockport Offerton Palace
24. Manchester – Southern Sporting Club
25. Manchester – Southern Sporting Club
26. Manchester – Devonshire
28. SIGNED DECCA RECORDS
30. Stockport – Offerton
31. Manchester – Southern Sporting Club

February 1964

1. Accrington – Town Hall with Mike Sax and the Vikings (See poster)
2. Levenshulme
5. Nelson – Imperial
6. Offerton
7. Manchester – Southern Sporting Club

8. Manchester – Southern Sporting Club
9. Manchester – Plaza
12. Bury – Palais. Although not noted in the diaries it has been reported that this was Derek Thornhill's last gig, it seems Ian Wallace was in the audience for the gig and was asked to join the band
13. Stockport – Offerton
14. Southern – Sporting Club
15. Manchester – Southern Sporting Club and in the afternoon Blackburn – Mecca
16. Manchester – Devonshire
17. Blackburn – Mecca
20. Stockport – Offerton Palace
21. Manchester – Southern Sporting Club
22. Manchester – Southern Sporting Club
23. Manchester – Southern Sporting Club
    Derek Thornhill decides to leave the band but agrees to record at Decca as per his contract. Ian Wallace agrees to join the band
26. London – Decca, Record Studios. Travel down for the recording session
27. London – Decca Studios 10.00am – 2.30pm – 5.30pm. Staying in a hotel in London in Sussex Gardens where they met the band The Animals.
    Ian Wallace recollects:
    'I was really nervous and spent most of the session in the toilet.'
28. Manchester – Southern Sporting Club
29. Manchester – Southern Sporting Club

March 1964

1. Burnley – Mecca
2. Blackburn – Mecca
4. Nelson – Imperial
5. Stockport – Offerton
6. Manchester – Southern Sporting Club
7. Manchester
8. Levenshulme
11. Accrington – St Augustine's
12. Stockport – Offerton
13. Manchester – Southern Sporting Club
14. Manchester – Southern Sporting Club
15. Manchester – Devonshire
18. Bury – Palais
19. Stockport – Offerton
20. Manchester – Southern Sporting Club
21. Blackburn – Mecca
22. Levenshulme
24. Derek leaves
26. Leyland – Motor Club
27. Manchester – Southern Sporting Club
28. Manchester – Southern
29. Manchester – Devonshire
30. Manchester – Plaza

April 1964

1. Manchester – Southern Sporting Club
2. Stockport – Offerton
3. Nelson – St John's Youth Club
4. Manchester – Devonshire, Palace Club Church
4. The Beatles records occupy the first five spots on the American singles chart
5. Blackburn – King Georges Hall
7. London to chat about the movie *Just for You* in Wardour Street with agent Phil Soloman
8. London – Shepperton Studios for the filming of *Just for You*, filmed 7 am – 4 pm
9. Stockport – Offerton

10. Chorley – Leyland Club
11. Burnley – Mecca
12. Nelson – Imperial
15. Accrington – Christ Church
16. Stockport – Offerton
18. Nelson – Imperial
19. Blackburn – Mecca
22. Manchester – Southern Sporting Club ... £10.00
23. Stockport – Offerton
24. Manchester – Devonshire
25. Levenshulme? Blackburn Mecca? Blackburn Door Club?
26. Manchester – Devonshire
30. Burnley – Mecca

May 1964

2. Levenshulme
3. St Pauls Church cancelled
7. Wigan – Sportsman Club
8. Nelson – Imperial Ballroom supporting Marianne Faithfull
9. Nelson – Imperial
11. Blackburn – Mecca
12. London – Decca Records
13. Rawtenstall – Astoria?
14. Stockport – Offerton
15. Swinton – Playa / Plaza
16. Manchester – Southern Sporting Club
17. Nelson – Imperial with Little Richard
18. Accrington – Conservative Club
19. London – Decca
21. Stockport – Offerton
22. Eccles – Taylor Brothers
23. Nelson – Imperial with Eden Kane
24. Manchester – Southern Sporting Club
25. Manchester – Southern Sporting Club
28. Stockport – Offerton
29. Manchester – Cavern
31. Birmingham – Lucky Stars

June 1964

Manchester – Cathedral concert playing to hundreds of fans, the set was 'He's Got the Whole World in His Hands', 'Blowin in the Wind', 'All Things Bright and Beautiful', 'Father Hear the Prayer we Offer (In the manner of the police TV series *Z Cars'* theme tune)

1. Blackburn – Mecca
4. Burnley – Mecca
5. Manchester – Devonshire
   Release date of The Warrior's single
6. London – *Thank Your Lucky Stars*. TV show along with Peter and Gorden, The Four Pennies, Craig Douglas, The Migil Five, Dusty Springfield, The Mods and Andee Silver. The Manchester Devonshire was recorded as an evening gig the same day
7. Nelson – Imperial
8. Manchester – Southern Sporting Club
9. West Houghton gig was cancelled. The local paper has The Warriors as their headline story
10. Colne – Dolphin Club
11. Stockport – Offerton Cancelled
12. Manchester – Southern Sporting Club
13. Manchester – Devonshire gig evening. In the day time, The Warriors signing for their single at Mary's Record Shop and The Record Centre. [Both are local stores]
14. Levenshulme
15. Manchester – Southern Sporting Club

17. Colne – Dolphin Club
18. Stockport – Offerton
19. Manchester – Devonshire
20. Rawtenstall – Astoria?
22. Manchester – Southern Sporting Club
24. Colne – Dolphin Club
25. Stockport – Offerton
26. Manchester – Southern Sporting Club, AEI DANCE, New Century Hall, CIS Buildings
27. Nelson – Imperial – Cancelled
28. Nelson – Imperial
29. Manchester – Southern Sporting Club

July 1964

3. Manchester – Devonshire
5. Manchester – Devonshire
11. Rawtenstall – Astoria
    Mike recalled: 'The first van we had, we painted orange. On the back we painted 'No Hand Signals, Only Smoke Signals (Warriors)'. We were driving into Manchester one night, and there was this dead guy on the road! We saw these policemen a little while away, and they looked at us and the van and just dismissed it really, but there was this dead bloke in the road.'
12. Manchester? Oasis bar

August 1964

2. Nelson – Imperial
15. Nelson – Imperial
16. Blackpool – Opera House

September 1964

2. Nelson – Imperial with Bill Haley & Gene Vincent
26. Blackburn – St Stephens

October 1964

1. Southport – Aldridge's. The Paramounts, The Warriors, The Vampires all play the Thursday night for the entrance fee of 6/6. Advertised as the 'Beat Scene 64'. The band has the introduction on the rare poster as: DECCA, FILM AND T.V. RECORDING GROUP THE WARRIORS.

December 1964

26. Rawtenstall – Astoria
    The rare surviving poster read 'Fabulous Christmas Eve Attraction – THE FOUR PENNIES, SATURDAY, DEC 26, BOXING DAY DANCE Featuring the Decca Disc Group THE WARRIORS plus THE SWASHBUCKLING – MUTINEERS and THE VITALIZING – VINCENTS. 7.30 – 11.45 Licenced Bar, advanced 6'6 – at Door 7'6
31. Bolton – Navada Ball. Dave Foster said: 'We played on New Year's Eve at a ball, I think we did 'Won't Be Long' by the Beatles, they were very influential to us.'
    Accrington, Antley Methodist Church. The band met up with the Methodist minister Fletcher Richardson at Antley Church and started a Rock Gospel movement called 'Rock Goes to Church'. The Warriors played here in December 1964. Fletcher Richardson was happy to let them play and rehearse and to make as much noise as they wanted. Fletcher Richardson eventually joined the BBC from the Methodist Church, where, in the 1960s with his long hair, he was known as the 'Rockin' Vicar'. He later became a presenter on *Radio Blackburn*.

1965

January 1965

Not a busy schedule for the band but now and again they would get to play the famous Cavern Club. The other venues that had the big groups playing at was The Peppermint Lounge, situated on Fraser Street, off London Road, Liverpool 3

March 1965

16. Liverpool, The Cavern Club with The Clayton Squares and The US Limited. This was the Accrington Cavern Club, on the corner of Milnshaw Lane and Castle Street
    Jon Anderson remembered this gig:
    I'd been down the Cavern and seen a lunchtime session and I was determined to play the place and when we got a booking, it was a dream come true. The atmosphere was amazing, and we did a lot of Everly Brothers songs and could sound quite like The Beatles. I turned professional, and I've never done anything else since then.

May 1965

28. Liverpool, The Cavern Club, The Feelgoods plus The Measles were a few of the 24 bands to appear at a benefit show, which ran from 12 noon until midnight. Paul McCartney's brother Mike also appeared on the bill as a member of Scaffold

June 1965

12. Nelson – Imperial supporting Donovan. Some 12 years later it would be Donovan supporting Jon in Yes on the *Going for the One* tour!
26. Nelson – Imperial, supporting Tom Jones (see the poster)

September 1965

Bolton: Beachcomber Club. Live. It was here that the only released live recording of the band was recorded, made available in three versions on CD. (See collectables section)

November 1965

3. *Bolton Evening News* Newspaper. Warriors article
12. *Bolton Evening News* shows a Beachcomber advert
13. *Bolton Evening News* shows a Beachcomber advert

December 1965

10. *Bolton Evening News*. Bury – Palaise de Dance advert

1966

January 1966

1. Dumfries with the Walker Brothers
2. Dunfermline
6. Stockport
7. Castleford
8. Worsley Civic Hall, Beat Dance Night with Heinz and The Wild Boys and Rede, 8 shillings entrance fee
9. Ashton – Palais
10. Chester
13. Litherland
14. Berwick – Red Lion
15. Edinburgh – Top Storey Club. Jon recalled the crazy reception they had from the fans up north and said there was nothing quite like the Scottish girls screaming all the way through their set. It had them all in the band realising how The Beatles must have felt.
    It is possible that on this day also the band played at the London Olympia for the BBC DJ Pete Murray. Performing a short promotional set, and supporting the legendary Bill Halley
17. Blackburn – Mecca
21. Leigh – Beachcomber Club with The Who and The Rocking Vickers
22. Berwick – Hageston
23. Castleford
25. Leigh – Beachcomber Club (special offer on the evening – A shilling for girls)
26. Leigh – Beachcomber Club
27. Bolton – Palais a dancing night out
28. Liverpool
    Mike leaves the band

February 1966

1. Bolton – Bamboo Club. Diary notes from a fan 'Jon ruined the first half with his showing off! I think they are going down the drain'. The band was paid £10
3. Sale – Locarno, have also seen adverts for a gig at the Bolton Palais
4. Liverpool
5. Rochdale. A fan said they played three new songs tonight. There was a local paper advert for the 7th gig in Bolton
6. Preston
7. Bolton – Palais
9. London. Some reports to say that the band went to do a recording session for their next possible single 'Run to Me'. Their manager Don Reed accompanied them; this is a much earlier date than on the eventual acetate produced
10. Ripley – Regal
13. Manchester – Jigsaw Club. (Rog) Fan's diary noted they wore grey jackets with red buttons and half belts
14. Warrington
15. The local paper has an advert for the forthcoming gig at the Beachcomber Club along with The Koobas, who featured the drummer Tony O'Reilly
16. Wythenshawe – St John's. The local paper has an advert for the following night's gig in Bolton
17. Bolton – Casino
18. Newcastle
19. Billingham – KD
20. Grimsby
21. Wolverhampton with the Kinks
23. Britannia
25. Bingley – T.C. with Gina
26. Leigh – Beachcomber Club
27. Sheffield – the gig where Joe Cocker guested?
28. Warrington

March 1966

1. Liverpool – Grafton (cancelled Bolton gig possible) West Derby Road, Liverpool. Seven acts on the bill with The Warriors seventh!
3. Blackpool – Mecca
4. Nottingham. Was this the evening when they crashed the van?
5. Bolton – Conservative Club then Sheffield
6. Stockport
7. Bolton – Palais
8. Manchester – Oasis club
9. London – I.B.C Studios (Travel to see Don Reed and sessions talk)
11. Sunderland with Sounds Inc and Heinz
13. Jungfran?
16. Newcastle
17. York
18. Sheffield – Ice Rink
19. Berwick
20. Bolton – Beachcomber

21/22. Maureen/Sue West Hendon Police Station!

23. London
24. Sale – Locarno
25. Middleborough
    By this date it was reported that 'You Came Along' had sold 10,000 copies
26. Bolton – Nevada
27. Mr Smiths?
28. Bolton – Palais [Author: Every time I put a Bolton date in think, gosh, I was about seven years old and only three miles away! Why didn't someone tell me about this band playing in town?]

April 1966

1. Stoke

2. Manchester – Universities
3. Rochdale
5. Liverpool
7. Coventry Locarno
9. Newcastle
10. Palais – Casino
15. Droylesden
17. Aston
18. Bolton Palais
20. Newcastle – Agogo
22. Berwick
23. Manchester C.J.S.
24. Chesterfield
27. Farnworth
28. Coventry
29. Penge?
30. Bolton – Nevada?

May 1966

1. Bolton – Palais
6. Nottingham This could have been the date of the van's crash
7. Leeds
8. Bolton – Palais
13. St Bernadette's
14. Henley
15. Carlisle – Cosmo on Central Avenue
16. Bolton – Palais (fan's diary said they were being watched by a man from Hamburg, who seemed to be impressed)
17. Cheadle Hulme
20. Middlesbrough
21. Newcastle – Agogo £30.00
22. Whitley Bay
23. Newcastle – Quay £15.00
24. Hansey Smith! £25.00
26. Warrington – Carlton £15.00
27. Oxford £30.00
28. Cromford £30.00
29. Chesterfield £25.00
30. Bolton – Palais £20.00
31. Birmingham

June 1966

1-6 Birmingham

7. Lostock
8. Warrington
9. Bolton
10. Birmingham – Elbow Room
11. Britannia
12. Whitley Bay
13. Bolton – Casino
15. Manchester – Smiths

    Manchester – Bell Vue, date unknown.

    Mike Brereton remembers a lucky evening for Jon:

    Bell Vue zoo was were the club was. It was not posh at all but big. They had gambling on the side too, dice, roulette. They used to give us some money to play and get people in, so if they saw someone playing, others would come in then. [They probably gave us] ten quid. We had to drag Johnny out one night because he was winning too much. He won and won and won...we had to tell him to put it all on the black to lose it. We needed him on stage. He didn't.
16. Unclear venue entered in the diary

17. Warrington
18. West Bromwich – Elbow Room £30.00
19. Burton on Trent
20. Bolton – Palais
22. Newcastle – Agogo
24. Chesterfield (50%)
25. Ashton £30.00
26. Birmingham
27. Chester
29. Drive down to Dover
30. Germany 06:00 sailing from Dover, Rod said, 'Everyone was SICK! I must remember to drive on the right side of the road next time too.'

July 1966

1. Cologne – Storyville Club they play 6 pm – 2 am!

Over the next two pages a pen drawing of someone!

5. London – Haggerston Hall, supporting the Small Faces
9. Newcastle – Agogo
10. Whitley Bay
11. Black Casino
12. Liverpool – Peppermint Lounge
13. Greyhound
15. Frankfort A Main!
17. Chester – Victoria
18. Bolton – Palais
19. Droylesden
22. Stoke – Storch
28. Bolton – Palais

29-30. Rodney did some more doodling in the diary of a silly head with a hat! Travel to Germany

30. Germany. The England football team win the world cup. The Warriors play shows in Germany to very angry crowds!

August 1966

1. Bolton – Palais
2. Accrington – Town Hall (cancelled)
3. Bolton – Nevada
5. London – Haggerston Hall – No dancing!
6. Newcastle – Agogo
7. Whitley Bay
8. Hassocks – Brighton Downs Hotel
11. Blackpool – Casino
12. Liverpool – Peppermint Lounge
13. Greyhound
17. The ??? Place
20. London – Tiles Club 79-89 Oxford Street. The Warriors support the band Felders Orioles. 7.30 – 11.30. Members pay five shillings, guests seven shillings and sixpence
21. London – Tiles Club (gig not confirmed)
24. The date shown on the acetate disc for the tracks 'The Doll House is Empty' and 'Run to Me', which was meant to be their follow-up single

September 1966

2. Accrington – 1966 Miss Accrington Dance

October 1966

8. London – Haggerston (Rod: 'I remember odd trips to London where we'd play a gig at a club and then go home, maybe Tiles Club?')
13. Liverpool – Cavern Club,Liverpool with the band Look Twice (probably a Friday)
14. Leeds – B.G. (this could be a girl's initials)
15. London – Tiles

16. Esquire Club
18. Liverpool – Peppermint Lounge
19. Newcastle – Agogo Club – ‘Loved the Agogo Club, we worked there with loads of acts, I particularly remember 10 Years After.’ ~ Rod
21. Birmingham – Elbow Room (The night the band had a cracking gig and was the place where they met a gangster packing a gun)
23. Bolton – Casino
24. Bolton – Palais
15. RED
26. Morley
27. Birmingham – Rum Runners Club (I think this is where we met Mandy Rice Davis. I must admit I do get confused with this and the Elbow Room)
28. Liverpool – Peppermint Lounge
29. Accrington – Technical Collage
30. Accrington – Wheatsheaf Pub

November 1966

2. Lancaster – Alexander Hotel (50%)
3. Newcastle – Grapes £25.00
4. Birmingham £30.00
5. Tunstall – Goldech Torch £40.00 Rod recalls: ‘Classic gig place – always a real pleasure and all the best bands played there. I remember seeing Butterfield Blues Band here and partying with them. Later, after Yes began, I roadied for them at a gig here.’
6. Bell Pub..?? £30.00
7. Darlington – Majestic 50%
11. Birmingham City £30.00
12. NOT BRIT B5
13. Oldham
16. Place £20.00
17. Sale
18. Oldham £25.00
19. Liverpool – Sutton Hall £45.00
21. Golden Torche £25.00
23. Newcastle – Agogo £25.00
24. Barlow £22.00
26. Carlisle
27. Whitley £20.00
28. Bolton – Palais
29. Off to Germany sailed from Dover 12.30

Looking at these listings after many years, Rod Hill commented: ‘This list demonstrates how much we were working, from my memory every month August, September, October, after we came back from that first trip to Cologne and Frankfurt was this busy.’

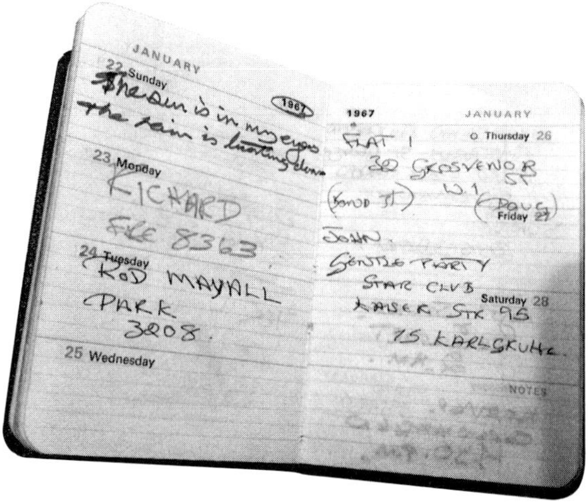

Right: January 1967. Entries for Jon and The Gentle Party at the Star Club, some old mates contact details plus some new lyrics. *(Rod Hill – David Watkinson Collection)*

December 1966

Germany – Cologne, Storyville Club – Played an all month's residency
3. Played with the Rocking Berries
4. Played with the Rocking Berries
5. Played with the Rocking Berries
6. Played with the Rocking Berries
10. 1.000 DM (Any amounts in numbers did not necessarily have DM after the entered number, most likely amounts paid over the week or month with some calculations shown of monies grouped together)
17. 1.000 DM Rochester Avenue, Breightmet, Bolton. (This was a few streets away from where the author grew up in Withins Drive, Breightmet, Bolton)
24. Radathal Jorgen 1.300 DM
Notes – 4.800 Jurgens Grandparents

1967

January 1967

Germany – Frankfurt residency all month for The Warriors
1. Two bands to go and see – Thoughts and the Koobas in Frankfurt

Other notations in the diary re the Koobas included the contact details for ROY-ARROWBROOK – 6055 and TONY/CLA -1437 – LIVERPOOL.

2. Thoughts band went home... Joe Crame?
3-4. Dave Jacobs, 14A Gunter Grove, Chelsea, London, S.W.10 (Rodie)
5-7. John Bull c/o B.F.B.S
8. A Party at Angelica's with Karen
9-10. Dave Jacobs
11. Artwoods – Wes 3377
12. Pete Cole, East Ham
13. Mog, Frank Boxlan – Dublin 3
15. Nanni & Marianne...Gulda...Jan
19. Sent some money back home...sunni, tery, eric books
23. Richard 8363
24. Rod Mayall – park 3208
26. Flat 1, 32 Grosvenor Street, London W1. Bond Street. (Doug)
27-28. JOHN & GENTLE PARTY, STAR CLUB, KAISER STRBE 95, 15 KARLGRUHZ
This detail above is the only proof so far of Jon meeting and singing with The Gentle Party band. So even though it was a good while from the end of The Warriors it shows he was keen to explore other musicians and styles.
29. JOHN ANDERSON, GASTHANS, ST GEORGE, 8721, OBERWERRN, GERMANY
30. Sunny...2863522
31. LEFT STORYVILLE AND FRANKFURT 2.A.M.

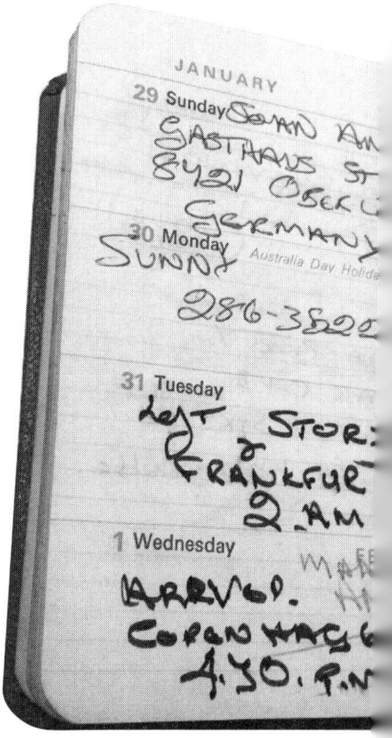

Above: Rod's diary entries which show were Jon was staying and gigs for the band. *(Rod Hill – David Watkinson Collection)*

The last week saw the band go to London to meet Joe Meek and record a session. Turning out to be a wasted trip in the end, as Joe Meek was going through a mental illness, culminating in his murder of his landlady and suicide on 3 February 1967

February 1967

1. ARRIVED COPENHAGEN 4.30 P.M.
5. John M. Claxton, 14 Talbot Square, Sussex Gardens, London W2
6. PAD 5962
7. PETER DYER, PONTHOUSE STUDIOS, 32, BARONS COURT ROAD, LONDON W14
10. KEN BAXTER 9536 (Carl Douglas)

11. Neville
17. 1300 DM
24. 1500 DM
27. Club
28. Denmark – Carousel Club. A long month's residency in the middle of the red-light district!

March 1967

1. Cologne – Storyville Club residency all month again
   (Earning around 200 DM a week each, details of some of the payments received were recorded, but not all are reproduced here.)
3. March – A quick visit home to Accrington
4. 1.000 plus 400 DM travelling
11. 1,000 DM
18. 1,000 DM
25. 1,000 DM

April 1967

1. Back to ENGLAND for short stay, rest and family
22. Germany – Frankfurt for a week's residency

May 1967

1. München!
5. 250 DM?
6. 1,000 DM?
13. 2.000 DM?
16. Munich – PN Hithouse Club. (DJ Nikki)
16. Munich – Big Apple Club with Jimi Hendrix
18. Germany – Stadhalle JIMI HENDRIX
19. 500 DM
20. 3.000 DM
27. 4.000 DM
29. Munich – PN Hithouse. (DJ Nikki)
30. The band spend time in the studios in Germany. Recording the track 'She's Gone'. This being one of the last recordings of Jon Anderson with The Warriors

June 1967

1. Hamburg
9. 1.000 DM

11-19. There are eight separate calculations showing simple, numbered amounts being added up. All look like monthly amounts written down, with a whole week's diary entry days written over in what looks like a winding up of accounts for The Warriors

19-26. These are the dates that have been given for the TV show *Beat! Beat! Beat!* appearance in Germany along with The Move and The Creation. One is the recording date, and the other is the broadcast date

July 1967

1. DENMARK – COPENHAGEN

2-8. Once again, eight diary pages are taken up with various weekly, monthly and grand sum totals.

The Warriors played gigs along with the band The Big Sound

August 1967

The Warriors played gigs along with the band the Big Sound

27. The Beatles' manager Brian Epstein dies

Jon Anderson played his last show with The Warriors in August 1967 at the Storyville Club in Frankfurt Germany.

31. Finished in Frankfurt

Brian, Jon and Dave at the Storyville Club in 1967. *(M. Evans)*

September 1967

1. On this Friday two names are entered but difficult to make out. Possibly friend's names Maggie and Frieson
3. Written large in ink in Rod's diary: 'I think something's happening with the band.'
4. Left for home, England
5. Arrived about 5 pm
6. Dave and Jon told me about the group! (THE WARRIORS FINISH)

Around this time The Syn became Mabel Greer's Toyshop with Chris Squire

7. London – Happening 44 Club Mabel Greer's Toyshop
9. Here the notes could say 'Jon back' but unsure and hard to make out
11. Jon Anderson rang, Brian came up
12. Mike came around to the house
13. Mike came around and saw Eileen
14. Jon Anderson rang and went to Bolton
15. Went to Blackburn
16. Diary has M.M music symbols written down!
17. Went to London
18. London went to the 100 club to see the Artwoods (John Lord of Deep Purple fame)
19. London B.B.C. with the Artwoods and met Alexis Korner
20. London Picture's (Cinema) with Dave Foster to watch Boney and Clyde
20. London Keith West gig – Tomorrow (Yes' Steve Howe)
21. At Dave's again
24. Undecided as yet! (what to do about it all now no band)
25. Around this time Jon had received his invitation to join a group The Gentle Party in Germany

The following section shows key Yes dates for historic purposes. Not all concerts for the years are shown.

October 1967

10. London – Middle Earth Club. Mabel Greer's Toyshop
21. London – Middle Earth Club. Mabel Greer's Toyshop
25. The last entry in Rod Hill's diary entries is a little vague but says… 'Brian and Jon came around'. (Address unknown)

The Warriors band members had hoped to continue playing somehow through the remainder of 1967/8, but they finally parted ways and didn't play together again.

November 1967

4. London – Marquee Club London with Neat Change and support act The Open Mind
13. London – Marquee Club London with The Nice and but support act The Open Mind

December 1967

We have this month emerging Yes connections with Neat Change and Mabel Greer's Toyshop playing gigs. Later in the month, Jon is thought to have gone back to Accrington in Lancashire to see family and friends for Christmas.

5. London – Marquee Club. The Open Mind play as a support act
9. London – Marquee Club. Neat Change and Mable Greer's Toyshop
11. London – Marquee Club. Simon Dupree and the Big Sound / JON
    Considering Jon had known the band The Big Sound, it's definitely a timely coincidence that a solo artist support act called JON was on the same bill.
23. London – Marquee Club Neat Change and support act The Open Mind

January 1968

Jon was in and around the clubs and bars of London looking for the deals and breaks

1. London – Marquee Club. Mabel Greer's Toyshop
6. London – Marquee Club. Mabel Greer's Toyshop
15. London – Marquee Club. The Open Mind
20. London – Marquee Club. Mabel Greer's Toyshop
23. London – Marquee Club. The Open Mind

February 1968

Jon was in and around the clubs and bars of London looking for the deals and breaks
Les Cruches gig – a one off? Jon can't recall it, and the venue is unknown.

1. London – Marquee Club featured an artist named JON.
2. London – Middle Earth Club. Mabel Greer's Toyshop
3. London – Marquee Club. The Open Mind
5. London – Middle Earth Club. Mabel Greer's Toyshop
19. London – Marquee Club. The Open Mind

March 1968

Jon was rehearsing with Gun for three weeks, before a short run of gigs
9. The review of the Hans Christian single appears in the UK music paper *Melody Maker*
9-21. London Marquee Club – the Open Mind
15. The release of the single 'Never My Love' / ' All of The Time' as Hans Christian
Les Cruches gig in Tilburg, Holland?

April 1968

3. Mabel Greer's Toyshop appear on *Nightride* (the whole program) courtesy of John Peel. It is the night before Clive's 18th birthday.
6. London – Marquee Club. Jon Anderson & Gun, supported by Family
13. The band called Grapefruit has an advert out for their single called Yes, the imagery is very similar to how the first Yes logo would look.
22. London Marquee Club. The Open Mind

May 1968

Jon and Chris meet with Jon joining in on the 2 May 68

2. London – Archway Club. Mabel Greer's Toyshop with The Nice. Jon Anderson, Chris Squire, Clive Bayley, Peter Banks and Bob Hagger
18. London – St Joseph's Hall, Highgate Archway. Mabel Greer's Toyshop supported by Action. This is reportedly Bob Hagger's last gig. The line up is Chris Squire, Clive Bayley, Peter Banks and Bob Hagger
    Bob Hagger says: 'I do recall playing The Marquee Club and a venue in Highgate with The

Action. After that, they changed the band's name to Mighty Baby.

24. The release of the Hans Christian second single '(The Autobiography of) Mississippi Hobo' / 'Sonata of Love'

June 1968

After Bob Hagger leaves Mabel

7. Bill Bruford reportedly meets Mabel / Yes at The Lucky Horseshoe Café and went on to play at Rachel Macmillan College in Deptford. Bill Bruford has this date documented as his first gig with Jon and Chris Squire for Mabel / Yes. Some say it's the first Yes gig, but generally it's not recognised as such although Bill has always said he never joined Mabel Greer's Toyshop, only Yes

9/14/19/24/29. Mabel Greer's Toyshop rehearsed

13. London – Marquee Club Jon Anderson & Gun
It is suggested that Jon rehearses with Mabel Greer's Toyshop at some point in the day time. It is thought that they rehearsed at a big concrete warehouse in Shepherds Bush for a couple of weeks, as recalled by Clive Bayley. Interviewed in 2017 he said:

> We rehearsed at a big concrete warehouse in Shepherd's Bush for a couple of weeks, Jon introduced a potential manager for the band who came up with the inspirational request that we dyed our hair green to match Chris Squire's Green Anele and Davide custom made boots! We were rehearsing 'America', 'Eight Miles High', 'Carpetman' and the left-over Mabel Greer's songs like 'Beyond and Before', 'Sweetness', 'Jeanetta', 'Sweetness', 'Electric Funeral', 'Get Yourself together' and 'Images of You and Me'

July 1968

In London this month the mysterious performer 'JON' disappears from any listings

6. London – Middle Earth Club. Gun play down the bill at this one-night summer celebration of the new Roundhouse, along with the headliners, The Byrds. 10.30 – dawn

Not confirmed, but in this month, Jon may have joined in with some of the gigs played by Mabel Greer's Toyshop

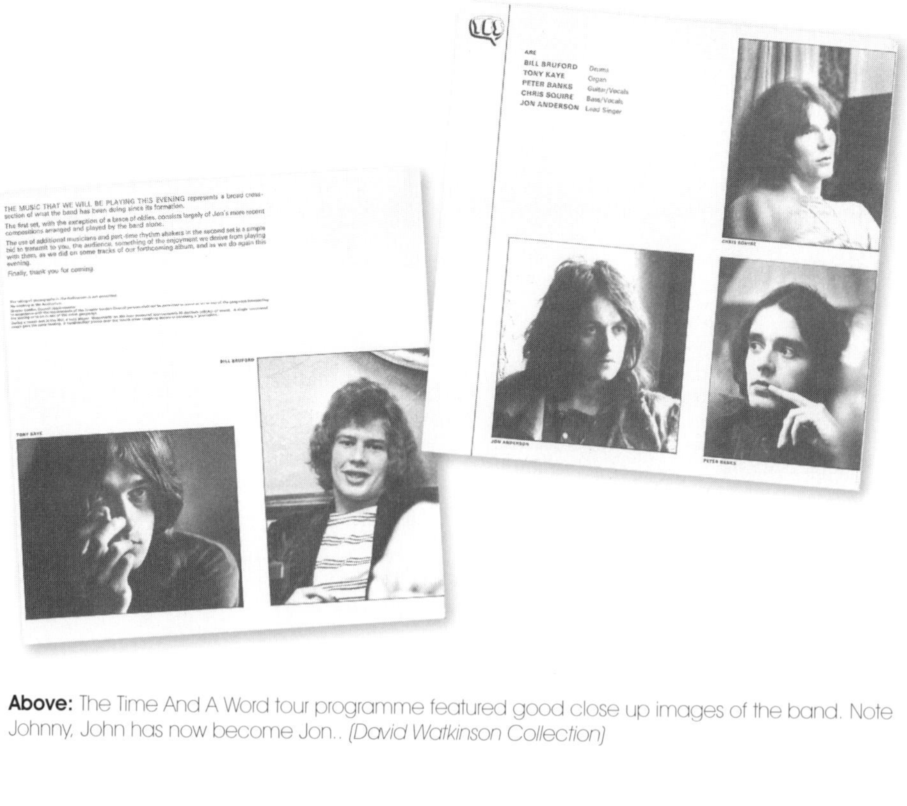

Above: The Time And A Word tour programme featured good close up images of the band. Note Johnny, John has now become Jon.. *(David Watkinson Collection)*

20. London – Kingston Market Hall, Kingston-upon-Thames, Mabel Greer's Toyshop
Clive Bayley added in 2017, 'I'm sure Jon performed at this one, I think around this time we also played Coronation Hall in Kingston, and we all went around to my parent's house in Kingston after the gig.'
26. Bracknell – Sports Centre. Mabel Greer's Toyshop. Not 100% clear if went ahead
27. Newmarket – Municipal Hall. Mabel Greer's Toyshop, not 100% clear if went ahead
31. London – Mabel Greer's Toyshop / Yes rehearse at the Lucky Horseshoe Cafe in Shaftsbury Avenue
(N.B. The 1971 movie *Gumshoe* shows the inside of the Horseshoe Cafe which had not changed since 1968, and even fifty years later it has the same windows. This can be viewed on YouTube)

August 1968

1. London – Mabel Greer's Toyshop / Yes rehearse at the Lucky Horseshoe Cafe
2. London – Mabel Greer's Toyshop / Yes rehearse at the Lucky Horseshoe Cafe

Yes – YES – The Yes – Yes!

Jon Anderson, Chris Squire, Bill Bruford, Tony Kaye, Peter Banks

Michael Tait (Yes' Tour Manager, sound and lighting engineer): 'Looking back at the beginning of Yes, we would turn up at a gig and people's jaws would drop! No one had heard anything like it, Yes were stunning. People in those days would listen to the band, really listen.'

Key gigs

August 1968 – YES

3. Essex – East Mersey Youth Camp
Yes play their first gig out of town as a warm-up for the main first show in London two days later on the 5th. (A venue photo is shown in the Plexus Publishing book *Yes: Perpetual Change*, 2001)
5. London – Marquee Club. Yes supporting the Nite People. This became the most important venue for Yes. As they started their careers, this was the most prestigious venue, where everyone played, including all the biggest artists of the day. Yes went on to play 38 times at the venue

September 1968

15. London Blaises Club
Yes' first break came from the manager of The Nice. He recommended Yes to replace Sly and The Family Stone, who couldn't get in from the USA at customs, and so were a no-show. Following that gig, Yes began to get noticed by managers and producers. Roy Flynn offered to manage the band on the same evening, an offer which was accepted.

November 1968

15. London – Roundhouse – The all-night show featuring The Who, Joe Cocker & The Grease Band, Small Faces, Crazy World of Arthur Brown, Mindbenders
16. Leeds – University gig, Bill Bruford comes back to watch Yes, is shocked by their current replacement drummer and is asked to re-join the band, which he does
26. London – Royal Albert Hall support to Cream, who played their farewell concert

December 1968

17. London – Marquee Club.
The Who's Christmas Party. Yes opened with Traffic's 'Heaven is in Your Mind'. Reported as another great show, topped off by the announcement they were to begin a Wednesday residency at the club in January 69. They had to endure a bit of barracking by a handful of Who fans, who were really taken to task by Pete Townshend after The Who came on! Pete had already become a big fan over those early months
19. London – Royal Albert Hall support to Janis Joplin
A short set but any chance to play in front of such a huge audience was a bonus for Yes

For a continuation of information on Yes concerts and history, please find a copy of the *Yes: Perpetual Change* by David Watkinson (Plexus books) which has an excellent guide covering

Yes gigs for around 35 years. Two editions were printed with the second edition having added information. Visually the only way to tell the difference between the copies is that the second edition has magazine reviews printed on the back cover. For up to date information on gigs played and set lists for the rest of Yes' career take a look at: *forgotten-yesterdays.com* and Steve *Sullivan's Yesgigs 1966-1980* web sites.

Yes in 1969, and just one year old as a band thank the then manager Roy Flynn by presenting him with a gold-plated Dunhill made lighter. It reads: 'To Roy Flynn, who has done more for us than anybody else in the business. We hope this small gift will enlighten you as much as you have enlightened us.' Ironically, six months later he was dumped as their manager.

The major influence in Yes' career would be their second manager Brian Lane. He began his involvement with Yes just before the release of The Yes Album. Attending a gig at The Marquee with friend and client Jack Wild, Brian recalled the gig in *Prog* magazine, interviewed by Daryl Easlea:

> The place was jam-packed, and they were fantastic. I heard a whisper that they had just fired their manager, Roy Flynn, and were looking for a new manager. Jack and I went backstage and met Jon Anderson. I told him I'd like to have a shot at being their manager and gave him my verbal CV about the bands I'd broken. Jon was impressed by those two magic words 'The Pink Floyd' and said they would give me a shot. He said they had a new album coming out in three weeks called The Yes Album, and that I had three months, if they went to Number one, I could have the job.

Although they did not achieve their goal of getting to number one in the UK with The Yes Album, Lane visited the Oxford Street Virgin record store and bought enough Yes albums to ensure that it was a number-one-selling record in that store. The third Yes album did it: it made Yes a name to remember.

Appendix 7 Set Lists

In just a year, the difference in the setlists performed by Jon was massive. Changing from those played by The Warriors, in September 1967 to Yes in September 1968 was a big jump. There was a completely new setlist for Yes with a broader, more eclectic mix of songs. For the most part, Yes dropped the real pop songs, except for their love of Beatles material, for a more experimental, complicated, fuller sound. Lovely harmonies filled the air, but the musicianship had improved, the sounds were better, the equipment was newer. The Beatles' influence, along with the cinematic grandeur and inspiration from Simon and Garfunkel were evident. They created material that could be played with, extended and given the Yes touch. Still a copy-band finding their way with arrangements and with new sounds, Yes were beginning to understand what they wanted to be, although it was just a little too early to say for certain what that was.

We do know for sure though that they were going to work hard at it. 'Practice makes perfect' is an old saying and Yes most certainly did that. When they weren't practising, they were gigging or planning and working on getting new gigs.
There was no time to rest for Yes, they had a world to conquer.

The Little John Skiffle Group

'Don't You Rock Me Daddy-O' (Lonnie Donegan)
'Rock Island Line' (Lonnie Donegan)
'Little Brown Jug' (Glenn Miller)
'Bugle Boy' (The Andrews Sisters)
Speaking of Lonnie Donegan: 'He was the first person we had heard of from Britain to get to the coveted number one in the charts, and we studied his records avidly. We all bought guitars to be in a skiffle group. He was the man.' – Paul McCartney.
Typical instruments needed: Washboard, jugs, tea chest, bass, kazoo, cigar-box, fiddle, musical saw, comb and paper and a guitar or banjo.

The Warriors

Various Elvis songs;
I'm Down'
'Don't Make Me Blue'. (Dave Fosters first ever song)
You Came Along' (A side single release)
'I Found You' (sessions only)
'It's Up to You'
'Night of a Thousand Eyes'
'Like I've Never Been Gone'
'That's What Love Will Do'
'How Do You Do It?'
'It Won't Be Long''Blowing in the Wind'
'Not Fade Away''Autumn Leaves'
'Bo Didley'
'Sticks & Stones'
'The Girl Who Sang the Blues'
'Goldfinger'
'Hold on I'm Coming' (Sam & Dave)
'You`re Always on My Mind'
'No One Can Make Sunshine Smile'
'Jump Back'
'You Can`t Lie to a Liar'
'I'm Down'
'Cathy's Clown'
'Bye Bye, Love'
'Twist and Shout'
'Run-around Sue'
'Crying in the Rain'
'Hit the Road Jack'
'She`s a Woman'
'Fortune Teller'
'Too Much Monkey Business'
'Don`t You Dig this Kind-a-Beat'
'Hey Baby''A Fool Such as I'
'So Sad''Be My Baby'
'Bad Bad Times'
'Love is Where You Find It'
'Summer Girl'
'Turn to Me'
'Hey Good Lookin'
'Something's Got a Hold on Me'
'Will You Still Love Me Tomorrow'
'Anyway You Want Me' ('That's the Way I'll Be')
The Theme from 'The Traitors' movie
'All Things Bright and Beautiful'
'Can't Live it Down'
'Cry Over Love'
'God Save the Queen'
'Edelweiss' – solo Jon with Marianne
'Sabre Dance'
'Savage'
'Run to Me'
'He's Got the Whole World in His Hands'
'Father Hear the Prayer we Offer' (in the manner of the police TV series Z Cars theme tune).
'She Loves You'
'What Can this Hour Given Me?'
The list was edited along with Rod Hill and Derek Thornhill from the band. It has been said that they covered songs by the Four Seasons, The Beach Boys and Tamla Motown, mostly because of Jon's voice.

Jon Anderson & Gun set list

'Remember' (Walking in the Sand) (The Shangri-las) Jon singing solo
'Eight Miles High' (The Byrds)
'A Day in the Life' (The Beatles)

Yes 1968/9

'Heaven is in Your Mind'
'Beyond and Before'
'Paper Cup'
'Mr Fantasy'
'Everydays'
'Sweet Dreams'
'Then'
'Dear Father'
'No Opportunity Necessary, No Experience Needed'
'In the Midnight Hour'
'Carpetman'
'Eleanor Rigby'
'I'm Only Sleeping'
'Every Little Thing'
'You Keep Me Hanging On'
'I See You'
'Eight Miles High'
'I Can Hear the Grass Go'
'Sweetness'
'Harold Land'
'Survival'
'It's Love'
'Number 14 Bus' (Peter Banks Solo) Jon and Peter on acoustic guitars
'Looking Around'
'Something's Coming'

The band are rumoured to have played a very fast version of 'For Your Love' (the Yardbirds tune) as early as their first few gigs. Some of the tracks went on for fifteen to twenty minutes longer than their natural length, due to the extended soloing that came from Peter Banks and Chris Squire. An organ solo from Tony Kaye and a drum solo from Bill Bruford sometimes got a look in too.

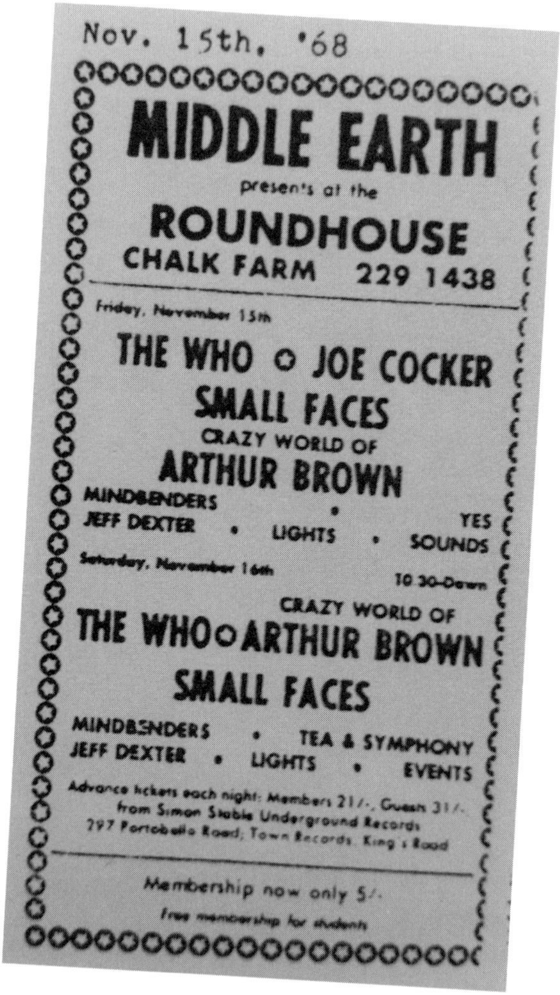

Above: November 15 1968 sees Yes placed just above the DJ on the bill. *(David Watkinson Collection)*

Appendix 8 The Collectables

The Little John Skiffle Group

Vinyl 12-Inch 78 Rpm Record (Homemade)
'Don't You Rock Me Daddy-O'
This appears to be Jon Anderson's first-ever record. It is a homemade vinyl 78, put together with friends and family. In it they perform in their front room in Norfolk Street, Accrington. Presumably, there was only one ever made. Unusually, it was made with a stick-on-vinyl, which covered and fit any 12-inch record, so it would be stuck over the top of a 12-inch, 78rpm vinyl record of the time. Its whereabouts are unknown.

The Warriors

'You Came Along' (Mason/Reed) A-side F11926
'Don't Make Me Blue'. (David Foster) B-side
UK Decca Records June 1964
Vinyl 7-Inch Standard Release Single 45rpm
The band only had one single released, and that was on 6 June 1964. Selling well locally, it sold around 40,000 copies in the end, but it did little nationally. Other attempts were made in the recording studios, but they never made a final vinyl disc release.

'You Came Along' (Mason / Reed) A-side
'Don't Make Me Blue'. (David Foster) B-side
Vinyl 7-Inch Demo Single 45rpm
A promotional copy of the single was released for the DJs. It was essentially the same 45 with the addition of the wording 'DEMONSTRATION SAMPLE NOT FOR SALE' along with a large letter 'A'.

'You Came Along' b/w 'Sad Story (All I Can Do Is Cry)' written by George Bean. Decca. F11926
This very rare demo seven inch single came to light in 2020.

'Anything That's a Part of You'
Vinyl 12-Inch 78 Rpm Record (Homemade)
Derek Thornhill recalls an early event, 'We did the track in someone's house because we loved Elvis. I remember we recorded a song, Tony sang lead vocal on it, 'Anything That's a Part of You', 'Only You', or something like that. It was our first recording, but unfortunately, I haven't got it.'

This one would have been produced in the same manner as the first Little John Skiffle Group single, listed at the beginning of the collectables. Its whereabouts are unknown.

'Too Much' (2.21), 'Can't Live It Down' (2.44), 'Summer Girl' (1.54)
Acetate 7-Inch Vinyl 45rpm
This acetate is an unreleased single. Acetates they were made for assessing whether the music had been successfully transferred to disc. Unlike a mass-produced vinyl record, these were usually hand-cut and tended to be less durable than standard vinyl discs. From this point the actual record could be produced if the quality has been agreed. They are the rarest form of a collectable single, as very small numbers were produced, and sometimes they represent the only existing copy of a record, due to the recording being rejected and the acetate version being the only one to survive.

A double-sided 7-inch vinyl single Emidisc, this particular record is an acetate with handwritten details in the centre. Only one example is known to survive and is owned by the author. I took this along to the Abbey Road studios on the 18 May 2017, to see if the acetate had any kind of salvageable content. The first (and only) needle drop on the vinyl revealed that the tracks could be saved and that there was something there, as, after 50 years, there might have been nothing left. Transferring them to digital format, along with cleaning and EQ-ing the recordings means they have been saved. Working with mastering engineer Andrew Walter at Abbey Road was indeed a wonderful experience, and I hope our saved production of a somewhat damaged and very poor-quality recording has been worthwhile. It is thought that these earliest never-before-heard demo recordings by Jon Anderson will be made available in some format to tie in with the publication of this book in 2020.

Mike Brereton recalls the making of single, saying 'We did it with a producer called Ray and we accidentally smashed his tape recorder up and lost it!'

'Too Much' (2.21)

This was actually a version of a song called 'Please Don't Feel Too Bad', written by Alan Clarke of the Hollies. It is clearly the most lively of the three on this acetate, with Tony and Jon very strong in both lead and back-up vocals. It is a song about staying away too much from a loved one. Channelling their best Paul McCartney sounds, Tony shouts 'Hey' at the appropriate times. Jon can be heard backing his brother strongly in the choruses.

'Can't Live it Down' (2.44)

This sounds a lot like the Beatles with different time changes and fine harmonies. A guitar solo midway through by Rod is light and reflects the mood, but is not particularly exciting. Tony has an excellent lead vocal in what is a bit of a plodder of a song. It's still catchy – a smoochy type of song and the good harmonies save the record, like all Warriors material. In all these mixes, the backline of David Foster and Ian Wallace are far back in the mix, steady and solid, although I don't think they really shine through in the quality of the demos that are left. The song was written by Geoff Stephens.

'Summer Girl' (1.54)

Mike Brereton remembered, '"Lonely Summer Girl" was by David Box from America. Decca, at the time, got records from the states and tried to put a slant on it. It should be called 'Poor Little Summer Girl', having a Buddy Holly feel. I can see it now as Mike Leander (producer) showing how he wanted it to sound in the studio, he shouted, "play higher up the scale".'

Starting with a ten-second Shadows-style guitar intro, it happily leads into a strong Tony vocal. It continues with a Buddy Holly 'Peggy Sue'-feel, although it sounds muddy on this take. It's a song about school breaking up and teens wanting to be together. Jon can be heard backing Tony here, but it's hard to imagine a starring role coming from this.

Acetate 7-Inch Vinyl 45rpm 1966

'The Doll House is Empty' (1.59)

A single-sided 7-inch single unreleased vinyl Emidisc acetate. Numbers left are unknown but most likely just this one only surviving. The handwritten details on the disc are: 'The Doll House Is Empty', 24-8-66, c/o Don Read, 45 RPM 2.00. Warriors.

The above details refer to the song title, the date of the recording, c/o the manager Don Read, a 45 RPM single being the speed of play and the length of the track being two minutes. Warriors and the number two are written at the bottom of the centre, which could indicate two copies being made.

The other writings on the acetate are: Made in GT. Britain, Emidisc, Recording Blank, Keep Surface Clean, Use lightweight Pick Up, Emi Tape Limited, Hayes, Middlesex, England.

Acetate 7-Inch Vinyl 45rpm 1966 (Version 1)

'Run to Me' (2.21)

The handwritten details on the disc are: 'Run to Me', 4-8-66, 45 RPM, 2:24, Warriors and the number 2 are written at the bottom of the centre.

The above details mean the song title, the date of the recording, a 45 RPM single speed of play and the length of the track being two minutes and twenty-four seconds, Warriors and the number 2 are written at the bottom of the centre, which could indicate that two copies were made.

The other writings on the acetate are: Made in GT. Britain, Emidisc, Recording Blank, Keep Surface Clean, Use lightweight Pick Up, Emi Tape Limited, Hayes, Middlesex, England.

Acetate 7-Inch Vinyl 45rpm 1966 (Version 2)

'Run to Me' (2.21)

This version came to light in April 2018. An unreleased single-sided Emidisc UK acetate single. More than likely produced on, 24-8-66, along with the version 1 above. 'Run to Me' was planned as their follow up single.

The proposed second single had much more of a rock sound to it than 'You Came Along'. The guitars are stronger all-round, opening with power chords, the bass standing out with clearer drums. The track goes straight into a Beatle- inspired harmony-drenched pop song with Tony high in the mix. Jon's backing vocal is deep in the mix, and the track is pulled together by Brian Chatton's organ work, along with the 'hey' shouted out in the background. It's a harmless boy-meets-girl love-song, with lyrics about being on a train journey, wanting to be back together with the girl and how he would never leave her ever again and is longing for her kiss. For its time, it was decent, but not a great follow up, and it never saw the light of day, not to be heard until 52 years later, when it came up for sale.

This acetate was written by another Manchester musician DJ called Ray Teret who performed under the name Ugli (Ugly) Ray Teret. It is believed that The Warriors even supported him at a few gigs. The acetate was pressed by Decca Records at the Emidisc studios. It came from a record company executive's collection. Handwritten on the centre label is 45 rpm, 'Run to Me', (Ray Teret) and in bold The Warriors. The other writings on the acetate are: Made in GT. Britain, Emidisc, Recording Blank, Keep Surface Clean, Use lightweight Pick Up, Emi Tape Limited, Hayes, Middlesex.

The Warriors also recorded for the Immediate Record label with the producer/DJ Ray Teret, recording the tracks 'Run To Me' and 'No Longer A Lover'. It was reported that the two tracks were laid down in the studio in a brisk one hour and ten minutes.

Acetate 10-Inch Vinyl 45rpm

'Cry Over Love' / 'Turn to Me'

Written details on the centre are: Emidisc, 2' 19", Nield & Hardy Ltd, 45 RPM, The Warriors, 'Cry Over Love'. This acetate is known to exist and was known to be sold online on the open market around 2013, with no other details

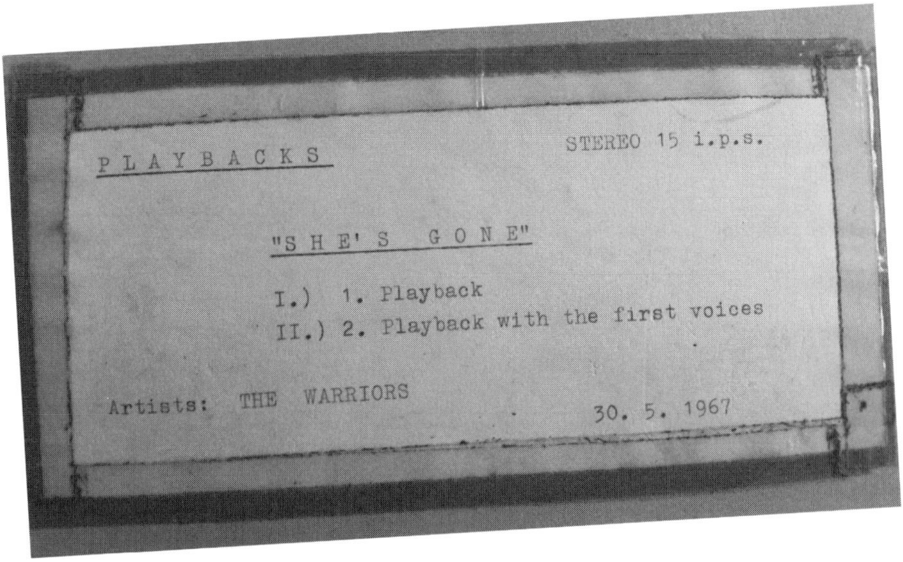

Above: A close – up of the text on the tape box. *(David Watkinson Collection)*

available other than a visual which can be tracked down on the internet. The owner is unknown, and the numbers left of this item would again be very small. This is likely to be the only one.

The other writings on the acetate are: Made in GT. Britain, Emidisc, Recording Blank, Keep Surface Clean, Use lightweight Pick Up, Emi Tape Limited, Hayes, Middlesex.

Plastic Record Disc 7-Inch 45rpm (One Only Made)

'Any Way You Want Me' / 'Too Much'
This was recorded by the lads on this cheap, throwaway format, a staple of the 1960s. The whereabouts are unknown, and it cannot be confirmed whether it survives or not. Derek Thornhill spoke about its recording, and final produced numbers are not known.

Taped Recording Sessions 1

Reported in the Lancashire press in 1964 and at a later stage probably in 1966, the band members recall having been in studios to record tracks in various locations. It seems likely that a four or five-track demo was made featuring some of the following tracks: 'Out of Reach' / 'Sabre Dance' (instrumental) / 'Marianne Bella' / 'Mr Nobody Nothing' / 'I Found You' / 'Will She' / 'Sweets for My Sweet' / 'She's Gone'. Rod recalled in 2016 that:

> We recorded in Salford near Manchester, in what looked like a dentist's place as the engineers all wore white coats! We recorded, I think, four songs including 'Sweets for My Sweet'. We did the acetate at Decca records of five songs – I can't remember exactly which they were, but all our own arrangements, I think.

'Out of Reach'
This song was written and arranged by The Hollies who it is believed supervised the seven-hour recording session within a Stockport recording studio.

The local paper said: 'A copy of the disc is now in the hands of record company executives in London.' The piece records the band's ages as Johnny (21), Tony (22), Mike (19), Rodney (18), Ian (18), Dave (18).

'Sabre Dance'
This was a guitar instrumental in the manner of The Shadows – it was fast and furious. Rod added: 'It was later released by the band, Gun, who had a hit with it too, renamed as 'Race with the Devil'. We were well pissed off about that, I can tell you.' In a little touch of irony, Jon Anderson also went on to sing with Gun.

'Marianne Bell' (Bella)
This was a song created about a girl the band all liked. She was a fan of Jon's and followed his career for decades. Her name was Marianne Dung, a friend from Bonn, who the band met in Cologne.

'Mr Nobody Nothing'
The track was written by Jon Anderson, Brian

Chatton and Rodney Hill. The band can be seen playing it in Germany, on YouTube.

'I Found You'
A band-written song, this was proposed as the follow-up single for the band.

'Will She'
An unheard band-written song.

'Sweets for My Sweet'
Written by the song writing team of Doc Pomus and Mort Shuman, and also recorded by The Drifters, The Searchers and many more.

Taped Recording Sessions 2

'She's Gone' (2.02)
Thanks to Rodney, the studio tapes came to light in 2017, having been hidden away for 50 years in his loft. The tape came in a cardboard sleeve and was in fair condition. Dated 30 May 1967, this would mean these were the last recordings by Jon Anderson with The Warriors. Rod recalls working late on a couple of tracks in the German studios:

> We recorded it during the week on the date mentioned. We did three songs; it was a session done through the night. We were playing at the PN Hit House, Munich and this was organised through someone who was in the club. We had just played for 4 or 5 hours (45 min with 15-minute breaks). We played the backing track through before listening) to it – it was probably about 4 am by this time – then put on the vocals. Ian took control of the mixing. On listening back, there was one track which Ian hadn't realised had a second verse and he got a little 'psychedelic' and missed the vocals out! I don't remember which it was. It was all done for free. We were still quite happy together although the workload was a bit heavy and we'd done the Frankfurt TV just before (or maybe just after) this recording. Tracks are 'Mr Nobody Nothing', 'Marianne Bell' and 'She's Gone', I seem to think this was the best, I can't remember why. As you can see this must have been one of the last things we did before splitting. We went to Hamburg for June then Frankfurt in July for a while, where we split in August. I was in London by late September. I hung on to this just to have something from those days.

Writing on the AGFA tape reel:
Playback – the playback with voices – Stereo 15 i.p.s
The other labelling on the reel box:
PLAYBACKS, Stereo 15 i.p.s (Inches Per Second) 'She's Gone'. Artists: THE WARRIORS, 30 May 1967
It is hoped that this can be saved along with the acetate music and made available for fans at some point. This item was featured in the *UK Record Collector* magazine along with a feature on Jon Anderson in August 2018.

On the 21 June 2019, the tape, along with two acetates was worked on at FX Rental studios in

Above: The inside sleeve for the CD *Bolton Club 65*. (*Voiceprint*)

London by the author, where we transferred these three songs to digital format. 'She's Gone' was the best sounding of the tracks from the sessions. Two copies are known to exist, one copy with the author and one which was passed to Jon Anderson sometime in the 70s along with other two tapes from Rodney Hill.

Official Compilation Vinyl Albums and CDs

The Warriors featured in various recordings through the years, on both legal and unofficial bootleg offerings. Here are the ones that are known at the time of writing, although others are possible in the future.

Pop Inside the Sixties (1963-69)

(LP, Compilation) See: For Miles Records Ltd. SEE 243 UK 1988

22-track vinyl album LP features both sides of The Warriors' single 'You Came Along' and 'Don't Make Me Blue'. The Warriors' name is on the cover and track listing on the back cover.

Pop Inside the Sixties (1963-69)

(CD, Compilation) Polygram, See: For Miles Records Ltd. SEECD386 UK 1993

A 20-track CD featuring The Warriors' track 'You Came Along'

I guess the startlingly non-politically correct sleeve cover would be the easiest way to find this in your local record store. It pictures four attractive women in their bras! More sexist commentary is written at the bottom of the front cover but I've chosen not to reprint that here.

Sixties Lost and Found. Volume 4

See: For Miles Records Ltd. – SEE 215, UK, Vinyl, LP, Compilation 1987

A 20-track album with Yes connections, as there is a track by the Federals', who had Tony Kaye on keyboards and Paul Korda, Jon's producer with Hans Christian Anderson.

Hans Christian: 'Never My Love'

Rock Rare Collection

EMI – TOCP-71486, CD, Compilation, Japan, Released: 06 Feb 2013

This is an eighteen track CD, featuring the single.

Hans Christian: 'Never My Love'

Just for You (Film soundtrack)

Decca Records Mono LP 4620/ 1964

'Don't Make Me Blue' (Foster)

The film soundtrack, a single vinyl LP. The Warriors' name features on the front cover along with an image taken on the film set for the back cover. On side two, track four, is the song written by Dave Foster.

Hard Up Heroes

'You Came Along' (Mason, Reed)

Decca Records DPA 3009/10. UK. Music from 1963 – 68

Left: Jon in full swing pictured on the back cover of the bootleg *Bolton live 65* CD made by the infamous Highland company. *(David Watkinson Collection)*

This was released as a double gatefold vinyl album compilation in the UK, Belgium, Germany, Canada and France. The French and Belgian editions had a completely different cover in the colour red with the same track listing. Decca DA 225/26 (LP) 2 DAC 225 (Cassette). This version has the brothers named as Anthony and Jon Anderson.

The inner sleeve has a small band profile with a group photograph. The band profile reads as follows:

> The Warriors were a typical £25 pound per gig ballroom pop band. They could be seen most nights of the week around Bolton, Bury, Blackburn, Rochdale and Manchester in their smart little suits. Jon Anderson is now with Yes and his financial status has somewhat improved.

It was re-released in 1974 on King Records of Japan along with a lyrics sheet and an obi strip (information). Decca – DA-225/26 Mono, a cassette version was also released. Jon Anderson has a credit in the special thank you notes in the inner sleeve.

Hard Up Heroes

'You Came Along' (Mason, Reed)
An Australian Star Trax label released 23 track various artists CD compilation. 845 178-2, also on the Mercury label – 845 178-2. 1990.

Idols

Decca – DC 15052/3 / 2 × Vinyl, LP, 24 track LP Compilation 1974
'You Came Along'
The album was basically the same as the *Hard Up Heroes* LP, with a different cover for the Spanish market.

Live and Bootleg CDs

As with any illegal recording, I do not advocate going out and supporting the business of bootlegging material, i.e. creating pirate recordings. I have included them here as I did in the *Yes: Perpetual Change* book, as a reference only. Three different versions of the live performance by The Warriors from 1965, in Bolton, have been released. The original recordings were jointly held by Rod Hill and Dave Foster. David went on to release the recording privately and through a record company. A bootleg version was also made. It came to light in 2016 that there was another recording of a live performance out there somewhere, which had never been heard. A long-term friend of the band confirmed it was made in Germany and that Dave Foster likely owned it at some point. The author is on the case to find this one as you read.

Warriors 65

The first and only known live recording to be released of the band was in the 1990s. This first edition was a David Foster privately- produced, 21 track CD, in very limited in numbers, although the actual number unknown. It has a homemade feel to it with simple paper inserts in the CD case. Each CD came signed by Dave Foster on the back cover, with the front cover image being a stage shot in black and white, taken at the Bolton Beachcomber Club, which clearly shows Jon singing. This, and all the different CD versions inserts have the following words written in the CD insert: *WARRIORS 65*. It was originally recorded on a small two-track tape recorder placed at the rear of the Bolton Beachcomber Club in September 1965. The quality of the recording leaves a lot to be desired – it's a mass of distorted noise. However, it has been cleaned up considerably, enough to hear the comical and sometimes rude banter between the songs. As the night wore on, the band got more and more drunk, the resulting performance slowly degenerating into something of a revel. However, the soundtrack gives the listener a real taste of a cellar gig played by a northern band of the era. Tracks are:

'You're Always on My Mind'
'No-one Can Make My Sunshine Smile'
'Jump Back'
'You Can't Lie to a Liar'
'I'm Down'
'Runaround Sue'
'Crying in the Rain'
'Hit the Road Jack'
'She's a Woman'
'Fortune Teller'
'Too Much Monkey Business'
'Unidentified'
'Don't You Dig this Kinda Beat'
'Hey Baby'
'A Fool Such as I So Sad'
'Be My Baby'
'Bad Bad Time'
'Love is Where You Find It'
'Summer Girl'

Bolton Club 65 Voiceprint VP268CD / November 2003

This 23 track Voiceprint official release came with the bright red cover with a picture of the band on it. The image used was of the band at the time of the movie (Just for You) release. We see them messing about on a stage which is believed to be at the local cinema just before the movie started. Inside the fold-out sleeve there are multiple images taken over the various line-up changes with Jon featuring centre image, wearing a suit, he is leaning on the white car used to transport the band around. The back cover insert picture is another photo given a shot of red colour which again shows Jon singing.

Voiceprint – Newsprint Sampler – Promo-VP2003 – CD

The Warriors 'Too Much Monkey Business'
This is a UK compilation, released in 2003. The CD comes in a clear PVC sleeve with no track listing.

Apart from the official CD release on Voiceprint, this is the only live recording put out separately from the original disc. The recording is taken from Bolton Club 65 Voiceprint VP268CD/2003.

Jon and Tony Anderson do their very best to sound like Elvis Presley and what comes across is the real fun that the band had as the show went on. The compilation has eighteen tracks, including one by the future Yes guitarist Trevor Rabin. The CD came with a magazine, including a page feature written about each artist. The Warriors' brief history was compiled by the author, along with a selection of vintage images.

The Warriors / Bolton Club 65 (Hl535) Bootleg / Private Pressing

This 22 track CD labelled HIGHLAND ORIGINAL MASTER seems to be the only bootleg version made of the gig. Coming from the prolific eastern bootleg supplier Highland, it is attractively cased with the front cover showing the band's photo (with a purple tint) of the lads outside in a park – Jon sporting a cravat! Inside images are either close - up or seated shots, in a location that appears to be outside a London tower block. The back-cover photo shows Jon in a close-up, clearly in the moment with eyes closed and hands in the air.

The variations in number of tracks credited on the discs is because some of the songs include an introduction. All the CDs are the same musically, but they all have different sleeve notes regarding the tracks themselves. Track 12 on all the variations is labelled as 'unknown' – but it is, in fact, a variation of the 'Colonel Bogey March', altered to feature comedy lyrics. The tune was borrowed in the UK for the Second World War propaganda song, 'Hitler has Only Got One Ball'. The song was generally sung as a four-line verse and originates from 1939. Other little snippets played around the normal tracks are 'God Save the Queen', a ventriloquist act, and for some inexplicable reason Jon becomes a stand-up comedian (or Goons-type character) telling us nonsense about his smelly feet!

CD review

The live performances are a wonderful way of going back in time and it is quite amazing how Jon went from a young full-of-fun teenager, playing innocent basic rock 'n roll style music with his mates, to *Close To The Edge*, and *Tales From Topographic Oceans* within five years, followed by the phenomenal *Olias of Sunhillow* and *Relayer* a couple of years later.

Writing this while listening to the CD, I am amazed that I was only three miles away in Bolton, playing in the streets as a young boy, while all this was happening. Did I somehow hear it drifting over the town and filtering into my brain? Jon's music, either solo or in Yes, has had a massive influence on me over the years. Put the CD on, play it loud and just imagine what it was like in that club that night. I bet it puts a smile on your face. I'm smiling now, at the familiar moment when Jon sings (screams) 'I'm Down' on track 22. Yes fans will recognise that Jon delivered the same powerful version in the 70s and in the 80s at live performances with Yes

Bootleg compilation CD albums with The Warriors and Hans Christian Tracks

The Beat Scene

Deram Decca Originals label 844 799-2 (1998) (2005)
'Don't Make Me Blue' (Foster)
A 25-track single CD with an 11-page booklet giving brief overviews of the bands included. These 25 tracks have been culled from a host of mid-1960s artists on the UK-based Decca Records label as part of their critically and enthusiastically lauded 'Decca Originals' series. The very disparaging liner notes report the following:

> 'You Came Along', 'Don't Make Me Blue' was the sole offering from this Manchester beat combo, who would have disappeared into total obscurity were it not for a cameo in the movie Just For You and the fact that Jon Anderson later fronted prog legends, Yes.

The Goddess of Mercy

Highland 1963-68 HL405/406,2CD (1999)
The Warriors – 'You Came Along' (Mason/Reed) 2:09, 'Don't Make Me Blue' (Foster) 2:08

Hans Christian – 'Never My Love' (Addrissl / Addrissl) 2:28, 'All of The Time' (Korda) 2:16, '(The Autobiography of) Mississippi Hobo' (Korda) 2:36, 'Sonata of Love' 2:58 (Korda), 'Out of My Mind' (Korda) 1:06, 'Someone in Heaven Knows' (Korda) 1:33
The cover featured the original Yes logo, interspaced with four images of some of the pre-Yes bands. Throughout the CD, most of the recordings are studio versions coming from vinyl records or acetates, and within this twin pack of CDs, it covers all the main future Yes men in their pre-Yes days. The Jon Anderson tracks featured, are in varying quality.

Before the Birth of Yes

(Seymour SR-021/022)
Pre-Yes tracks 1963-79 Studio Recordings by various members.
This very well produced double CD pack is a real treat. It covers 42 tracks from all the key Yes members before Yes. Production is excellent with quality printed discs using Roger Dean's lettering. Cases show the classic Roger Dean logos in multi-colour. The cover artwork is suitably spacey in feel with a subtle centre logo.
The Warriors – 'You Came Along'
Hans Christian – '(Autobiography of) Mississippi Hobo', 'Sonata of Love'
In the 1970s, Jon Anderson was visiting WMMR radio station in Philadelphia, a real 'Yes' east coast city. A friend of DJ, Ed Sciaky's (himself a fan and friend of the band), Gerry Abear, brought the Hans Christian single in and played it for Jon live on the radio. Jon pleaded with Ed to take it off, which he did. Jon has never been a fan of this short shot at pop stardom.

The Movie – Just for You

The Warriors featured in the UK version of the film *Just for You*, released 28 June 1964 in the UK, contributing to the movie score with the song 'Don't Make Me Blue', the B-side of The Warriors' single written by David Foster. This was an odd choice considering it was not the song they wanted to plug. Only the UK version of the film featured The Warriors, with them removed from the re-named Disk-O-Tek versions and later DVD versions. It was released on video through selected specialist 1960s music sites in the 1990s, but these are hard to find. The *Just for You* movie was shown all over Europe and it was rumoured that The Warriors' clip was shown on its own in Spain at one point.

Other release dates include 1 June 1966 in the USA, 7 July 1966 in Denmark, as *Just for You*, in Denmark *Beat-Hit-Paraden*. In the UK it is also known as *Discotheque Holiday* and in the USA *Disk-O-Tek Holiday*.

The tag line for the movie was 'The Happiest Film of Them All: Today's Stars – Tomorrows Hits'. The movie was released on DVD in 2014 on Network, at 62 minutes long, PG-rated, in English, for Region 2. The Warriors are not listed on the cover. The actors are Casey Paxton and Katherine Quint. An accompanying *Just for You* magazine was produced to promote the film. In full colour, this is a commercial light read of its time. Full of photos, it gives an overview of the movie. The Warriors most certainly were not the most important musicians included, and they only make a page near the back. However, it does include this short but fun band line-up overview:

> There is always a beautiful blonde to be found on a film set, so The Warriors find inspiration for their new song – 'Don't Make Me Blue'.
> The Warriors consist of:
> Rodney Hill (aged 17), nicknamed 'Pill'. He has dyed red-gold hair and likes horror books.
> Jonnie Anderson (aged 19). He has dyed auburn hair, likes cars and dislikes candy floss.
> Tony Anderson (aged 22 and Jonnie's brother). He has dyed brownish blond hair, likes omelettes and dislikes elevators.
> Mike Brereton (aged 19). He has natural bright red hair and likes E-type Jaguars.
> Ian Russell Wallace (aged 17). He likes dogs.
> The Warriors like to dress in mod clothes, and they have one ambition – to reach the top of the ladder together.

Live TV Appearances

Thank Your Lucky Stars

ABC Television
Featured on 6 June 1964, Season five, Episode 37, where The Warriors were voted third best act on the programme, with the first and second spots going to the Beatles and the Rolling Stones respectively. The third spot behind two of the most influential bands in the UK music history, and the world's music scene is not bad for a small Lancashire band. The following artists have been recorded as appearing on the episode. Hosted by Brian Matthew, guests included Peter and Gordon, The Four Pennies, Dusty Springfield, Craig Douglas, The Migil Five, The Mods, Andree Silver, The Warriors, and Janice Nicholls. Guest DJ was Tony Hall. The sheer expense of the equipment and large reels of 2' quad videotape, meant that only the most important events or performance would be considered good enough to keep. If the budget was tight, then the policy was to wipe the tape. The Beatles were one of the few who survived the trash can. The Warriors didn't.

Juke Box Jury – BBC TV

No audio or video recordings have come forward showing The Warriors, as at the time the BBC had a policy of wiping the tapes of its programmes and often didn't record live shows. It seems that even now, only three episodes of *Juke Box Jury* have been saved in their complete form. They are:

- A Merseyside special broadcast December 1963, with the Beatles topping the bill, recorded on the afternoon of Sunday, 15 December 1963 at the Alpha Television Studios in Aston, Birmingham.
- An edition from May 1966 featured two numbers from the Rolling Stones.
- Goodbye Lucky Stars, the final edition broadcast in June 1966.

Juke Box Jury was chaired by David Jacobs, the then famously mild-mannered DJ presenter. Each week he played a selection of 7-inch' singles on a large jukebox to a panel of four celebrities. As the music played the camera moved over the faces of the panellists and the audience so the viewer could gauge their reaction. The panellists then gave their opinion of the discs and voted them a hit or a miss. If there was a tie, a jury of teenagers drawn from the audience would have the deciding vote. Each week a mystery performer was revealed after the panel had voted on his or her disc, to the joy or embarrassment of the panel.

Beat! Beat! Beat!

German TV Music Show 1967
'Mr. Nobody Nothing' / 'Tango'
This Frankfurt-based TV show ran from 1966 to 1969. It featured all the best current chart music, including the likes of the Hollies, Chris Farlowe, the Small Faces and the Troggs. 26 episodes of naïve, charming stage performances alongside some library cartoon sequences, in black and white were filmed, with the bands performing their hit or prospective hits – of the day. The show contained an eclectic mix of music as it ran through the 1960s, and should not to be confused with the *Beat Club* German music programme which had started a little earlier. The *Beat! Beat! Beat!* audience were generally made up of German and American teenagers, with performances being filmed at the airbases, town hall or schools in and around Frankfurt. The Warriors performance on the show can be seen, thanks to this rare footage being uploaded to YouTube. Their song 'Mr. Nobody Nothing' is available with sound, as is, 'Tango' (an Isley Brothers song) which came to light after some 50 years in February 2019, found by a Japanese fan.

A show has survived on tape which will be of interest to Warriors' fans, one complete *Beat! Beat! Beat!* show has made the rounds of collectors in the past ten years. It features The Warriors, the Move, the Creation, Don and Dottie, Graham Bonney and the house band of Waner and Storer.
Both The Warriors and Tony Anderson's band Los Bravos, played on the *Beat! Beat! Beat!* TV Show, and their performances were lovingly reviewed on *www.perfectsoundforever.com* as follows:

> The Warriors from Manchester performed the quasi-psychedelic 'Mister Nobody Nothing' and 'Tango.' By the standards of the mid-sixties, their hair was long. The drummer (Ian Wallace) was a dead ringer for the band MC5's Rob Tyner. The organist (Brian Chatton) and the bass player. (David Foster) wore gaucho hats and capes. The lead guitarist (Rod Hill) wore what looked like a marching band hat. The lead singer had Roger McGuinn glasses and an Iron Cross Medallion. They had a very cool comportment and went over well with the audience. Their harmonies were good and loud too, and remember that this was all live.

In the October 1966 show with The Small Faces, for example, Mal Sondock was the MC, and the show also featured the Untamed, Los Bravos (featuring Tony Anderson) and Tony Sheridan.

Above: A poster for the 1 October 1964 gig at the Southport Aldridge's club. A great night's entertainment for the entrance fee of 6/6.

Bootleg lists have been bulging with *Beat! Beat! Beat!* audio and video items for years and fragments of the shows have been broadcast on German TV and throughout Europe in the 1980s and the 1990s in half-hour specials. Complete episodes are also brought back and aired from time to time in Germany and other countries. In 1997, VH1's UK subsidiary bought the rights and aired a mini-series featuring many of the *Beat! Beat! Beat!* best and most exciting moments, highlighting the cheesier elements of the show. The company TV.com offers about five or six prime shows for downloading to PC. One show that is definitely available dates from May 1967 and features the Jimi Hendrix Experience, Sandie Shaw, Simon Dupree and the Big Sound, who later morphed into progressive rock band Gentle Giant, plus Dave Dee, Dozy, Beaky, Mick and Tich. *Videobeat.com* offers ten or 15 shows all from 1966 and 1967- they are 2-shows on one DVD or VHS tape with bonus items. Collectors won't want to pass up the Kinks in January 1966, the Small Faces in October 1966 or the Yardbirds in the spring of 1967.

Live Radio Appearance's – Manchester Cathedral

'All Things Bright and Beautiful', 'He's Got the Whole World in His Hands', 'Blowin In the Wind', 'All Things Bright and Beautiful', 'Father Hear the Prayer We Offer' – In the manner of the police TV series Z Cars theme tune.

The Warriors Manchester Cathedral gig was broadcast locally on Lancashire radio. There was an article in the *Radio Times* around the time which depicted the band in a photo, showing them from the back with the audience in front of them. I don't believe any recording was kept and the Cathedral doesn't have any history of it. The local press did cover it well and it was attended by hundreds of fans, many whom could not get in.

Cover Songs

In 1965 The Warriors' song 'You Came Along' was covered by the German band The Krauts. Released on the Bellaphon label, it was the B-side to their A-side 'I Can Understand'. Catalogue: BL 1024, September 1965, Format: 7' 45 RPM, Vinyl. Their cover of the track was also featured on the CD compilation *Die Frankfurt Szene*. A various artist, single-CD Digipak, which includes a 32-page booklet and 22 tracks in all. It was released in 2002, on the Bear Family record label.

Perhaps due to the structure of the single or just the musical times in which it was made and creative processes available, the single sounds uncannily like The Warriors. They have changed little or nothing in tempo, arrangement, sound or production, which means it is a very similar sounding featuring harmonies, a foot-tapping beat and overall a very jolly sounding record.

Memorabilia

The band was together around five years, and most of the memorabilia is represented in this book. The Warriors' original promotion postcards were distributed, with around three different versions made. They all had the band's photo on the front and details of the single on the back. The official fan club address for the band was 6 Oswald Street, Accrington, this was sometimes added to the promo cards. Both the London and Accrington addressed versions have been seen. Mike, the band's guitarist, recalled: 'We must have been a good band, we used to have somebody that ran our fan club. She was called Wendy, and she lived in Bolton. Yeah, we actually had a fan club!' Aileen Darroch started the fan club in the beginning. It was covered in newspaper articles that the band had signing events and plenty of autograph books – popular in those days – were signed. Although I haven't come across any books, they must be out there somewhere. In 2019 a signed newspaper cutting came on the market for sale, this was likely to be the earliest signature by Jon and the band as it came from 1963, this is shown in this book. The earliest poster so far found is from 1964 and is also shown.

The Warriors Posters

A small amount of original concert posters had been made which are now very rare indeed. I know of around five different ones, with most in private collections. Most of the posters come from the small Lancashire town of Nelson, where the dance hall called the Imperial Ballroom (Imp) packed them in every weekend, it must have fun.

1. Accrington Town Hall, Saturday 1 February 1964, 'HYNDBURN BEAT 64, with Mike Sax and the Vikings. (David Watkinson Collection)
2. Accrington, a very rare poster from perhaps late 1965 early 1966. Very English in design which would mean it was to promote the band in the UK still and not Germany. The earliest known poster to feature an image of Jon Anderson along with the band's images. This one also has the management details on it saying – Sole Representation Don Read Agency 24-28 Bank Street Bolton Lancs 0804 – 26277-8. Over a black background, The Warriors writing and faces of the band are in

pink. Pictured resting all close together with head in their hands. It shows Brian Chatton on this, so it was the last year or so of the band. Rodney Hill thinks it may have been created by the *Bolton art club* and believes it's probably the only one left, and when Brian Chatton saw it, he said 'Wow!' The image was credited to M. Chapman. The dancing couple image at the top of the poster would be reminiscent of Jon's parents in their heyday as ballroom dancers. (David Watkinson Collection)
3. Southport, Aldridge's, Thursday 1 October 1964, BEAT SCENE 64, The Paramount's, The Warriors, The Vampires, entrance fee of 6/6. DECCA, FILM AND T.V. RECORDING GROUP THE WARRIORS. White background, blue framed with green and black writing. (Unknown owner)
4. Rawtenstall Astoria 26 December 1964, 'Fabulous Christmas Eve Attraction – THE FOUR PENNIES, SATURDAY, DEC 26 BOXING DAY DANCE. Featuring the Decca Disc Group, THE WARRIORS' plus The Swashbuckling – MUTINEERS and The Vitalizing – VINCENTS. 7.30 – 11.45 Licenced Bar, advanced 6'6 – At Door 7'6 (seven shillings and sixpence). With a bright yellow background and Warriors writing in red, this looks impressive. (Dave Ridge)
5. Nelson Imperial, 26 June 1965 supporting the dynamic Tom Jones plus The Warriors and The Elders. Tickets 7/6, 7.30 – 11.30 pm. This larger outside venue poster has more details covering the night before also. (Unknown owner)

Flyer and Posters

There must have been hundreds of mini-posters and flyers produced, but now only a small number have survived.
1. November 1963 Nelson Imperial supporting BILLY. J. KRAMER and the DAKOTAS, describes the band as the sensational, contest-winning WARRIORS. A replica is owned by the author. (David Watkinson Collection)
2. Nelson Imperial, 2 September 1964 Bill Haley ROCK SHOW, Bill Haley and The Comets with Gene Vincent, plus The Dynamic WARRIORS. A replica is owned by the author. (David Watkinson Collection)
3. Nelson Imperial, 12 June 1965, supporting Donovan with the band the Quare Fellows supporting The Warriors. Some twelve years later it would be Donovan supporting Jon in Yes on the *Going for The One* tour. A replica is owned by the author. (David Watkinson Collection)
4. Nelson Imperial, 26 June 1965 supporting the dynamic Tom Jones plus The Warriors and The Elders. Tickets 7/6, 7.30 – 11.30 pm. A replica is owned by the author. (David Watkinson Collection)
5. Nelson Imperial, 8 May 1964. Showing the band supporting Marianne Faithfull. A replica is owned by the author. (David Watkinson Collection)
6. The Grafton Rooms, 1 March 1966, POPS GALORE, featuring the Realm and five other bands and special guest stars THE WARRIORS. Tickets 3/6. (David Watkinson Collection)

The rare Warriors' song lyric sheet music was released by Decca with a wonderful front cover image, inside the transcription of the single 'You Came Along'.
The movie *Just for You*, produced lobby cards, a poster and made various small appearances in film magazine features. The *Bolton Beat Scene* magazine covered the area's events and was produced in small amounts in the mid-1960s. I don't believe The Warriors made it into the magazine.

Book Projects and other sources of information

In around 1998, David Foster along with a friend Andrew Blake worked on a book project based on David's musical life, including his time with The Warriors, called *Yours is No Disgrace – a Rock and Roll Memoir*. It was not released. Brian Chatton released his biography in 2018 which contained a chapter of his memories in the band, the most that had been

Above: An early Yes programme featuring the Atlantic logo. *(David Watkinson Collection)*

written up to that point. Called *Rolling with Rock Royalty*, it is a rollicking and fun read about his long and successful 50-year career in the music business.

Jon Anderson released the first chapter of his memoirs on the 29 August 2019. This chapter related to The Warriors years and was fifteen pages long. His Memoirs called Survival and Other Stories, was presented as a down load, it is not clear in what format other versions it will be made available in. Jon's only other published collaboration in the book world so far was with Wendy Vig. Fountains of Gold, a paperback was released in 1997. It featured poems by the author Wendy along with Jon Anderson providing a foreword and paintings. Published by Heaven Bone Press, it had 28 pages. Jon was also involved with some children's book projects, but it isn't clear what stage they are at. Another musician from The Warriors' times who knew the band and Jon Anderson, who has put pen to paper recalling his rock and roll life stories from the 1960s is Dave 'Wammy' Walmsley, whose autobiography Delivering The Goods talks about the highs and lows of being in and around the crazy 1960 s music scene. For interesting photos of Jon (then in Yes) and Tony Anderson around this time check out *www.wammy-uk.com*

The Warriors' history for the last 50 years had only ever really been covered in books on Yes. Generally, their story has only had a few lines or at best a page or two. Those and the Voiceprint full page write up for the live CD insert by the author is pretty much all that covers The Warriors' history in print form up to 2018, when Brian Chatton released his book. Two Accrington mini visual photo books called *the Accrington Life* were printed showing the history of Accrington, which featured two photographs by Garth Dawson of the band. He was a local newspaper photographer during the 1960s and was the main photographer of The Warriors. The books show full-page photographs of The Warriors.

After discussions with previous Warriors' band members, it seems items from the band such as photographs, cuttings, reel to reel tapes and possibly other items were in the possession of various band members. It is not clear if any of it will be seen or used again in any format, although investigations continue. Rod had originally owned some of the material such as the reel to reel tapes with the tracks 'Marianne Bella' and 'Mr Nobody Nothing' – the latter recorded in a studio in Munich.

Rod remembers, 'I gave three tapes to Dave Foster and two to Jon. We used to have a demo with four or five tracks on it, one being the 'Sabre Dance' instrumental which he gave to a friend.'

While researching photographs, I was lucky enough to see some rare photos which were taken in and around Germany at the time The Warriors first arrived there.

Having seen these images of the band at work and play in the Storyville Club and in Cologne clubs, some show Brian Chatton and Jon Anderson in the local park, messing around on see-saws, and others show various members on stage. In the same collection of material there comes a letter written to a fan from Jon, which I am afraid I can't show here, but it does include a sketch, words and a signature by Jon as 'Jon' in 1967.

Other images seen and unpublished are of Jon and Brian with girlfriends, and band members drinking in bars, also with some of them on stage. They take the viewer on a fascinating journey to the 60s and show Jon as a normal young man way before stardom, some of them are within this book.

One framed item has a letter to a fan from Jon in 1966 reads:

> Hi
> It's me JON...do you remember me. It's so nice to write to you, love is all you NEED
> JON

The word NEED was spelt in capitals and took up half the page, and with the spelling of Jon as JON. This again is proof that Jon was aiming to change his Christian name way before previously had been thought. He seems to have been practising it, to see how it looked.

Other interesting items came from Bonham's auction house in the UK in December 2009, these coming from the Roy Flynn collection, their first Yes manager. This included a group of handwritten lyrics by Jon Anderson and David Foster. The writing team of Jon and David regrouped after The Warriors split and worked on Yes material circa 1969. The items comprised of four sheets of lined notepaper by Jon Anderson, one entitled Go!!, each with writing on the reverse (with one side by David Foster), and four sheets in blue ballpoint by David Foster, titles being 'Melancholy Day', 'Cotton Candy Universe', 'Reasons Child', 'Rock', '3rd Floor Song', 'Miriam', 'See You Again', 'In Between' and 'Hoping You'll Understand', with typewritten copies. Other memorabilia on offer from the collection of Roy Flynn included press releases, posters and handwritten lyrics for the tracks, 'Harold Land', 'Beyond and Before', 'Looking Around' and 'Sweetness'.

The *Accrington Life* magazine published

two features on Jon Anderson in 2017. These covered Jon's early days in the town and included interviews, photos and memorabilia and Jon was pictured on the cover of one of the issues.

Hans Christian collectables

Promotional images are all I have been able to track down. Clive Bayley from Mabel Greer's Toyshop spoke about a promotional poster being made in 1968 with Hans Christian on it. No copies of this have been found to my knowledge. Some music press reviews were written in the *Melody Maker* and possibly the *New Musical Express.* Record company press photographs came out but a full press release pack I haven't seen. Adverts also appeared in the UK record music paper press. As with The Warriors, other trips to the studio lead to some demo recordings being made. These although not released, have sometimes surfaced, while others disappeared over time. Both singles were released into a world not ready for Jon's sound, which is possibly why they crashed and burned. Demonstration and acetate versions would have been made for all produced vinyl singles. I have documented here the ones I have found to be in circulation or in collections world-wide. There is an image of Jon Anderson as Hans Christian on the cover of his Lost Tapes box set of rare collectable music, released on Voiceprint records in 2006.

Hans Christian on the Odeon label. A German copy of the interestingly titled 'The Autobiography of Mississippi Hobo'. *(David Watkinson Collection)*

Vinyl 7-Inch 45rpm Standard Release Singles

1 'Never My Love' / 'All of The Time'
1968 Parlophone 45 UK: R 5676. 19677X CE 19133-1 / 7X CE 19134-1
2 ('The Autobiography of) Mississippi Hobo' / 'Sonata of Love'
Parlophone 45 UK, R 5698, 24 May 1968.
Supplied with a Parlophone outer sleeve and with the centre intact.

Vinyl promo special double 'A' sided promo 45rpm

1 '(The Autobiography of) Mississippi Hobo' 23 842 7XCE 2113 8-1 rpm.
2 'Never My Love' XCE 19133-1.
Odeon label: Made in Germany, no centre and in a plain sleeve.

The writing credits on the singles are as follows: 'Never My Love'. (Don & Dick Addrissi), 'All of The Time' (Korda), 'Sonata of Love' (Korda), ('The Autobiography of) Mississippi Hobo' (Korda).

Acetate Vinyl 7-Inch Promo Single 45rpm

'(The Autobiography of) Mississippi Hobo'
Known to exist is the one-sided Emidisc acetate, with the handwritten white centre label. Featuring the title, artist, length at 2.32, the speed of 45 RPM and letters MWS. Showing the wording: Made in GT Britain recording blank.

Acetate Vinyl 7-Inch UK Pre-Production Metal Acetate Single 45rpm

'Never My Love'
An Emidisc acetate came up for sale in October 2018. The centre has a written cream coloured label, with age-related staining. Featuring the title, artist, length at 2.20, the speed of 45 RPM and letters MWS. The B Side is blank. Showing the wording: Made in GT Britain recording blank. Advertised as 'possibly a different unissued cut, by frontman of Yes, real name John Roy Anderson. This is a short 1: 45-minute extract and did sound very clear with only minor crackling. It is not known if there was any difference to the final release.

Vinyl 7-Inch UK Demo Single 45rpm (1968)

'(Autobiography of) Mississippi Hobo' (2.33) / 'Sonata of Love' (2.57)
Parlophone 5698 / 7XCE 21136 or 7X CE 21138-145 / 7X CE 21139-1
UK demo versions do come up from time to time on the web sales sites such as eBay. Printed in the centre of this bright green record centre is the date 24/5/68. Along with NOT FOR SALE and DEMONSTRATION RECORD

with a large letter 'A' covering the whole centre. KORDA PUBLISHING LIMITED is spelt out in full to the left of centre. Parlophone record company used the green coloured sleeve with the white swirl coming out of the centre.

Vinyl 7-Inch Demo Single 45rpm

'Never My Love' R5676 7XCE19133-1 'All of The Time' 7XCE19134-1
It was supplied with a Parlophone outer sleeve, and with the centre intact.

Vinyl 7-Inch Germany Demo Single 45rpm

Not surprisingly there were attempts to promote Jon as Hans Christian (Anderson) in Germany through the very well-known Odeon label.
'(Autobiography of) Mississippi Hobo' / 'Never My Love'
ODEON O2 38 42 45-0-29 627 (2.30)

Vinyl 7-Inch USA Demo Single 45rpm

'Never My Love' / 'All of The Time'
TOWER 409 1968, white label promo only

It perhaps comes as a surprise that the USA would have picked up on the Hans release at all, but they did, and it seems that there are two promo versions of the single out there on the Tower label. Tower Records was an American record label from 1964 to 1970. A subsidiary of Capitol Records, Tower often released music by artists who were relatively low profile in comparison to those released on the parent label, including a number of artists such as The Standells and The Chocolate Watchband, later recognised as 'garage bands'. For this reason, Tower is often associated with the garage rock phenomenon of the 1960s.
Two versions of the US promo single, 'Never My Love' / 'All of The Time' single have come to light. The white label NOT FOR SALE centres differ with some versions having the letter 'A' on them obviously dictating the main play side. Other differences are some have single centres and others not. Publishing credits also differ with the following shown on one or the other.
Tamerlan Music, BMI – 409 (45 X 62063)
U.S. pub not assigned 409 (45 X 62064)

Acetate, 8" Vinyl USA 45rpm Single-Sided

'Never My Love' (Instrumental)

This is one that has been found and displayed on the internet. It is not 100% clear if it is indeed a backing track before Jon's vocals being added, in time that may be clarified. It is likely to be an unreleased instrumental version,

Above: The rare and interesting bootleg/private pressing CD of pre – Yes bands

Right: A very early ticket stub. *(David Watkinson Collection)*

possibly a one-off acetate. The Eldorado Studio in Hollywood, California had been in business since the 1950s and could have done something with this track in the late 60s. The Tamerlane Music company changed hands in April 1967 and now is owned by Warner.

Details shown on the label: Eldorado Studio, 1717 North Vine Street, Hollywood 28, California. Hollywood 7-6131, 45, INST, Never My Love, Tamerlane Music Inc.

Acetate 7-Inch Vinyl 45rpm 1967

'Out of My Mind' / 'Someone in Heaven Knows'

These recordings are generally difficult to find and own, having been produced in such small quantities. It is, however, possible to search and find an audio link to them, with most being on youtube.com

Different single variations were made from the various record companies. A variety of different covers are out there to collect. None show any images of Hans Christian or Jon.

TOWER / PARLOPHONE / ODEAN / PLAIN DEMO / COLOURFUL FOUR PICTURED COVER OF VARIOUS IMAGES (New York / Greece / Tokyo / Aeroplane) Not Jon / MUSICAL INSTRUMENTS IMAGES/ FACTORY SAMPLE

Hans Christian Featured Tracks on Compilation Vinyl Albums

Back Beat – See for Miles Records Ltd, SEE 39, UK, 1985

This 20 track LP mostly features artists from 1958 through to 1968, including an early Slade in the form of The 'N' Betweens, The Federals have the Yes connection as Tony Kaye played in the band and at No 19 on the playlist is Hans Christian. The album cover features a promotional photograph of Jon Anderson as Hans Christian, which is the only vinyl album to do so. Featured track 'Never My Love'.

Hobo Sounds Sonidos, Vagabundos – cat No 12595, PATHE 4048 Argentina in 1968

Surprisingly, Hans Christian was one of the artists featured on the compilation album released at the same time as the single. Released by Eve Graham it has the superb psychedelic art cover showing a naked woman's painted back, the imagery is very 1960s. The other artists featured are The Cats, Deena Webster, The Nocturnes and Treetops. Featured track '(The Diary of) A Mississippi Hobo'

Hans Christian Featured Tracks on Compilation CDs

British Pop Psych and Other Flavours – 1966-1969

A twenty track CD, featuring minor bands and artists, released on the UK Particles label in 2014, PARTCD4036, the Piccadilly Sunshine series, Part Seventeen.

Track No 4: Hans Christian – 'All of the Time'

Rock Rare Collection

A CD released on the EMI label, TOCP-71486CD. A compilation released in Japan, 06 Feb 2013, Track No 12: Hans Christian – 'Never My Love'

Jon Anderson with Gun

Nothing has come to light showing photos with this line-up. There are only mentions of Gun on Marquee flyers. A review is shown early in this book of the Gun gig with Jon. Maybe a gig flyer or a mention of the said gig, Jon Anderson and Gun will appear one day?

Mabel Greer's Toyshop

The Mabel Greer's Toyshop era was a very brief time with Jon. It seems nothing has survived

or has come to light from that short period. Clive Bayley did, however, reveal in 2017 that much of what has been searched for was in his suitcase in New York at one point, only to be lost at an airport.

For details on collectables by Yes and Jon Anderson in the following years, do investigate the book *Yes: Perpetual Change* by David Watkinson.

Left: Jon and Jack Barrie, owner of La Chaisse and an early champion of the band, enjoy a catch up in London. *(Chris Welch)*

Below: Marketing materials for the Blaises Club, where Yes practiced during their first months. *(David Watkinson Collection)*

Right: A rare early poster for a gig on 11 May 1969 in Kidderminster. *(David Watkinson Collection)*

JON ANDERSON and THE WARRIORS THE LOST DEMOS EP

This rare and exciting material came from the various lofts and trunks around the world. Hidden away for more than fifty years, the condition of some of the material was very poor. The material had jumps, scratches and even stopping completely in places. In my attempt to bring these recording to life again, on a few tracks I made the decision not to over produce them, leaving in crackles and other deficiencies. With others, however, I was surprised at how clear the music sounded. The band sounds very accomplished, and you can hear just how well rehearsed they were, The Warriors being among the best beat group acts in the country at the time.

The EP Features seven demo tracks from the band at different times in their career, from Lancashire at the rise of their local stardom to the end of the road in Germany, in 1967. Six of the tracks are with the full band, featuring Jon as both a backing and as a lead vocalist Just one track as an instrumental.

It was released as a limited-edition picture sleeve vinyl EP. A seven inch record, played at 33rpm. The format tips it's hat to the days in the 1970s when Yes would produce EPs in a similar style. This long-lost material gives the Jon Anderson and Yes fans a new insight into these beat music years.

David Watkinson

Track listing:

1. **'Too Much (Please Don't Feel Too Bad)'** (The Hollies / Alan Clarke) (2.21)

2. **'Can't Live It Down'** (Geoff Stephens) (2.44)

3. **'Summer Girl (Poor Little Lonely)'** (David Box and Roland Pike)(1.54)
These three tracks were originally taken from an Acetate three track seven-inch vinyl from 1964. A double-sided 7-inch vinyl single acetate Emidisc, with handwritten details in the centre. After fifty years hidden in Rodney's loft, these songs were worked on at the great Abbey Road studios in London on the 18 May 2017. Line-up: Jon Anderson, Tony Anderson, Rodney Hill, Mike Brereton, Dave Foster, Ian Wallace

4. **'The Doll House Is Empty'** (The Everley Brothers)(1.59)
This track was originally a single-sided seven-inch single unreleased vinyl Emidisc acetate from August 1966. Line-up: Jon Anderson, Brian Chatton, Rodney Hill, Dave Foster, Ian Wallace

5. **'Run To Me'** (Ray Teret)(2.21)
This was originally a seven inch vinyl acetate from August 1966. Recorded in London. Line-up: Jon Anderson, Brian Chatton, Rodney Hill, Dave Foster, Ian Wallace

6. **'She's Gone'** (Jon Anderson/Brian Chatton/Rodney Hill) (2.08) (instrumental version)

7. **'She's Gone'** (Jon Anderson/Brian Chatton/Rodney Hill) (2.02) (with vocals)
Reel to reel tape recording, 30 May 1967. Recorded in Munich, Germany. Line-up: Jon Anderson, Brian Chatton, Rodney Hill, Dave Foster, Ian Wallace

Researched, Mastering, co-ordinated, liner notes, images and production by David Watkinson
Sleeve design by David Watkinson and Chris Topham
Mastering at Abbey Road Studios London, 18 May, 2017 and FX Group London, 21 June 2019
Chris Topham – Plane Groovy Records.
Cat No: OLIAS90127

Also from Sonicbond Publishing

On Track series

Queen Andrew Wild 978-1-78952-003-3
Emerson Lake and Palmer Mike Goode 978-1-78952-000-2
Deep Purple and Rainbow 1968-79 Steve Pilkington 978-1-78952-002-6
Yes Stephen Lambe 978-1-78952-001-9
Blue Oyster Cult Jacob Holm-Lupo 978-1-78952-007-1
The Beatles Andrew Wild 978-1-78952-009-5
Roy Wood and the Move James R Turner 978-1-78952-008-8
Genesis Stuart MacFarlane 978-1-78952-005-7
Jethro Tull Jordan Blum 978-1-78952-016-3
The Rolling Stones 1963-80 Steve Pilkington 978-1-78952-017-0
Judas Priest John Tucker 978-1-78952-018-7
Toto Jacob Holm-Lupo 978-1-78952-019-4
Van Der Graaf Generator Dan Coffey 978-1-78952-031-6
Frank Zappa 1966 to 1979 Eric Benac 978-1-78952-033-0
Elton John in the 1970s Peter Kearns 978-1-78952-034-7
The Moody Blues Geoffrey Feakes 978-1-78952-042-2
The Beatles Solo 1969-1980 Andrew Wild 978-1-78952-042-2
Steely Dan Jez Rowden 978-1-78952-043-9
Pink Floyd Solo Mike Goode 978-1-78952-046-0
Hawkwind Duncan Harris 978-1-78952-043-9
Fairport Convention Kevan Furbank 978-1-78952-052-1
Iron Maiden Steve Pilkington 978-1-78952-061-3

On Screen series

Carry On... Stephen Lambe 978-1-78952-004-0
Powell and Pressburger Sam Proctor 978-1-78952-013-2
Seinfeld Seasons 1 to 5 Stephen Lambe 978-1-78952-012-5
Francis Ford Coppola Cam Cobb and Stephen Lambe 978-1-78952-022-4
Breaking Bad Roman Colombo 978-1-78952-045-3
Monty Python Steve Pilkington 978-1-78952-047-7

Other Books

Not As Good As The Book Andy Tillison 978-1-78952-021-7
The Voice. Frank Sinatra in the 1940s Stephen Lambe 978-1-78952-032-3
Maximum Darkness Deke Leonard 978-1-78952-048-4
The Twang Dynasty Deke Leonard 978-1-78952-049-1
Maybe I Should've Stayed In Bed Deke Leonard 978-1-78952-053-8

and many more to come!